ACA
ETHICAL STANDARDS
CASEBOOK

Fifth Edition

Barbara Herlihy, PhD, LPC, NCC
Loyola University of New Orleans

Gerald Corey, EdD, ABPP, NCC
California State University, Fullerton

AMERICAN
COUNSELING
ASSOCIATION
5999 Stevenson Avenue
Alexandria, VA 22304-3300

American Counseling Association
5999 Stevenson Avenue
Alexandria, VA 22304

ACA ETHICAL STANDARDS CASEBOOK
Fifth Edition

10 9

American Counseling Association
5999 Stevenson Avenue
Alexandria, VA 22304

Acquisitions and Development Editor
Carolyn Baker

Managing Editor
Michael Comlish

Copyeditor
Lucy Blanton

Cover design by Brian Gallagher

Library of Congress Cataloging-in-Publication Data

American Counseling Association
    ACA ethical standards casebook / [edited by] Barbara Herlihy, Gerald Corey. —
5th ed.
       p.   cm.
    Rev. ed. of: AACD ethical standards casebook. 4th ed. c1990.
    Includes bibliographical references.
    ISBN 1-55620-150-8
    1. American Counseling Association. 2. Counseling—Moral and ethical aspects—United States. 3. Counselors—Professional ethics—United States. 4. Counseling—Moral and ethical aspects—United States—Case studies. 5. Counselors—Professional ethics—United States—Case studies. I. Herlihy, Barbara. II. Corey, Gerald. III. American Association for Counseling and Development. AACD ethical standards casebook. IV. Title.
BF637.C6A37 1995
174'.915—dc20
                                                  95-41682
                                                   CIP

DEDICATION

To Scott, whose internal compass is true.

*To Heidi Jo and Cindy, stalwart skippers
in all kinds of weather.*

*And to our student readers — the next generation
of counseling professionals who will guide us
through some uncharted waters.*

Contents

ACKNOWLEDGEMENTS

T his fifth edition of the casebook is truly the product of the collaborative efforts of many people over time.

We want to begin by acknowledging individuals who contributed to the development of the 1995 ACA Code of Ethics and Standards of Practice that form the basis of the book. ACA Ethics Committee members who worked on writing and revising the documents during their various terms of service are Thomas E. Davis, Beth A. Durodoye, Holly Forester-Miller, Jorge Garcia, Barbara Herlihy, Wayne C. Huey, Richard Mukowski, Mark Salo, Diane Shepard-Tew, and Janice L. Smith.

Many, many ACA members also gave helpful input during the comment periods for early drafts of the Code of Ethics and Standards of Practice. Although we cannot thank them all by name, this is their book, too.

Theodore P. Remley, Jr., Executive Director of ACA from 1990 to 1994, was a guiding and organizing presence whose contributions were absolutely invaluable.

Other ACA headquarters staff members, particularly Harriet L. Glosoff and Pat Schwallie-Giddis, provided substantial support and facilitated the work in many ways.

The casebook, like the ethical standards, is a collaborative effort that reflects the work of numerous individuals. Graduate students at the University of Houston-Clear Lake who contributed some of the illustrative vignettes that appear in Part II are Karen Bryant, Julie C. Engelking, Leah Ibarguen, Patricia LaPoint, Dawn M. Penny, and Lynn Tolles.

Five individuals served as prepublication reviewers. They thoroughly read and reacted to the casebook in draft form. We are grateful for the extremely helpful comments and suggestions made by Sheila Bell (graduate student in social work, University of Southern California), Harriet Glosoff (University of Southern Mississippi), Michelle Muratori (graduate student in counseling psychology, Northwestern University), Pam Paisley (University of Georgia), and Janice L. Smith (Columbus College).

As always, it has been a joy to work with the capable and conscientious publications staff at ACA. Copy editor Lucy Blanton's thorough and meticulous work is appreciated, as is Carolyn Baker's prompt and careful attention throughout the production process.

And finally, we wish to acknowledge the authors and editors of previous editions of the casebook: Robert Callis, Mary E. DePauw, Larry Golden, and Sharon K. Pope. They gave us the foundation on which to build.

ABOUT THE AUTHORS

Barbara Herlihy, PhD, NCC, LPC, is an associate professor of counseling at Loyola University of New Orleans. She has served on the ACA Ethics Committee as chair (1987-89) and as a member (1986-87, 1993-94), as chair of the Ethics Committee of the Texas Counseling Association, as cochair of the Ethics/Professional Practices Network of the Association for Counselor Education and Supervision, and as a member of the Ethics Committee of the Association for Specialists in Group Work. She is the author of numerous articles and co-author of two previous books on ethical issues in counseling: the ACA *Ethical Standards Casebook*, 4th edition (1990), with Larry Golden; and *Dual Relationships in Counseling* (1992) with Gerald Corey. She is a frequent presenter of seminars and workshops on ethics across the United States, including ACA Professional Development National Workshops in 1995-96.

Gerald Corey, EdD, ABPP, NCC, is a professor of human services and counseling at California State University, Fullerton. He is a diplomate in counseling psychology and a fellow of the American Psychological Association and a fellow of the Association for Specialists in Group Work. He is recipient of the California State University — Fullerton Outstanding Professor of the Year Award in 1991 and an honorary doctorate in humane letters from National Louis University in 1992. Gerald Corey is the author or coauthor of 12 textbooks in counseling that are currently in print. In the past 20 years he has conducted workshops for mental health professionals at many universities in the United States as well as in Canada, Mexico, China, Germany, Belgium, and Scotland.

Virginia B. Allen, EdD, is professor of counselor education, Idaho State University, Pocatello, and former chair of the ACA Ethics Committee.

Michael L. Baltimore, PhD, is assistant professor of counseling and clinical programs, Columbus College, Columbus, Georgia.

Thomas E. Davis, PhD, is associate professor, School of Applied Behavioral Sciences and Educational Leadership, Ohio University, Athens, and a member of the ACA Ethics Committee 1994-97.

Beth A. Durodoye, EdD, is assistant professor of counselor education, University of North Texas, Denton, and a member of the ACA Ethics Committee 1993-96.

Lynda L. Fielstein, EdD, is associate professor, Department of Psychology and Counseling, University of Central Arkansas, Conway.

Holly Forester-Miller, PhD, is associate professor of counseling, West Virginia Graduate College, and cochair of the ACA Ethics Committee 1995-97.

Jorge Garcia, PhD, is associate professor of counseling, George Washington University, District of Columbia, and cochair of the ACA Ethics Committee 1993-95.

Harriet L. Glosoff, PhD, is assistant professor of counseling psychology, University of Southern Mississippi, Hattiesburg.

Larry Golden, PhD, is associate professor of counseling and guidance, University of Texas at San Antonio, and a former member of the ACA Ethics Committee.

Wayne C. Huey, PhD, is director of counseling, Lakeside High School, DeKalb County, Georgia, and a former member of the ACA Ethics Committee.

Geri Miller, PhD, is assistant professor, Department of Human Development and Psychological Counseling, Appalachian State University, Boone, North Carolina.

Mary E. Moline, PhD, is professor of family psychology, Seattle Pacific University, Seattle, Washington.

Theodore P. Remley, Jr., JD, PhD, is professor and coordinator of the Counseling Graduate Program, University of New Orleans, Louisiana.

Mark Salo, MEd, is a counselor at Chief Joseph Middle School in Bozeman, Montana, and cochair of the ACA Ethics Committee 1994-96.

James P. Sampson, Jr., PhD, is professor and codirector of the Center for the Study of Technology in Counseling and Career Development, Florida State University, Tallahasee.

Janice L. Smith, PhD, is assistant professor of counseling and clinical programs, Columbus College, Columbus, Georgia, and cochair of the ACA Ethics Committee 1992-94.

Derald Wing Sue, PhD, is professor of psychology, California School of Professional Psychology-Alameda, and California State University, Hayward.

George T. Williams, EdD, is professor, Department of Counseling, California State University, Fullerton.

J. Melvin Witmer, PhD, is professor emeritus, Ohio University, Athens.

Robert E. Wubbolding, EdD is professor of counseling, Xavier University, Cincinnati, Ohio, and director of the Center for Reality Therapy.

Daniel L. Yazak, DED, is assistant professor and chair, Counseling and Human Services, Montana State University-Billings.

Mary Ellen Young, PhD, CRC, is assistant professor, Department of Physical Medicine and Rehabilitation, Baylor College of Medicine, and associate director, Brain Injury Research Center, The Institute for Rehabilitation and Research, Houston, Texas.

MAKING THE BEST USE OF THE CASEBOOK

We hope that both students and seasoned practitioners of counseling will find this casebook to be a valuable resource. We believe the casebook can be effectively utilized in an ethics course or in a practicum or internship experience to help future members of our profession learn about their ethical responsibilities. Reading the incidents that illustrate the standards can help to clarify their intent, and discussing and debating the case studies can provide opportunities to deal with some of the complexities that students will later encounter in their work. Students have often told us that they had never thought about certain ethical questions until they were confronted with cases that raised difficult issues or posed dilemmas that could not be neatly resolved.

For experienced counselors, we hope that the casebook serves as a vehicle for continuing education and that you use the material to further your aspirational ethics. As you read, reflect, and discuss the material with your colleagues, we hope you will ask yourselves questions like, "How can I best monitor my own behavior?" "How can I apply relevant standards to situations I encounter?" "How can I develop increased ethical sensitivity?" "How can I ensure that I am thinking about what is best for my clients, or students, or supervisees?"

We believe that ethics is best viewed from a developmental perspective. We may look at issues in one way as students; later, with time and experience, our views are likely to have evolved. Ethical reasoning takes on new meaning as we encounter a variety of ethical dilemmas. Professional maturity entails our willingness to question ourselves, to discuss our doubts with colleagues, and to engage in continual self-monitoring.

INTRODUCTION

INTRODUCTION

Foundations of Codes of Ethics

The codes of ethics of the various professional organizations serve a number of purposes. Perhaps their most basic function is to educate members about sound ethical conduct. As professional counselors, we rely on the ethical standards of the American Counseling Association (ACA) to guide us in our work. Reading and reflecting on the standards can help us to expand our awareness, clarify our values, and subsequently inform clients about our professional responsibilities. Applying the standards to our own practices can assist us to raise significant questions, many of which may not have simple or definitive answers. The application of ethical guidelines to particular situations demands a keen ethical sensitivity.

A second function of ethical standards is to provide a mechanism for professional accountability. The ultimate end of a code of ethics is to protect the public. The American Counseling Association, through enforcement of its ethics code, holds its members accountable to the standards it has set forth. As professional counselors, we have an obligation not only to monitor our own behavior but also to encourage ethical conduct in our colleagues.

Codes of ethics also can serve as a catalyst for improving practice (Herlihy & Corey, 1994). No ethics code, no matter how lengthy or precisely worded, can address every situation that counselors might encounter in their work. Therefore, it is crucial that we read the code with an eye to both its letter and its spirit, and that we strive to understand the intentions that underlie each standard. This requires us to consider both mandatory and aspirational ethics. There is a very real difference between merely following the ethical codes and living out a commitment to practice with the highest ideals. *Mandatory ethics* is a term that describes a level of ethical functioning at which counselors merely act in compliance with minimal standards. By complying with these basic *musts* and *must nots*, counselors can meet the letter of the ethical standards of their profession. *Aspirational ethics*, a term that describes the highest standards of conduct to which professional counselors can aspire, requires that we do more. Practicing according to aspirational ethics entails an understanding of the spirit behind the code and of the principles on which it rests.

Five general principles guide the ethical conduct of professional counselors in their relationships with those whom they serve, including clients, students, and supervisees:

✦ *Autonomy* refers to independence and self-determination. Under this principle, counselors respect the freedom of clients to choose their own directions, make their own choices, and control their own lives. We have an ethical obligation to decrease client dependency and foster independent decision making. We refrain from imposing goals, avoid being judgmental, and are accepting of different values.

✦ *Nonmaleficence* means to do no harm. As counselors, we must take care that our actions do not risk hurting clients, even inadvertently. We have a responsibility to avoid engaging in practices that cause harm or have the potential to result in harm.

✦ *Beneficence* means to promote good, or mental health and wellness. This principle mandates that counselors actively promote the growth and welfare of those they serve.

✦ *Justice* is the foundation of our commitment to fairness in our professional relationships. Justice includes consideration of such factors as quality of services, allocation of time and resources, establishment of fees, and access to counseling services. This principle also refers to the fair treatment of an individual when his or her interests need to be considered in the context of the rights and interests of others.

✦ *Fidelity* means that counselors make honest promises and honor our commitments to clients, students, and supervisees. This principle involves creating a trusting and therapeutic climate in which people can search for their own solutions, and taking care not to deceive or exploit clients.

The ethical standards of ACA are grounded in a commitment to honoring these moral principles. They set forth minimally acceptable expectations (mandatory ethics) and describe the ideals of best practice (aspirational ethics).

Evolution of the ACA Ethical Standards and the Casebook

In 1953 Donald Super, then president of the newly formed American Personnel and Guidance Association (APGA), charged the association to develop a code of ethics. Work was commenced, and the first code of ethics for APGA was adopted 8 years later, in 1961, by its board of directors. In 1963 the Ethics Committee began to solicit and compile incidents having ethical implications, both positive and negative, that could illustrate the standards. The first edition of the *Ethical Standards Casebook* was published in 1965, 4 years after the ethical standards were adopted.

About 1972 it was recognized that the ethical standards needed to be revised, and that the casebook would also require revision. To reduce the time lag between publication of the standards and the accompanying casebook, two committees were appointed to work simultaneously: one to revise the standards and the other to collect illlustrative incidents for the casebook. The revised APGA Ethical Standards were adopted in 1974, and a single editor collated the collected incidents and prepared the second edition of the casebook, which was published in 1976.

Since the first revision of the code of ethics in 1974, the code has been revised every 7 years. The APGA Ethical Standards were revised and adopted in 1981. The editor of the second edition of the casebook prepared the third edition with the assistance of two co-editors. This third edition was published in 1982.

The association, then the American Association for Counseling and Development (AACD), adopted another revision of the code of ethics in 1988. Two lessons learned from previous experience were that a casebook should be published as soon as possible after the ethical standards are revised, and that the casebook editors must be aware of the thought processes that go into the revisions of the standards. Therefore, soon after the adoption of the revised code of ethics, the chair and a member of the Ethics Committee undertook the revision of the casebook. Input was solicited from a wide variety of sources to determine what changes were needed in the casebook to maximize its usefulness. The fourth edition was published in 1990.

The 1995 ACA Code of Ethics and Standards of Practice

Work toward preparing the current revision of ACA's ethical standards began in the fall of 1991, when a meeting was held to consider both the process of revising the code and general changes that might be needed in its content. The Ethics Committee embarked on an extensive revision process with several goals in mind: to develop a comprehensive set of ethical standards, to produce a user-friendly document, and to conduct an open revision process that could allow all ACA members opportunities to give input.

Recognition of the need for a comprehensive set of standards grew out of a concern that there has been a proliferation of ethics documents for counselors. Historically the ACA ethical standards were generic and did not include the unique concerns of ACA divisions, and as a result several divisions published their own sets of ethical guidelines. It has also been necessary for the national voluntary certifying bodies that credential counselors as well as for the counselor licensure boards in various states to establish their own codes of ethics. The existence of multiple codes of ethics has created a situation that is confusing both for professional counselors and for consumers of our services and is counterproductive to efforts to establish counseling as a unified profession (Herlihy & Remley, in press.) Therefore, the Ethics Committee carefully studied the ethics documents of ACA divisions and of other mental health professional associations, with a goal of incorporating standards that were applicable to all counselors into a single, comprehensive document. The 1995 Code of Ethics and Standards of Practice are intended to be a comprehensive set of standards that are acceptable to all groups of professional counselors that currently have their own sets of standards.

A second identified need was to reorganize the ACA ethical standards into a more readable format. Specific standards on issues such as confidentiality were scattered throughout the document, and members found the code difficult to read. The Ethics Committee began by identifying the major sections that a comprehensive code needed to include. The result was a new organization that includes sections on the counseling relationship; confidentiality; professional responsibility; relationships with other professionals; evaluation, assessment, and interpretation; teaching, training, and supervision; research and publication; and resolving ethical issues. Within the sections, each standard has a heading and is cross-referenced as appropriate.

A final consideration was the desire of the Ethics Committee to have an inclusive revision process that could allow opportunities for members, leaders, and relevant professional groups to give input and suggestions. A first draft of the proposed revised ethical standards was published to the membership in September 1993 and underwent a lengthy comment period. A second draft that reflected input and suggestions was published a year later, in September and October 1994. A final version was adopted in April 1995 and went into effect on July 1, 1995.

At the beginning of the revision process, applications for the position of editor of the fifth edition of the casebook were solicited, the editors were selected by the ACA Media Committee, and work was begun on the casebook in conjunction with the standards revision process.

The 1995 ACA Code of Ethics and Standards of Practice together address both mandatory and aspirational ethics. The rationale for creating not only an ethics code but also practice standards has not been clear to some ACA members. The Standards of Practice were developed in response to the needs of nonmembers of ACA to understand our minimal expectations for ethical behavior and to enforce these expectations in legal arenas. Increasingly, courts of law and state licensure boards are demanding that the counseling profession define its minimal standards to which all counselors may be held accountable. The Standards of Practice are comparatively brief and specify minimal behaviors required of professional counselors (mandatory ethics) that can be understood and evaluated by individuals outside the counseling profession. The Code of Ethics is lengthier, gives more detailed guidance regarding the standards of practice, and includes statements describing the best practice that represents the ideals of the profession (aspirational ethics).

Enforcement of the Code of Ethics

All ACA members are required to adhere to both the Code of Ethics and the Standards of Practice. (For the complete text see Part I of this casebook or ACA, 1995.) The Code of Ethics serves as the basis for processing complaints of ethical violations against members.

The ACA Ethics Committee is responsible for the enforcement of the Code of Ethics (ACA, 1994). Because this aspect of the committee's work is strictly confidential, many ACA members may not be aware of how the committee performs this function.

Dealing With Complaints. The committee considers a complaint if the individual who is the subject of the complaint is a current member of ACA or was a member when the alleged violation(s) occurred. The ACA Ethics Committee has no jurisdiction over nonmembers. Only written complaints, signed by complainants, are considered. The Ethics Committee does not act on anonymous complaints. Members of the general public, ACA members and other professionals, and the cochair of the Ethics Committee may initiate complaints.

If you believe that an ACA member has acted or is acting unethically, according to the ACA Code of Ethics you have an ethical responsibility to take action (Standard H.2.a.). Your first step should be to try to resolve the issue informally, directly with the individual in question, if this is feasible in the situation and you can do so without violating the confidentiality rights involved. If informal resolution is not feasible or if it is attempted without success, you should write a letter to the Ethics Committee outlining the nature of the complaint, signing it and sending it in an envelope marked *confidential*. You then receive back a formal complaint that identifies all the ACA ethical standards that might have been violated if the accusations are true. You are asked to sign the complaint (or suggest modifications if needed) and a release-of-information form. With your authorization, the accused member then receives copies of the formal complaint and any evidence or documents you have submitted in support of the complaint.

After the accused member has responded to the charges and all pertinent materials have been gathered, the Ethics Committee meets to deliberate and decide on the complaint. Each complaint is given the most careful consideration. Because most complaints are complex, alleging violations of multiple standards and often including a considerable amount of documentation, discussions of each case are typically lengthy and involved. All perspectives are fully examined before a decision is reached. The Ethics Committee has the following options for disposition of a complaint:

+ dismiss the complaint or dismiss charges within the complaint; or
+ determine that ethical standards have been violated and impose sanctions.

Possible sanctions include a reprimand, probation or suspension for a specified period of time subject to Ethics Committee review of compliance, permanent expulsion from ACA membership, or other corrective action. Remedial requirements may be imposed along with a reprimand, probation, or suspension. A decision to expel a member requires a unanimous vote. After the appeals process has been completed or the deadline for appeal has passed, the sanctions of suspension and expulsion are published to the membership.

For detailed information and the complete text of Policies and Procedures for Processing Complaints of Ethical Violations, see Appendix A (or ACA, 1994, 1995).

What to Do If a Complaint Is Filed Against You. Few events in a counselor's professional life can be more distressing than to learn that he or she has been charged with an ethics violation. Although most counselors spend their lifelong careers without having to deal with this situation, a few suggestions are offered here to help counselors be better prepared to respond.

First, take the complaint seriously. Although you may believe that the charges are unwarranted, it is not in your best interest to ignore them or to respond in a casual manner. We have occasionally heard counselors make statements like, "Why worry about an ethics complaint to the professional association? The worst that could happen is that I would lose my membership." Although it is true that the most severe sanction available to the ACA Ethics Committee is permanent expulsion from the association, it is important to know that when a sanction of suspension or expulsion is imposed, notifications are made to counselor licensure, certification, or registry boards, other mental health boards, the ACA Insurance Trust, and other entities. This could very well trigger an investigation by a state licensing board that could result in loss of license to practice.

Second, respond fully to the charges. You are required to cooperate with the Ethics Committee in its investigation (Standard H.3.). You should also keep in mind that the Ethics Committee members who will be deciding the outcome of the complaint do not know you personally and can deliberate only on material they have before them. We suggest that you write your response as deliberately and dispassionately as possible. Although you may be tempted to write an emotional, impassioned defense, the committee must deal with the factual material provided. The Ethics Committee is charged to compile an objective, factual account of the dispute and make the best possible recommendation for its resolution.

Attend to the details of the complaint "with scrupulous attention" (Crawford, 1994, p. 92). Gear your response to the specific charges, addressing each section of the ACA Code of Ethics you have been accused of violating, and submitting documentation. For instance, if you have utilized a powerful technique (one that might be considered experimental) with a client who has filed a complaint, it is useful to submit documentation that you are trained in the specific technique, are working under supervision, have regularly consulted about the case with an expert in the technique, and/or have taken other precautions to prevent harm as specified in the Code of Ethics.

Third, even if you are surprised that a client or colleague has made an accusation against you, you should not attempt to contact the complainant to discuss the situation. Despite your best intentions, doing so could be deemed as an attempt to coerce or unduly influence the client or colleague (Crawford, 1994). Instead, you might consider notifying your professional liability insurance carrier that a complaint has been made.

Finally, it is prudent to consult with an attorney who can help you prepare your response and provide you with legal counsel. Although an ethics committee is not a court of law, an attorney who is familiar with due process and is skilled at formulating responses to charges of wrongdoing can be a helpful resource.

Developing a Personal Ethical Stance

As we have noted, ethically conscientious counselors require more of themselves than simply following the letter of the ethical standards. Their decisions are not motivated by a desire to avoid charges of unethical or unprofessional conduct but rather by a desire to provide the best possible services to clients, students, or supervisees. Thus, although it is important for us to familiarize ourselves thoroughly with the ethical codes, it is also necessary for each of us to develop a personal ethical sense. We need to examine our own practices, looking for subtle ways that we might not be acting as ethically as we could. Certainly, gross unethical conduct can be detected, and enforcement is possible. Yet there are many less obvious situations in which counselors can fail to do what is appropriate. A few examples of ways that counselors might engage in ethically questionable behavior, which would be difficult for others to detect and thus difficult to enforce, include

+ prolonging the number of counseling sessions to satisfy the counselor's emotional needs or financial considerations;

+ being unaware of countertransference reactions to a client, student, or supervisee, thus inadvertently increasing resistance and thwarting growth;

+ imposing values, goals, or strategies on clients that are not congruent with their cultural background;

+ using techniques or strategies that are comfortable for the counselor rather than those that are aimed at helping clients achieve their therapeutic goals; and

+ practicing with little enthusiasm or tolerating boredom and apathy.

As Golden (1992) has noted, the work of the counselor is fraught with ambiguities. When we find ourselves navigating in waters that are not clearly charted by our profession's ethical codes, we must be guided by an internal ethical compass.

We hope that counselors use the 1995 ACA Code of Ethics, and this casebook, as a means to further their own aspirational ethics. As we have noted, ethics codes do not make decisions for us. Although the codes do help to guide us, in the final analysis each of us is responsible for our own actions. We must be willing to grapple with the gray areas, raise questions, discuss our ethical concerns with colleagues, and monitor our own behavior.

An Ethical Decision-Making Model

Counselors are often faced with situations that require sound decision-making ability. Determining the appropriate course to take when faced with a difficult ethical dilemma can be a challenge. To assist ACA members in meeting this challenge, the ACA Ethics

Committee has developed *A Practitioner's Guide to Ethical Decision Making* (ACA, 1996). This guide, written by committee members Holly Forester-Miller and Thomas E. Davis, incorporates the work of Van Hoose and Paradise (1979), Kitchener (1984), Stadler (1986), Haas and Malouf (1995), Forester-Miller and Rubenstein (1992), and Sileo and Kopala (1993) into a practical, sequential, seven-step model. The steps of this ethical decision-making model (as excerpted from *A Practitioner's Guide to Ethical Decision Making*, by Holly Forester-Miller and Thomas E. Davis — ACA, 1996) are as follows:

1. **Identify the problem.** Gather as much information as you can that will illuminate the situation. In doing so, it is important to be as specific and objective as possible. Writing ideas on paper may help you gain clarity. Outline the facts, separating out innuendoes, assumptions, hypotheses, or suspicions. There are several questions you can ask yourself: Is it an ethical, legal, professional, or clinical problem? Is it a combination of more than one of these? If a legal question exists, seek legal advice.

   Other questions that it may be useful to ask yourself are Is the issue related to me and what I am or am not doing? Is it related to a client and/or the client's significant others and what they are or are not doing? Is it related to the institution or agency and their policies and procedures? If the problem can be resolved by implementing a policy of an institution or agency, you can look to the agency's guidelines. It is good to remember that dilemmas you face are often complex, so a useful guideline is to examine the problem from several perspectives and avoid searching for a simplistic solution.

2. **Apply the ACA Code of Ethics.** After you have clarified the problem, refer to the ACA Code of Ethics to see if the issue is addressed there. If there is an applicable standard or several standards and they are specific and clear, following the course of action indicated should lead to a resolution of the problem. To be able to apply the ethical standards, it is essential that you have read them carefully and that you understand their implications.

   If the problem is more complex and a resolution does not seem apparent, then you probably have a true ethical dilemma and need to proceed with further steps in the ethical decision-making process.

3. **Determine the nature and dimensions of the dilemma.** There are several avenues to follow in order to ensure that you have examined the problem in all its various dimensions:

   ✦ Consider the moral principles of autonomy, nonmaleficence, beneficence, justice, and fidelity. Decide which principles apply to the specific situation, and determine which principle takes priority for you in this case. In theory, each principle is of equal value, which means that it is your challenge to determine the priorities when two or more of them are in conflict.
   ✦ Review the relevant professional literature to help ensure that you are using the most current professional thinking in reaching a decision.
   ✦ Consult with experienced professional colleagues and/or supervisors. As they review with you the information you have gathered, they may see other issues that are relevant or provide a perspective you have not considered. They may also be able to identify aspects of the dilemma that you are not viewing objectively.
   ✦ Contact your state or national professional associations to see if they can provide help with the dilemma.

4. **Generate potential courses of action.** Brainstorm as many possible courses of action as possible. Be creative and consider all options, without evaluating the ideas at this point. If possible, enlist the help of at least one colleague to help you generate options.

5. **Consider the potential consequences of all options and determine a course of action.** Considering the information you have gathered and the priorities you have set, evaluate each option and assess the potential consequences for all parties involved. Ponder the implications of each course of action for the client, for others who will be affected, and for yourself as a counselor. Eliminate the options that clearly do not give the desired results or cause even more problematic consequences. Review the remaining options to determine which option or

combination of options best fits the situation and addresses the priorities you have identified.

6. **Evaluate the selected course of action.** Review the selected course of action to determine if it presents any new ethical considerations. Stadler (1986) suggested applying three simple tests to the selected course of action to ensure that it is appropriate. In applying the test of justice, assess your own sense of fairness by determining whether you would treat others the same in this situation. For the test of publicity, ask yourself whether you would want your behavior reported in the press. The test of universality asks you to assess whether you could recommend the same course of action to another counselor in the same situation.

   If the course of action you have selected seems to present new ethical issues, then you need to go back to the beginning and reevaluate each step of the process. Perhaps you have chosen the wrong option, or you might have identified the problem incorrectly. If you can answer in the affirmative to each of the questions suggested by Stadler (thus passing the tests of justice, publicity, and universality) and you are satisfied that you have selected an appropriate course of action, then you are ready to move on to implementation.

7. **Implement the course of action.** Taking the appropriate action in an ethical dilemma is often difficult. The final step involves strengthening your ego to allow you to carry out your plan. After implementing your course of action, it is a good practice to follow up on the situation to assess whether your actions had the anticipated effect and consequences.

   It is important to realize that different professionals may implement different courses of action in the same situation. There is rarely one right answer to a complex ethical dilemma. However, if you follow a systematic model, you can be assured that you will be able to give a professional explanation for the course of action you chose. Van Hoose and Paradise (1979) suggested that a counselor "is probably acting in an ethically responsible way concerning a client if (1) he or she has maintained personal and professional honesty, coupled with (2) the best interests of the client, (3) without malice or personal gain, and (4) can justify his or her actions as the best judgment of what should be done based upon the current state of the profession" (p. 58). Following this model will help to ensure that all four of these conditions have been met.

> ### The Ethical Decision-Making Model at a Glance
>
> 1. *Identify the problem.*
> 2. *Apply the ACA Code of Ethics.*
> 3. *Determine the nature and dimensions of the dilemma.*
> 4. *Generate potential courses of action.*
> 5. *Consider the potential consequences of all options, and determine a course of action.*
> 6. *Evaluate the selected course of action.*
> 7. *Implement the course of action.*

An Inventory of Your Attitudes and Beliefs About Ethical Issues

As a way to encourage you to think critically about the ACA Code of Ethics, we have created the following self-inventory to help you examine your reactions to many of the ethical issues that are addressed by the code. The items in the inventory relate directly to specific aspects of the code.

The inventory is different from the typical multiple-choice test in which there is one correct answer. This inventory is intended to promote critical thinking, and to identify and assess your beliefs about ethical guidelines. For each item, identify the letter (or letters) of the response (or responses) that most accurately identifies your thinking about the issue. There is a blank line for you to write your own response if none of the choices seems appropriate to you. If you think all the choices are appropriate, you can write *all of the above* on the blank line.

1. The counselor's primary obligation is to

    a. avoid a malpractice suit.
    b. enlist the family's involvement to help the client reach counseling goals.
    c. promote the values of society.
    d. respect the integrity and promote the welfare of the client.
    e. _____ .

2. Counselors who work with clients from backgrounds different from their own

   a. are likely to find a referral necessary because of basic conflicts in values.
   b. respect these differences.
   c. do all that they can to gain knowledge about the client.
   d. attempt to influence the client to adjust to the values of society.
   e. _____ .

3. It is ethically imperative to secure the client's informed consent

   a. except for clients who are unable to give consent.
   b. except for minor clients.
   c. except for involuntary clients.
   d. for all clients.
   e. _____ .

4. Informed consent implies that clients have a right to

   a. expect absolute confidentiality.
   b. have information about counseling explained to them.
   c. refuse any recommended services.
   d. expect a guarantee that counseling will be effective.
   e. _____ .

5. Counselors who meet their personal needs through their work are

   a. behaving ethically so long as they do not do so at the expense of their clients.
   b. behaving unethically.
   c. not altruistically motivated.
   d. likely to exploit their clients for personal gain.
   e. _____ .

6. With respect to the personal values of counselors, it is

   a. sometimes necessary for counselors to impose their values on clients.

   b. essential that counselors understand how their values influence the counseling process.

   c. a good policy for counselors to accept a client only if the client holds values similar to their own.

   d. important that counselors realize how their values and beliefs apply in a diverse society.

   e. _____ .

7. Dual relationships with clients, students, or supervisees are

   a. best avoided whenever possible.

   b. fraught with possibilities for exploitation and are, therefore, always unethical.

   c. generally unethical, illegal, and unprofessional.

   d. best decided in each situation, by balancing potential risks and benefits.

   e. _____ .

8. Sexual intimacies with current clients

   a. are unethical.

   b. are never justified.

   c. may be justified if the client initiates the relationship.

   d. represent a serious exploitation of the client's trust.

   e. _____ .

9. Counselors who offer group counseling have an ethical obligation to

   a. conduct a screening interview with potential group members.

   b. protect clients against physical and psychological trauma resulting from interactions within the group.

   c. provide follow-up assistance after termination, if needed.

   d. develop safety measures when using experimental methods.

   e. _____ .

10. In establishing fees for counseling services, counselors

   a. consider the financial status of clients in the local area.

b. decide how much they want to charge and never lower their set fee.

c. provide a referral for clients who cannot afford their fee.

d. may engage in bartering with clients who cannot afford the fee.

e. _____ .

11. If counselors determine that they are unable to be of professional assistance to a client

a. ethical practice dictates that they terminate the relationship.

b. they should refer the client.

c. they should discuss the situation with the client.

d. they should continue seeing the client if the client declines a suggested referral.

e. _____ .

12. Ethical practice dictates that counselors terminate a counseling relationship when

a. it is reasonably clear that the client is no longer benefiting.

b. counseling services are no longer necessary.

c. counseling no longer serves the client's needs or interests.

d. clients do not pay the fees charged.

e. _____ .

13. Counselors demonstrate their respect for privacy of their clients by

a. avoiding unnecessary disclosures of confidential information.

b. recognizing that the right to privacy belongs to counselors and may be waived if it is in the best interests of the client.

c. consulting with another mental health professional when they are unsure about legal exceptions to confidentiality.

d. securing the client's written permission before making any disclosure of confidential information.

e. _____ .

14. With respect to records of counseling sessions, counselors

    a. have no ethical obligation to maintain unnecessary records.
    b. maintain records that are necessary to render quality service to clients.
    c. must legally and ethically keep records for 10 years.
    d. obtain the client's permission to disclose or transfer records to third parties.
    e. _____ .

15. Counselors must practice within their boundaries of competence, which implies that they

    a. should develop a clearly defined specialty area.
    b. take steps to maintain competence in the skills they use.
    c. consult with other professionals when they have concerns about ethical and professional practice.
    d. practice strictly within the scope of their education and training.
    e. _____ .

16. When the personal problems or conflicts of counselors are likely to lead to harm to a client, counselors

    a. seek assistance for their own problems.
    b. may limit, suspend, or terminate their relationship with a client.
    c. are honest with their clients about their difficulties and engage in detailed self-disclosure with the client.
    d. make it a practice to consult with other professionals about the matter.
    e. _____ .

17. In recruiting clients, counselors should realize

    a. it is acceptable to split fees with another professional who has referred a client to a private practitioner.
    b. they have an ethical right to expect to receive a fee for making a referral to another counselor.
    c. they do not accept fees for referring clients.

    d. they should expect to receive referrals in return when they make referrals to another professional.

    e. _____ .

18. It is not ethical for counselors to discriminate based on differences in

    a. age.
    b. sexual orientation.
    c. religion.
    d. culture.
    e. _____ .

19. In selecting assessment techniques, making evaluations, and interpreting the performance of special populations, ethical practice involves

    a. proceeding with caution.
    b. recognizing the effects of age, color, culture, disability, ethnicity, race, gender, religion, sexual orientation, and socioeconomic status on test administration and interpretation.
    c. treating all clients exactly alike to ensure uniformity of practice.
    d. not allowing diversity issues to interfere with the quality of testing procedures.
    e. _____ .

20. With respect to dual relationships with their students, counselor educators

    a. serve as role models for professional behavior.
    b. are aware of the power differential and take steps to minimize any risks to students.
    c. explain to students the potential for such a relationship to become exploitive.
    d. always refrain from getting involved in any kind of dual relationship.
    e. _____ .

21. Counselor education programs should provide an orientation session prior to accepting students. The orientation should include information

    a. about the subject matter to be covered in the program.
    b. regarding training components that encourage or require self-growth and self-disclosure as part of the training process.
    c. about the history of the counseling profession.
    d. on up-to-date employment prospects for graduates.
    e. _____ .

22. It is an ethical responsibility of counselor education programs to

    a. present varied theoretical positions.
    b. teach a single theoretical position to minimize confusion among students about how theory translates into practice.
    c. insist that students master a single theoretical orientation early in their programs of study.
    d. provide information about the scientific bases of professional practice.
    e. _____ .

23. Regarding self-growth experiences as a part of a training program

    a. it is ethical to grade students on how self-disclosing and genuine they are in their interpersonal relationships in the classroom.
    b. it is important to develop safeguards so that risks to students are minimized.
    c. it is essential to have clear purposes in mind and maintain appropriate boundaries.
    d. these experiences are unethical because students can easily be put into situations that are uncomfortable for them.
    e. _____ .

24. In conducting research involving use of human subjects, ethical practice demands that counselors

    a. are sensitive to diversity issues with special populations.
    b. use deception only when good research design indicates its value.
    c. seek consultation and develop safeguards to protect the rights of research participants.
    d. obtain adequate informed consent of the research participants.
    e. _____ .

25. Involuntary participation in a research project is appropriate only when

    a. it can be demonstrated that participation will have no harmful effects on subjects.
    b. it is essential to the investigation.
    c. the participants are paid.
    d. the researcher is studying ways that involuntary participation might influence outcomes.
    e. _____ .

26. In reporting results of research, ethical practice involves

    a. presenting accurate results.
    b. reporting unfavorable results.
    c. disguising the identities of those who participated in the study.
    d. making available enough information so that other researchers could replicate the study.
    e. _____ .

27. When counselors have reasons to believe that another counselor is violating an ethical standard, an appropriate first step to take is to

    a. seek informal resolution.
    b. ignore the situation.
    c. report the suspected violation to an ethics committee.

   d. seek out clients of this counselor to discover more details about the suspected behavior.

   e. _____ .

28. If a counselor confronts a colleague about a suspected ethical violation and this informal process does not resolve the situation, the appropriate course for the counselor to follow is to
   a. respect the differences of opinion with the colleague.
   b. report the colleague to an ethics committee.
   c. seek consultation from a supervisor.
   d. continue talking with the colleague in hopes of changing his or her behavior.
   e. _____ .

29. The practice of bartering may be acceptable when
   a. the relationship is not exploitive.
   b. the client requests it.
   c. the counselor feels comfortable with the practice.
   d. a clear contract is established.
   e. _____ .

30. Counselors who refuse to offer pro bono service by giving some of their time and talent to endeavors for which there is little or no financial return
   a. should be considered unethical.
   b. should cancel their membership in ACA.
   c. are clearly motivated by self-interest and financial gain, and should leave the counseling profession.
   d. can be considered ethical if they are financially stressed.
   e. _____ .

PART I

ACA CODE OF ETHICS AND STANDARDS OF PRACTICE

Code of Ethics

The American Counseling Association is an educational, scientific, and professional organization whose members are dedicated to the enhancement of human development throughout the life-span. Association members recognize diversity in our society and embrace a cross-cultural approach in support of the worth, dignity, potential, and uniqueness of each individual.

     The specification of a code of ethics enables the association to clarify to current and future members, and to those served by members, the nature of the ethical responsibilities held in common by its members. As the code of ethics of the association, this document establishes principles that define the ethical behavior of association members. All members of the American Counseling Association are required to adhere to the Code of Ethics and the Standards of Practice. The Code of Ethics will serve as the basis for processing ethical complaints initiated against members of the association.

SECTION A: THE COUNSELING RELATIONSHIP

A.1. Client Welfare

a. *Primary Responsibility.*

The primary responsibility of counselors is to respect the dignity and to promote the welfare of clients.

b. *Positive Growth and Development.*

Counselors encourage client growth and development in ways that foster the clients' interest and welfare; counselors avoid fostering dependent counseling relationships.

c. *Counseling Plans.*

Counselors and their clients work jointly in devising integrated, individual counseling plans that offer reasonable promise of success and are consistent with abilities and circumstances of clients. Counselors and clients regularly review counseling plans to ensure their continued viability and effectiveness, respecting clients' freedom of choice. (See A.3.b.)

d. *Family Involvement.*

Counselors recognize that families are usually important in clients' lives and strive to enlist family understanding and involvement as a positive resource, when appropriate.

e. *Career and Employment Needs.*

Counselors work with their clients in considering employment in jobs and circumstances that are consistent with the clients' overall abilities, vocational limitations, physical restrictions, general temperament, interest and aptitude patterns, social skills, education, general qualifications, and other relevant characteristics and needs. Counselors neither place nor participate in placing clients in positions that will result in damaging the interest and the welfare of clients, employers, or the public.

A.2. Respecting Diversity

a. *Nondiscrimination.*

Counselors do not condone or engage in discrimination based on age, color, culture, disability, ethnic group, gender, race, religion, sexual orientation, marital status, or socioeconomic status. (See C.5.a., C.5.b., and D.1.i.)

b. *Respecting Differences.*

Counselors will actively attempt to understand the diverse cultural backgrounds of the clients with whom they work. This includes, but is not limited to, learning how the counselor's own cultural/ethnic/racial identity impacts her or his values and beliefs about the counseling process. (See E.8. and F.2.i.)

A.3. Client Rights

a. *Disclosure to Clients.*

When counseling is initiated, and throughout the counseling process as necessary, counselors inform clients of the purposes, goals techniques, procedures, limitations, potential risks, and benefits of services to be performed, and other pertinent information. Counselors take steps to ensure that clients understand the implications of diagnosis, the intended use of tests and reports, fees, and billing arrangements. Clients have the right to expect confidentality and to be provided with an explanation of its limitations, including supervision and/or treatment team professionals; to obtain clear information about their case records; to participate in the ongoing counseling plans; and to refuse any recommended services and be advised of the consequences of such refusal. (See E.5.a. and G.2.)

b. *Freedom of Choice.*

Counselors offer clients the freedom to choose whether to enter into a counseling relationship and to determine which professional(s) will provide counseling. Restrictions that limit choices of clients are fully explained. (See A.1.c.)

c. *Inability to Give Consent.*

When counseling minors or persons unable to give voluntary informed consent, counselors act in these clients' best interests. (See B.3.)

A.4. Clients Served by Others

If a client is receiving services from another mental health professional, counselors, with client consent, inform the professional persons already involved and develop clear agreements to avoid confusion and conflict for the client. (See C.6.c.)

A.5. Personal Needs and Values

a. *Personal Needs.*

In the counseling relationship, counselors are aware of the intimacy and responsibilities inherent in the counseling relationship, maintain respect for clients, and avoid actions that seek to meet their personal needs at the expense of clients.

b. *Personal Values.*

Counselors are aware of their own values, attitudes, beliefs, and behaviors and how these apply in a diverse society, and avoid imposing their values on clients. (See C.5.a.)

A.6. Dual Relationships

a. *Avoid When Possible.*

Counselors are aware of their influential positions with respect to clients, and they avoid exploiting the trust and dependency of clients. Counselors make every effort to avoid dual relationships with clients that could impair professional judgment or increase the risk of harm to clients. (Examples of such relationships include, but are not limited to, familial, social, financial, business, or close personal relationships with clients.) When a dual relationship cannot be avoided, counselors take appropriate professional precautions such as informed consent, consultation, supervision, and documentation to ensure that judgment is not impaired and no exploitation occurs. (See F.1.b.)

b. *Superior/Subordinate Relationships.*

Counselors do not accept as clients superiors or subordinates with whom they have administrative, supervisory, or evaluative relationships.

A.7. Sexual Intimacies With Clients

a. *Current Clients.*

Counselors do not have any type of sexual intimacies with clients and do not counsel persons with whom they have had a sexual relationship.

b. *Former Clients.*

Counselors do not engage in sexual intimacies with former clients within a minimum of 2 years after terminating the counseling relationship. Counselors who engage in such relationship after 2 years following termination have the responsibility to examine and document thoroughly that such relations did not have an exploitative nature, based on factors such as duration of counseling, amount of time since counseling, termination circumstances, client's personal history and mental status, adverse impact on the client, and actions by the counselor suggesting a plan to initiate a sexual relationship with the client after termination.

A.8. Multiple Clients

When counselors agree to provide counseling services to two or more persons who have a relationship (such as husband and wife, or parents and children), counselors clarify at the outset which person or persons are clients and the nature of the relationships they will have with each involved person. If it becomes apparent that counselors may be called upon to perform potentially conflicting roles, they clarify, adjust, or withdraw from roles appropriately. (See B.2. and B.4.d.)

A.9. Group Work

a. *Screening.*

Counselors screen prospective group counseling/therapy participants. To the extent possible, counselors select members whose needs and goals are compatible with goals of the group, who will not impede the group process, and whose well-being will not be jeopardized by the group experience.

b. *Protecting Clients.*

In a group setting, counselors take reasonable precautions to protect clients from physical or psychological trauma.

A.10. Fees and Bartering (See D.3.a. and D.3.b.)

a. *Advance Understanding.*

Counselors clearly explain to clients, prior to entering the counseling relationship, all financial arrangements related to professional services including the use of collection agencies or legal measures for nonpayment. (A.11.c.)

b. *Establishing Fees.*

In establishing fees for professional counseling services, counselors consider the financial status of clients and locality. In the event that the established fee structure is inappropriate for a client, assistance is provided in attempting to find comparable services of acceptable cost. (See A.10.d., D.3.a., and D.3.b.)

c. *Bartering Discouraged.*

Counselors ordinarily refrain from accepting goods or services from clients in return for counseling services because such arrangements create inherent potential for conflicts, exploitation, and distortion of the professional relationship. Counselors may participate in bartering only if the relationship is not exploitive, if the client requests it, if a clear written contract is established, and if such arrangements are an accepted practice among professionals in the community. (See A.6.a.)

d. *Pro Bono Service.*

Counselors contribute to society by devoting a portion of their professional activity to services for which there is little or no financial return (pro bono).

A.11. Termination and Referral

a. *Abandonment Prohibited.*

Counselors do not abandon or neglect clients in counseling. Counselors assist in making appropriate arrangements for the continuation of treatment, when necessary, during interruptions such as vacations, and following termination.

b. *Inability to Assist Clients.*

If counselors determine an inability to be of professional assistance to clients, they avoid entering or immediately terminate a counseling relationship. Counselors are knowledgeable about referral resources and suggest appropriate alternatives. If clients decline the suggested referral, counselors should discontinue the relationship.

c. *Appropriate Termination.*

Counselors terminate a counseling relationship, securing client agreement when possible, when it is reasonably clear that the client is no longer benefiting, when services are no longer required, when counseling no longer serves the client's needs or interests, when clients do not pay fees charged, or when agency or institution limits do not allow provision of further counseling services. (See A.10.b. and C.2.g.)

A.12. Computer Technology

a. *Use of Computers.*

When computer applications are used in counseling services, counselors ensure that (1) the client is intellectually, emotionally, and physically capable of using the computer application; (2) the computer application is appropriate for the needs of the client; (3) the client understands the purpose and operation of the computer applications; and (4) a follow-up of client use of a computer application is provided to correct possible misconceptions, discover inappropriate use, and assess subsequent needs.

b. *Explanation of Limitations.*

Counselors ensure that clients are provided information as a part of the counseling relationship that adequately explains the limitations of computer technology.

c. *Access to Computer Applications.*

Counselors provide for equal access to computer applications in counseling services. (See A.2.a.)

SECTION B: CONFIDENTIALITY

B.1. Right to Privacy

a. *Respect for Privacy.*

Counselors respect their clients' right to privacy and avoid illegal and unwarranted disclosures of confidential information. (See A.3.a. and B.6.a.)

b. *Client Waiver.*

The right to privacy may be waived by the client or his or her legally recognized representative.

c. *Exceptions.*

The general requirement that counselors keep information confidential does not apply when disclosure is required to prevent clear and imminent danger to the client or others or when legal requirements demand that confidential information be revealed. Counselors consult with other professionals when in doubt as to the validity of an exception.

d. *Contagious, Fatal Diseases.*

A counselor who receives information confirming that a client has a disease commonly known to be both communicable and fatal is justified in disclosing information to an identifiable third party, who by his or her relationship with the client is at a high risk of contracting the disease. Prior to making a disclosure the counselor should ascertain that the client has not already informed the third party about his or her disease and that the client is not intending to inform the third party in the immediate future. (See B.1.c and B.1.f)

e. *Court-Ordered Disclosure.*

When court ordered to release confidential information without a client's permission, counselors request to the court that the disclosure not be required due to potential harm to the client or counseling relationship. (See B.1.c.)

f. *Minimal Disclosure.*

When circumstances require the disclosure of confidential information, only essential information is revealed. To the extent possible, clients are informed before confidential information is disclosed.

g. *Explanation of Limitations.*

When counseling is initiated and throughout the counseling process as necessary, counselors inform clients of the limitations of confidentiality and identify foreseeable situations in which confidentiality must be breached. (See G.2.a.)

h. *Subordinates.*

Counselors make every effort to ensure that privacy and confidentiality of clients are maintained by subordinates including employees, supervisees, clerical assistants, and volunteers. (See B.1.a.)

i. *Treatment Teams.*

If client treatment will involve a continued review by a treatment team, the client will be informed of the team's existence and composition.

B.2. Groups and Families

a. *Group Work.*

In group work, counselors clearly define confidentiality and the parameters for the specific group being entered, explain its importance, and discuss the difficulties related to confidentiality involved in group work. The fact that confidentiality cannot be guaranteed is clearly communicated to group members.

b. *Family Counseling.*

In family counseling, information about one family member cannot be disclosed to another member without permission. Counselors protect the privacy rights of each family member. (See A.8., B.3., and B.4.d.)

B.3. Minor or Incompetent Clients

When counseling clients who are minors or individuals who are unable to give voluntary, informed consent, parents or guardians may be included in the counseling process as appropriate. Counselors act in the best interests of clients and take measures to safeguard confidentiality. (See A.3.c.)

B.4. Records

a. *Requirement of Records.*

Counselors maintain records necessary for rendering professional services to their clients and as required by laws, regulations, or agency or institution procedures.

b. *Confidentiality of Records.*

Counselors are responsible for securing the safety and confidentiality of any counseling records they create, maintain, transfer, or destroy whether the records are written, taped, computerized, or stored in any other medium. (See B.1.a.)

c. *Permission to Record or Observe.*

Counselors obtain permission from clients prior to electronically recording or observing sessions. (See A.3.a.)

d. *Client Access.*

Counselors recognize that counseling records are kept for the benefit of clients, and therefore provide access to records and copies of records when requested by competent clients, unless the records contain information that may be misleading and detrimental to the client. In situations involving multiple clients, access to records is limited to those parts of records that do not include confidential information related to another client. (See A.8., B.1.a., and B.2.b.)

e. *Disclosure or Transfer.*

Counselors obtain written permission from clients to disclose or transfer records to legitimate third parties unless exceptions to confidentiality exist as listed in Section B.1. Steps are taken to ensure that receivers of counseling records are sensitive to their confidential nature.

B.5. Research and Training

a. *Data Disguise Required.*

Use of data derived from counseling relationships for purposes of training, research, or publication is confined to content that is disguised to ensure the anonymity of the individuals involved. (See B.1.g. and G.3.d.)

b. *Agreement for Identification.*

Identification of a client in a presentation or publication is permissible only when the client has reviewed the material and has agreed to its presentation or publication. (See G.3.d.)

B.6.   Consultation

a. *Respect for Privacy.*

Information obtained in a consulting relationship is discussed for professional purposes only with persons clearly concerned with the case. Written and oral reports present data germane to the purposes of the consultation, and every effort is made to protect client identity and avoid undue invasion of privacy.

b. *Cooperating Agencies.*

Before sharing information, counselors make efforts to ensure that there are defined policies in other agencies serving the counselor's clients that effectively protect the confidentiality of information.

SECTION C: PROFESSIONAL RESPONSIBILITY

C.1.   Standards Knowledge

Counselors have a responsibility to read, understand, and follow the Code of Ethics and the Standards of Practice.

C.2.   Professional Competence

a. *Boundaries of Competence.*

Counselors practice only within the boundaries of their competence, based on their education, training, supervised experience, state and national professional credentials, and appropriate professional experience. Counselors will demonstrate a commitment to gain knowledge, personal awareness, sensitivity, and skills pertinent to working with a diverse client population.

b. *New Specialty Areas of Practice.*

Counselors practice in specialty areas new to them only after appropriate education, training, and supervised experience. While developing skills in new specialty areas, counselors take steps to ensure the competence of their work and to protect others from possible harm.

c. *Qualified for Employment.*

Counselors accept employment only for positions for which they are qualified by education, training, supervised experience, state and national professional credentials, and appropriate professional experience. Counselors hire for professional counseling positions only individuals who are qualified and competent.

d. *Monitor Effectiveness.*

Counselors continually monitor their effectiveness as professionals and take steps to improve when necessary. Counselors in private practice take reasonable steps to seek out peer supervision to evaluate their efficacy as counselors.

e. *Ethical Issues Consultation.*

Counselors take reasonable steps to consult with other counselors or related professionals when they have questions regarding their ethical obligations or professional practice. (See H.1.)

f. *Continuing Education.*

Counselors recognize the need for continuing education to maintain a reasonable level of awareness of current scientific and professional information in their fields of activity. They take steps to maintain competence in the skills they use, are open to new procedures, and keep current with the diverse and/or special populations with whom they work.

g. *Impairment.*

Counselors refrain from offering or accepting professional services when their physical, mental, or emotional problems are likely to harm a client or others. They are alert to the signs of impairment, seek assistance for problems, and, if necessary, limit, suspend, or terminate their professional responsibilities. (See A.11.c.)

C.3. Advertising and Soliciting Clients

a. *Accurate Advertising.*

There are no restrictions on advertising by counselors except those that can be specifically justified to protect the public from deceptive practices. Counselors advertise or represent their services to the public by identifying their credentials in an accurate manner that is not false, misleading, deceptive, or fraudulent. Counselors may only advertise the highest degree earned which is in counseling or a closely related field from a college or university that was accredited when the degree was awarded by one of the regional accrediting bodies recognized by the Council on Postsecondary Accreditation.

b. *Testimonials.*

Counselors who use testimonials do not solicit them from clients or other persons who, because of their particular circumstances, may be vulnerable to undue influence.

c. *Statements by Others.*

Counselors make reasonable efforts to ensure that statements made by others about them or the profession of counseling are accurate.

d. *Recruiting Through Employment.*

Counselors do not use their places of employment or institutional affiliation to recruit or gain clients, supervisees, or consultees for their private practices. (See C.5.e.)

e. *Products and Training Advertisements.*

Counselors who develop products related to their profession or conduct workshops or training events ensure that the advertisements concerning these products or events are accurate and disclose adequate information for consumers to make informed choices.

f. *Promoting to Those Served.*

Counselors do not use counseling, teaching, training, or supervisory relationships to promote their products or training events in a manner that is deceptive or would exert undue influence on individuals who may be vulnerable. Counselors may adopt textbooks they have authored for instruction purposes.

g. *Professional Association Involvement.*

Counselors actively participate in local, state, and national associations that foster the development and improvement of counseling.

C.4. Credentials

a. *Credentials Claimed.*

Counselors claim or imply only professional credentials possessed and are responsible for correcting any known misrepresentations of their credentials by others. Professional credentials include graduate degrees in counseling or closely related mental health fields, accreditation of graduate programs, national voluntary certifications, government-issued certifications or licenses, ACA professional membership, or any other credential that might indicate to the public specialized knowledge or expertise in counseling.

b. *ACA Professional Membership.*

ACA professional members may announce to the public their membership status. Regular members may not announce their ACA membership in a manner that might imply they are credentialed counselors.

c. *Credential Guidelines.*

Counselors follow the guidelines for use of credentials that have been established by the entities that issue the credentials.

d. *Misrepresentation of Credentials.*

Counselors do not attribute more to their credentials than the credentials represent, and do not imply that other counselors are not qualified because they do not possess certain credentials.

e. *Doctoral Degrees From Other Fields.*

Counselors who hold a master's degree in counseling or a closely related mental health field, but hold a doctoral degree from other than counseling or a closely related field, do not use the title "Dr." in their practices and do not announce to the public in relation to their practice or status as a counselor that they hold a doctorate.

C.5. Public Responsibility

a. *Nondiscrimination.*

Counselors do not discriminate against clients, students, or supervisees in a manner that has a negative impact based on their age, color, culture, disability, ethnic group, gender, race, religion, sexual orientation, or socioeconomic status, or for any other reason. (See A.2.a.)

b. *Sexual Harassment.*

Counselors do not engage in sexual harassment. Sexual harassment is defined as sexual solicitation, physical advances, or verbal or nonverbal conduct that is sexual in nature, that occurs in connection with professional activities or roles, and that either (1) is unwelcome, is offensive, or creates a hostile workplace environment, and counselors know or are told this; or (2) is sufficiently severe or intense to be perceived as harassment to a reasonable person in the context. Sexual harassment can consist of a single intense or severe act or multiple persistent or pervasive acts.

c. *Reports to Third Parties.*

Counselors are accurate, honest, and unbiased in reporting their professional activities and judgments to appropriate third parties including courts, health insurance companies, those who are the recipients of evaluation reports, and others. (See B.1.g.)

d. *Media Presentations.*

When counselors provide advice or comment by means of public lectures, demonstrations, radio or television programs, prerecorded tapes, printed articles, mailed material, or other media, they take reasonable precautions to ensure that (1) the statements are based on appropriate professional counseling literature and practice; (2) the statements are otherwise consistent with the Code of Ethics and the Standards of Practice; and (3) the recipients of the information are not encouraged to infer that a professional counseling relationship has been established. (See C.6.b.)

e. *Unjustified Gains.*

Counselors do not use their professional positions to seek or receive unjustified personal gains, sexual favors, unfair advantage, or unearned goods or services. (See C.3.d.)

C.6. Responsibility to Other Professionals

a. *Different Approaches.*

Counselors are respectful of approaches to professional counseling that differ from their own. Counselors know and take into account the traditions and practices of other professional groups with which they work.

b. *Personal Public Statements.*

When making personal statements in a public context, counselors clarify that they are speaking from their personal perspectives and that they are not speaking on behalf of all counselors or the profession. (See C.5.d.)

c. *Clients Served by Others.*

When counselors learn that their clients are in a professional relationship with another mental health professional, they request release from clients to inform the other professionals and strive to establish positive and collaborative professional relationships. (See A.4.)

SECTION D: RELATIONSHIPS WITH OTHER PROFESSIONALS

D.1. Relationships With Employers and Employees

a. *Role Definition.*

Counselors define and describe for their employers and employees the parameters and levels of their professional roles.

b. *Agreements.*

Counselors establish working agreements with supervisors, colleagues, and subordinates regarding counseling or clinical relationships, confidentiality, adherence to professional standards, distinction between public and private material, maintenance and dissemination of recorded information, work load, and accountability. Working agreements in each instance are specified and made known to those concerned.

c. *Negative Conditions.*

Counselors alert their employers to conditions that may be potentially disruptive or damaging to the counselor's professional responsibilities or that may limit their effectiveness.

d. *Evaluation.*

Counselors submit regularly to professional review and evaluation by their supervisor or the appropriate representative of the employer.

e. *In-Service.*

Counselors are responsible for in-service development of self and staff.

f. *Goals.*

Counselors inform their staff of goals and programs.

g. *Practices.*

Counselors provide personnel and agency practices that respect and enhance the rights and welfare of each employee and recipient of agency services. Counselors strive to maintain the highest levels of professional services.

h. *Personnel Selection and Assignment.*

Counselors select competent staff and assign responsibilities compatible with their skills and experiences.

i. *Discrimination.*

Counselors, as either employers or employees, do not engage in or condone practices that are inhumane, illegal, or unjustifiable (such as considerations based on age, color, culture, disability, ethnic group, gender, race, religion, sexual orientation, or socioeconomic status) in hiring, promotion, or training. (See A.2.a. and C.5.b.)

j. *Professional Conduct.*

Counselors have a responsibility both to clients and to the agency or institution within which services are performed to maintain high standards of professional conduct.

k. *Exploitive Relationships.*

Counselors do not engage in exploitive relationships with individuals over whom they have supervisory, evaluative, or instructional control or authority.

l. *Employer Policies.*

The acceptance of employment in an agency or institution implies that counselors are in agreement with its general policies and principles. Counselors strive to reach agreement with employers as to acceptable standards of conduct that allow for changes in institutional policy conducive to the growth and development of clients.

D.2. Consultation (See B.6.)

a. *Consultation as an Option.*

Counselors may choose to consult with any other professionally competent persons about their clients. In choosing consultants, counselors avoid placing the consultant in a conflict of interest situation that would preclude the consultant being a proper party to the counselor's efforts to help the client. Should counselors be engaged in a work setting that compromises this consultation standard, they consult with other professionals whenever possible to consider justifiable alternatives.

b. *Consultant Competency.*

Counselors are reasonably certain that they have or the organization represented has the necessary competencies and resources for giving the kind of consulting services needed and that appropriate referral resources are available.

c. *Understanding With Clients.*

When providing consultation, counselors attempt to develop with their clients a clear understanding of problem definition, goals for change, and predicted consequences of interventions selected.

d. *Consultant Goals.*

The consulting relationship is one in which client adaptability and growth toward self-direction are consistently encouraged and cultivated. (See A.1.b.)

D.3. Fees for Referral

a. *Accepting Fees From Agency Clients.*

Counselors refuse a private fee or other remuneration for rendering services to persons who are entitled to such services through the counselor's employing agency or institution. The policies of a particular agency may make explicit provisions for agency clients to receive counseling services from members of its staff in private practice. In such instances, the clients must be informed of other options open to them should they seek private counseling services. (See A.10.a., A.11.b., and C.3.d.)

b. *Referral Fees.*

Counselors do not accept a referral fee from other professionals.

D.4. Subcontractor Arrangements

When counselors work as subcontractors for counseling services for a third party, they have a duty to inform clients of the limitations of confidentiality that the organization may place on counselors in providing counseling services to clients. The limits of such confidentiality ordinarily are discussed as part of the intake session. (See B.1.e. and B.1.f.)

SECTION E: EVALUATION, ASSESSMENT, AND INTERPRETATION

E.1. General

a. *Appraisal Techniques.*

The primary purpose of educational and psychological assessment is to provide measures that are objective and interpretable in either comparative or absolute terms. Counselors recognize the need to interpret the statements in this section as applying to the whole range of appraisal techniques, including test and nontest data.

b. *Client Welfare.*

Counselors promote the welfare and best interests of the client in the development, publication, and utilization of educational and psychological assessment techniques. They do not misuse assessment results and interpretations and take reasonable steps to prevent others from misusing the information these techniques provide. They respect the client's right to know the results, the interpretations made, and the bases for their conclusions and recommendations.

E.2. Competence to Use and Interpret Tests

a. *Limits of Competence.*

Counselors recognize the limits of their competence and perform only those testing and assessment services for which they have been trained. They are familiar with reliability, validity, related standardization, error of measurement, and proper application of any technique utilized. Counselors using computer-based test interpretations are trained in the construct being measured and the specific instrument being used prior to using this type of computer application. Counselors take reasonable measures to ensure the proper use of psychological assessment techniques by persons under their supervision.

b. *Appropriate Use.*

Counselors are responsible for the appropriate application, scoring, interpretation, and use of assessment instruments, whether they score and interpret such tests themselves or use computerized or other services.

c. *Decisions Based on Results.*

Counselors responsible for decisions involving individuals or policies that are based on assessment results have a thorough understanding of educational and psychological measurement, including validation criteria, test research, and guidelines for test development and use.

d. *Accurate Information.*

Counselors provide accurate information and avoid false claims or misconceptions when making statements about assessment instruments or techniques. Special efforts are made to avoid unwarranted connotations of such terms as *IQ* and *grade equivalent scores.* (See C.5.c.)

E.3. Informed Consent

a. *Explanation to Clients.*

Prior to assessment, counselors explain the nature and purposes of assessment and the specific use of results in language the client (or other legally authorized person on behalf of the client) can understand, unless an explicit exception to this right has been agreed upon in advance. Regardless of whether scoring and interpretation are completed by counselors, by assistants, or by computer or other outside services, counselors take reasonable steps to ensure that appropriate explanations are given to the client.

b. *Recipients of Results.*

The examinee's welfare, explicit understanding, and prior agreement determine the recipients of test results. Counselors include accurate and appropriate interpretations with any release of individual or group test results. (See B.1.a. and C.5.c.)

E.4. Release of Information to Competent Professionals

a. *Misuse of Results.*

Counselors do not misuse assessment results, including test results, and interpretations, and take reasonable steps to prevent the misuse of such by others. (See C.5.c.)

b. *Release of Raw Data.*

Counselors ordinarily release data (e.g., protocols, counseling or interview notes, or questionnaires) in which the client is identified only with the consent of the client or the client's legal representative. Such data are usually released only to persons recognized by counselors as competent to interpret the data. (See B.1.a.)

E.5. Proper Diagnosis of Mental Disorders

a. *Proper Diagnosis.*

Counselors take special care to provide proper diagnosis of mental disorders. Assessment techniques (including personal interview) used to determine client care (e.g., locus of treatment, type of treatment, or recommended follow-up) are carefully selected and appropriately used. (See A.3.a. and C.5.c.)

b. *Cultural Sensitivity.*

Counselors recognize that culture affects the manner in which clients' problems are defined. Clients' socioeconomic and cultural experience is considered when diagnosing mental disorders.

E.6. Test Selection

a. *Appropriateness of Instruments.*

Counselors carefully consider the validity, reliability, psychometric limitations, and appropriateness of instruments when selecting tests for use in a given situation or with a particular client.

b. *Culturally Diverse Populations.*

Counselors are cautious when selecting tests for culturally diverse populations to avoid inappropriateness of testing that may be outside of socialized behavioral or cognitive patterns.

E.7. Conditions of Test Administration

a. *Administration Conditions.*

Counselors administer tests under the same conditions that were established in their standardization. When tests are not administered under standard conditions or when unusual behavior or irregularities occur during the testing session, those conditions are noted in interpretation, and the results may be designated as invalid or of questionable validity.

b. *Computer Administration.*

Counselors are responsible for ensuring that administration programs function properly to provide clients with accurate results when a computer or other electronic methods are used for test administration. (See A.12.b.)

c. *Unsupervised Test Taking.*

Counselors do not permit unsupervised or inadequately supervised use of tests or assessments unless the tests or assessments are designed, intended, and validated for self-administration and/or scoring.

d. *Disclosure of Favorable Conditions.*

Prior to test administration, conditions that produce most favorable test results are made known to the examinee.

E.8. Diversity in Testing

Counselors are cautious in using assessment techniques, making evaluations, and interpreting the performance of populations not represented in the norm group on which an instrument was standardized. They recognize the effects of age, color, culture, disability, ethnic group, gender, race, religion, sexual orientation, and socioeconomic status on test administration and interpretation and place test results in proper perspective with other relevant factors. (See A.2.a.)

E.9. Test Scoring and Interpretation

a. *Reporting Reservations.*

In reporting assessment results, counselors indicate any reservations that exist regarding validity or reliability because of the circumstances of the assessment or the inappropriateness of the norms for the person tested.

b. *Research Instruments.*

Counselors exercise caution when interpreting the results of research instruments possessing insufficient technical data to support respondent results. The specific purposes for the use of such instruments are stated explicitly to the examinee.

c. *Testing Services.*

Counselors who provide test scoring and test interpretation services to support the assessment process confirm the validity of such interpretations. They accurately describe the purpose, norms, validity, reliability, and applications of the procedures and any special qualifications applicable to their use. The public offering of an automated test interpretations service is considered a professional-to-professional consultation. The formal responsibility of the consultant is to the consultee, but the ultimate and overriding responsibility is to the client.

E.10. Test Security

Counselors maintain the integrity and security of tests and other assessment techniques consistent with legal and contractual obligations. Counselors do not appropriate, reproduce, or modify published tests or parts thereof without acknowledgment and permission from the publisher.

E.11. Obsolete Tests and Outdated Test Results

Counselors do not use data or test results that are obsolete or outdated for the current purpose. Counselors make every effort to prevent the misuse of obsolete measures and test data by others.

E.12. Test Construction

Counselors use established scientific procedures, relevant standards, and current professional knowledge for test design in the development, publication, and utilization of educational and psychological assessment techniques.

SECTION F: TEACHING, TRAINING, AND SUPERVISION

F.1. Counselor Educators and Trainers

a. *Educators as Teachers and Practitioners.*

Counselors who are responsible for developing, implementing, and supervising educational programs are skilled as teachers and practitioners. They are knowledgeable regarding the ethical, legal, and regulatory aspects of the profession, are skilled in applying that knowledge, and make students and supervisees aware of their responsibilities. Counselors conduct counselor education and training programs in an ethical manner and serve as role models for professional behavior. Counselor educators should make an effort to infuse material related to human diversity into all courses and/or workshops that are designed to promote the development of professional counselors.

b. *Relationship Boundaries With Students and Supervisees.*

Counselors clearly define and maintain ethical, professional, and social relationship boundaries with their students and supervisees. They are aware of the differential in power that exists and the student's or supervisee's possible incomprehension of that power differential. Counselors explain to students and supervisees the potential for the relationship to become exploitive.

c. *Sexual Relationships.*

Counselors do not engage in sexual relationships with students or supervisees and do not subject them to sexual harassment. (See A.6. and C.5.b)

d. *Contributions to Research.*

Counselors give credit to students or supervisees for their contributions to research and scholarly projects. Credit is given through coauthorship, acknowledgment, footnote statement, or other appropriate means, in accordance with such contributions. (See G.4.b. and G.4.c.)

e. *Close Relatives.*

Counselors do not accept close relatives as students or supervisees.

f. *Supervision Preparation.*

Counselors who offer clinical supervision services are adequately prepared in supervision methods and techniques. Counselors who are doctoral students serving as practicum or internship supervisors to master's level students are adequately prepared and supervised by the training program.

g. *Responsibility for Services to Clients.*

Counselors who supervise the counseling services of others take reasonable measures to ensure that counseling services provided to clients are professional.

h. *Endorsement.*

Counselors do not endorse students or supervisees for certification, licensure, employment, or completion of an academic or training program if they believe students or supervisees are not qualified for the endorsement. Counselors take reasonable steps to assist students or supervisees who are not qualified for endorsement to become qualified.

F.2. Counselor Education and Training Programs

a. *Orientation.*

Prior to admission, counselors orient prospective students to the counselor education or training program's expectations, including but not limited to the following: (1) the type and level of skill acquisition required for successful completion of the training, (2) subject matter to be covered, (3) basis for evaluation, (4) training components that encourage self-growth or self-disclosure as part of the training process, (5) the type of supervision settings and requirements of the sites for required clinical field experiences, (6) student and supervisee evaluation and dismissal policies and procedures, and (7) up-to-date employment prospects for graduates.

b. *Integration of Study and Practice.*

Counselors establish counselor education and training programs that integrate academic study and supervised practice.

c. *Evaluation.*

Counselors clearly state to students and supervisees, in advance of training, the levels of competency expected, appraisal methods, and timing of evaluations for both didactic and experiential components. Counselors provide students and supervisees with periodic performance appraisal and evaluation feedback throughout the training program.

d. *Teaching Ethics.*

Counselors make students and supervisees aware of the ethical responsibilities and standards of the profession and the students' and supervisees' ethical responsibilities to the profession. (See C.1. and F.3.e.)

e. *Peer Relationships.*

When students or supervisees are assigned to lead counseling groups or provide clinical supervision for their peers, counselors take steps to ensure that students and supervisees placed in these roles do not have personal or adverse relationships with peers and that they understand they have the same ethical obligations as counselor educators, trainers, and supervisors. Counselors make every effort to ensure that the rights of peers are not compromised when students or supervisees are assigned to lead counseling groups or provide clinical supervision.

f. *Varied Theoretical Positions.*

Counselors present varied theoretical positions so that students and supervisees may make comparisons and have opportunities to develop their own positions. Counselors provide information concerning the scientific bases of professional practice. (See C.6.a.)

g. *Field Placements.*

Counselors develop clear policies within their training program regarding field placement and other clinical experiences. Counselors provide clearly stated roles and responsibilities for the student or supervisee, the site supervisor, and the program supervisor. They confirm that site supervisors are qualified to provide supervision and are informed of their professional and ethical responsibilities in this role.

h. *Dual Relationships as Supervisors.*

Counselors avoid dual relationships such as performing the role of site supervisor and training program supervisor in the student's or supervisee's training program. Counselors do not accept any form of professional services, fees, commissions, reimbursement, or remuneration from a site for student or supervisee placement.

i. *Diversity in Programs.*

Counselors are responsive to their institution's and program's recruitment and retention needs for training program administrators, faculty, and students with diverse backgrounds and special needs. (See A.2.a.)

F.3. Students and Supervisees

a. *Limitations.*

Counselors, through ongoing evaluation and appraisal, are aware of the academic and personal limitations of students and supervisees that might impede performance. Counselors assist students and supervisees in securing remedial assistance when needed, and dismiss from the training program supervisees who are unable to provide competent service due to academic or personal limitations. Counselors seek professional consultation and document their decision to dismiss or refer students or supervisees for assistance. Counselors assure that students and supervisees have recourse to address decisions made to require them to seek assistance or to dismiss them.

b. *Self-Growth Experiences.*

Counselors use professional judgment when designing training experiences conducted by the counselors themselves that require student and supervisee self-growth or self-disclosure. Safeguards are provided so that students and supervisees are aware of the ramifications their self-disclosure may have on counselors whose primary role as teacher, trainer, or supervisor requires acting on ethical obligations to the profession. Evaluative components of experiential training experiences explicitly delineate predetermined academic standards that are separate and not dependent on the student's level of self-disclosure. (See A.6.)

c. *Counseling for Students and Supervisees.*

If students or supervisees request counseling, supervisors or counselor educators provide them with acceptable referrals. Supervisors or counselor educators do not serve as counselor to students or supervisees over whom they hold administrative, teaching, or evaluative roles unless this is a brief role associated with a training experience. (See A.6.b.)

d. *Clients of Students and Supervisees.*

Counselors make every effort to ensure that the clients at field placements are aware of the services rendered and the qualifications of the students and supervisees rendering those services. Clients receive professional disclosure information and are informed of the limits of confidentiality. Client permission is obtained in order for the students and supervisees to use any information concerning the counseling relationship in the training process. (See B.1.e.)

e. *Standards for Students and Supervisees.*

Students and supervisees preparing to become counselors adhere to the Code of Ethics and the Standards of Practice. Students and supervisees have the same obligations to clients as those required of counselors. (See H.1.)

SECTION G: RESEARCH AND PUBLICATION

G.1. Research Responsibilities

a. *Use of Human Subjects.*

Counselors plan, design, conduct, and report research in a manner consistent with pertinent ethical principles, federal and state laws, host institutional regulations, and scientific standards governing research with human subjects. Counselors design and conduct research that reflects cultural sensitivity appropriateness.

b. *Deviation From Standard Practices.*

Counselors seek consultation and observe stringent safeguards to protect the rights of research participants when a research problem suggests a deviation from standard acceptable practices. (See B.6.)

c. *Precautions to Avoid Injury.*

Counselors who conduct research with human subjects are responsible for the subjects' welfare throughout the experiment and take reasonable precautions to avoid causing injurious psychological, physical, or social effects to their subjects.

d. *Principal Researcher Responsibility.*

The ultimate responsibility for ethical research practice lies with the principal researcher. All others involved in the research activities share ethical obligations and full responsibility for their own actions.

e. *Minimal Interference.*

Counselors take reasonable precautions to avoid causing disruptions in subjects' lives due to participation in research.

f. *Diversity.*

Counselors are sensitive to diversity and research issues with special populations. They seek consultation when appropriate. (See A.2.a. and B.6.)

G.2.   Informed Consent

a. *Topics Disclosed.*

In obtaining informed consent for research, counselors use language that is understandable to research participants and that (1) accurately explains the purpose and procedures to be followed; (2) identifies any procedures that are experimental or relatively untried; (3) describes the attendant discomforts and risks; (4) describes the benefits or changes in individuals or organizations that might be reasonably expected; (5) discloses appropriate alternative procedures that would be advantageous for subjects; (6) offers to answer any inquiries concerning the procedures; (7) describes any limitations on confidentiality; and (8) instructs that subjects are free to withdraw their consent and to discontinue participation in the project at any time. (See B.1.f.)

b. *Deception.*

Counselors do not conduct research involving deception unless alternative procedures are not feasible and the prospective value of the research justifies the deception. When the methodological requirements of a study necessitate concealment or deception, the investigator is required to explain clearly the reasons for this action as soon as possible.

c. *Voluntary Participation.*

Participation in research is typically voluntary and without any penalty for refusal to participate. Involuntary participation is appropriate only when it can be demonstrated that participation will have no harmful effects on subjects and is essential to the investigation.

d. *Confidentiality of Information.*

Information obtained about research participants during the course of an investigation is confidential. When the possibility exists that others may obtain access to such information, ethical research practice requires that the possibility, together with the plans for protecting confidentiality, be explained to participants as a part of the procedure for obtaining informed consent. (See B.1.e.)

e. *Persons Incapable of Giving Informed Consent.*

When a person is incapable of giving informed consent, counselors provide an appropriate explanation, obtain agreement for participation, and obtain appropriate consent from a legally authorized person.

f. *Commitments to Participants.*

Counselors take reasonable measures to honor all commitments to research participants.

g. *Explanations After Data Collection.*

After data are collected, counselors provide participants with full clarification of the nature of the study to remove any misconceptions. Where scientific or human values justify delaying or withholding information, counselors take reasonable measures to avoid causing harm.

h. *Agreements to Cooperate.*

Counselors who agree to cooperate with another individual in research or publication incur an obligation to cooperate as promised in terms of punctuality of performance and with regard to the completeness and accuracy of the information required.

i. *Informed Consent for Sponsors.*

In the pursuit of research, counselors give sponsors, institutions, and publication channels the same respect and opportunity for giving informed consent that they accord to individual research participants. Counselors are aware of their obligation to future research workers and ensure that host institutions are given feedback information and proper acknowledgment.

G.3. Reporting Results

a. *Information Affecting Outcome.*

When reporting research results, counselors explicitly mention all variables and conditions known to the investigator that may have affected the outcome of a study or the interpretation of data.

b. *Accurate Results.*

Counselors plan, conduct, and report research accurately and in a manner that minimizes the possibility that results will be misleading. They provide thorough discussions of the limitations of their data and alternative hypotheses. Counselors do not engage in fraudulent research, distort data, misrepresent data, or deliberately bias their results.

c. *Obligation to Report Unfavorable Results.*

Counselors communicate to other counselors the results of any research judged to be of professional value. Results that reflect unfavorably on institutions, programs, services, prevailing opinions, or vested interests are not withheld.

d. *Identity of Subjects.*

Counselors who supply data, aid in the research of another person, report research results, or make original data available take due care to disguise the identity of respective subjects in the absence of specific authorization from the subjects to do otherwise. (See B.1.g. and B.5.a.)

e. *Replication Studies.*

Counselors are obligated to make available sufficient original research data to qualified professionals who may wish to replicate the study.

G.4.   Publication

a. *Recognition of Others.*

When conducting and reporting research, counselors are familiar with and give recognition to previous work on the topic, observe copyright laws, and give full credit to those to whom credit is due. (See F.1.d. and G.4.c.)

b. *Contributors.*

Counselors give credit through joint authorship, acknowledgment, footnote statements, or other appropriate means to those who have contributed significantly to research or concept development in accordance with such contributions. The principal contributor is listed first and minor technical or professional contributions are acknowledged in notes or introductory statements.

c. *Student Research.*

For an article that is substantially based on a student's dissertation or thesis, the student is listed as the principal author. (See F.1.d. and G.4.a.)

d. *Duplicate Submission.*

Counselors submit manuscripts for consideration to only one journal at a time. Manuscripts that are published in whole or in substantial part in another journal or published work are not submitted for publication without acknowledgment and permission from the previous publication.

e. *Professional Review.*

Counselors who review material submitted for publication, research, or other scholarly purposes respect the confidentiality and proprietary rights of those who submitted it.

SECTION H: RESOLVING ETHICAL ISSUES

H.1.   Knowledge of Standards

Counselors are familiar with the Code of Ethics and the Standards of Practice and other applicable ethics codes from other professional organizations of which they are member, or from certification and licensure bodies. Lack of knowledge or misunderstanding of an ethical responsibility is not a defense against a charge of unethical conduct. (See F.3.e.)

H.2.   Suspected Violations

a. *Ethical Behavior Expected.*

Counselors expect professional associates to adhere to the Code of Ethics. When counselors possess reasonable cause that raises doubts as to whether a counselor is acting in an ethical manner, they take appropriate action. (See H.2.d. and H.2.e.)

b. *Consultation.*

When uncertain as to whether a particular situation or course of action may be in violation of the Code of Ethics, counselors consult with other counselors who are knowledgeable about ethics, with colleagues, or with appropriate authorities.

c. *Organization Conflicts.*

If the demands of an organization with which counselors are affiliated pose a conflict with the Code of Ethics, counselors specify the nature of such conflicts and express to their supervisors or other responsible officials their commitment to the Code of Ethics. When possible, counselors work toward change within the organization to allow full adherence to the Code of Ethics.

d. *Informal Resolution.*

When counselors have reasonable cause to believe that another counselor is violating an ethical standard, they attempt to first resolve the issue informally with the other counselor if feasible, providing that such action does not violate confidentiality rights that may be involved.

e. *Reporting Suspected Violations.*

When an informal resolution is not appropriate or feasible, counselors, upon reasonable cause, take action such as reporting the suspected ethical violation to state or national ethics committees, unless this action conflicts with confidentiality rights that cannot be resolved.

f. *Unwarranted Complaints.*

Counselors do not initiate, participate in, or encourage the filing of ethics complaints that are unwarranted or intend to harm a counselor rather than to protect clients or the public.

H.3. Cooperation With Ethics Committees

Counselors assist in the process of enforcing the Code of Ethics. Counselors cooperate with investigations, proceedings, and requirements of the ACA Ethics Committee or ethics committees of other duly constituted associations or boards having jurisdiction over those charged with a violation. Counselors are familiar with the ACA Policies and Procedures and use it as a reference in assisting the enforcement of the Code of Ethics.

STANDARDS OF PRACTICE

All members of the American Counseling Association (ACA) are required to adhere to the Standards of Practice and the Code of Ethics. The Standards of Practice represent minimal behavioral statements of the Code of Ethics. Members should refer to the applicable section of the Code of Ethics for further interpretation and amplification of the applicable Standard of Practice.

SECTION A: THE COUNSELING RELATIONSHIP

Standard of Practice One (SP-1)
Nondiscrimination

Counselors respect diversity and must not discriminate against clients because of age, color, culture, disability, ethnic group, gender, race, religion, sexual orientation, marital status, or socioeconomic status. (See A.2.a.)

Standard of Practice Two (SP-2)
Disclosure to Clients

Counselors must adequately inform clients, preferably in writing, regarding the counseling process and counseling relationship at or before the time it begins and throughout the relationship. (See A.3.a.)

Standard of Practice Three (SP-3)
Dual Relationships

Counselors must make every effort to avoid dual relationships with clients that could impair their professional judgment or increase the risk of harm to clients. When a dual relationship cannot be avoided, counselors must take appropriate steps to ensure that judgment is not impaired and that no exploitation occurs. (See A.6.a. and A.6.b.)

Standard of Practice Four (SP-4)
Sexual Intimacies With Clients

Counselors must not engage in any type of sexual intimacies with current clients and must not engage in sexual intimacies with former clients within a minimum of 2 years after terminating the counseling relationship. Counselors who engage in such relationship after 2 years following termination have the responsibility to examine and document thoroughly that such relations did not have an exploitative nature.

Standard of Practice Five (SP-5)
Protecting Clients During Group Work

Counselors must take steps to protect clients from physical or psychological trauma resulting from interactions during group work. (See A.9.b.)

Standard of Practice Six (SP-6)
Advance Understanding of Fees

Counselors must explain to clients, prior to their entering the counseling relationship, financial arrangements related to professional services. (See A.10. a.-d. and A.11.c.)

Standard of Practice Seven (SP-7)
Termination

Counselors must assist in making appropriate arrangements for the continuation of treatment of clients, when necessary, following termination of counseling relationships. (See A.11.a.)

Standard of Practice Eight (SP-8)
Inability to Assist Clients

Counselors must avoid entering or immediately terminate a counseling relationship if it is determined that they are unable to be of professional assistance to a client. The counselor may assist in making an appropriate referral for the client. (See A.11.b.)

SECTION B: CONFIDENTIALITY

Standard of Practice Nine (SP-9)
Confidentiality Requirement

Counselors must keep information related to counseling services confidential unless disclosure is in the best interest of clients, is required for the welfare of others, or is required by law. When disclosure is required, only information that is essential is revealed and the client is informed of such disclosure. (See B.1. a.- f.)

Standard of Practice Ten (SP-10)
Confidentiality Requirements for Subordinates

Counselors must take measures to ensure that privacy and confidentiality of clients are maintained by subordinates. (See B.1.h.)

Standard of Practice Eleven (SP-11)
Confidentiality in Group Work

Counselors must clearly communicate to group members that confidentiality cannot be guaranteed in group work. (See B.2.a.)

Standard of Practice Twelve (SP-12)
Confidentiality in Family Counseling

Counselors must not disclose information about one family member in counseling to another family member without prior consent. (See B.2.b.)

Standard of Practice Thirteen (SP-13)
Confidentiality of Records

Counselors must maintain appropriate confidentiality in creating, storing, accessing, transferring, and disposing of counseling records. (See B.4.b.)

Standard of Practice Fourteen (SP-14)
Permission to Record or Observe

Counselors must obtain prior consent from clients in order to record electronically or observe sessions. (See B.4.c.)

Standard of Practice Fifteen (SP-15)
Disclosure or Transfer of Records

Counselors must obtain client consent to disclose or transfer records to third parties, unless exceptions listed in SP-9 exist. (See B.4.e.)

Standard of Practice Sixteen (SP-16)
Data Disguise Required

Counselors must disguise the identity of the client when using data for training, research, or publication. (See B.5.a.)

SECTION C: PROFESSIONAL RESPONSIBILITY

Standard of Practice Seventeen (SP-17)
Boundaries of Competence

Counselors must practice only within the boundaries of their competence. (See C.2.a.)

Standard of Practice Eighteen (SP-18)
Continuing Education

Counselors must engage in continuing education to maintain their professional competence. (See C.2.f.)

Standard of Practice Nineteen (SP-19)
Impairment of Professionals

Counselors must refrain from offering professional services when their personal problems or conflicts may cause harm to a client or others. (See C.2.g.)

Standard of Practice Twenty (SP-20)
Accurate Advertising

Counselors must accurately represent their credentials and services when advertising. (See C.3.a.)

Standard of Practice Twenty-One (SP-21)
Recruiting Through Employment

Counselors must not use their place of employment or institutional affiliation to recruit clients for their private practices. (See C.3.d.)

Standard of Practice Twenty-Two (SP-22)
Credentials Claimed

Counselors must claim or imply only professional credentials possessed and must correct any known misrepresentations of their credentials by others. (See C.4.a.)

Standard of Practice Twenty-Three (SP-23)
Sexual Harassment

Counselors must not engage in sexual harassment. (See C.5.b.)

Standard of Practice Twenty-Four (SP-24)
Unjustified Gains

Counselors must not use their professional positions to seek or receive unjustified personal gains, sexual favors, unfair advantage, or unearned goods or services. (See C.5.e.)

Standard of Practice Twenty-Five (SP-25)
Clients Served by Others

With the consent of the client, counselors must inform other mental health professionals serving the same client that a counseling relationship between the counselor and client exists. (See C.6.c.)

Standard of Practice Twenty-Six (SP-26)
Negative Employment Conditions

Counselors must alert their employers to institutional policy or conditions that may be potentially disruptive or damaging to the counselor's professional responsibilities, or that may limit their effectiveness or deny clients' rights. (See D.1.c.)

Standard of Practice Twenty-Seven (SP-27)
Personnel Selection and Assignment

Counselors must select competent staff and must assign responsibilities compatible with staff skills and experiences. (See D.1.h.)

Standard of Practice Twenty-Eight (SP-28)
Exploitive Relationships With Subordinates

Counselors must not engage in exploitive relationships with individuals over whom they have supervisory, evaluative, or instructional control or authority. (See D.1.k.)

SECTION D: RELATIONSHIP WITH OTHER PROFESSIONALS

Standard of Practice Twenty-Nine (SP-29)
Accepting Fees From Agency Clients

Counselors must not accept fees or other remuneration for consultation with persons entitled to such services through the counselor's employing agency or institution. (See D.3.a.)

Standard of Practice Thirty (SP-30)
Referral Fees

Counselors must not accept referral fees. (See D.3.b.)

SECTION E: EVALUATION, ASSESSMENT, AND INTERPRETATION

Standard of Practice Thirty-One (SP-31)
Limits of Competence

Counselors must perform only testing and assessment services for which they are competent. Counselors must not allow the use of psychological assessment techniques by unqualified persons under their supervision. (See E.2.a.)

Standard of Practice Thirty-Two (SP-32)
Appropriate Use of Assessment Instruments

Counselors must use assessment instruments in the manner for which they were intended. (See E.2.b.)

Standard of Practice Thirty-Three (SP-33)
Assessment Explanations to Clients

Counselors must provide explanations to clients prior to assessment about the nature and purposes of assessment and the specific uses of results. (See E.3.a.)

Standard of Practice Thirty-Four (SP-34)
Recipients of Test Results

Counselors must ensure that accurate and appropriate interpretations accompany any release of testing and assessment information. (See E.3.b.)

Standard of Practice Thirty-Five (SP-35)
Obsolete Tests and Outdated Test Results

Counselors must not base their assessment or intervention decisions or recommendations on data or test results that are obsolete or outdated for the current purpose. (See E.11.)

SECTION F: TEACHING, TRAINING, AND SUPERVISION

Standard of Practice Thirty-Six (SP-36)
Sexual Relationships With Students or Supervisees

Counselors must not engage in sexual relationships with their students and supervisees. (See F.1.c.)

Standard of Practice Thirty-Seven (SP-37)
Credit for Contributions to Research

Counselors must give credit to students or supervisees for their contributions to research and scholarly projects. (See F.1.d.)

Standard of Practice Thirty-Eight (SP-38)
Supervision Preparation

Counselors who offer clinical supervision services must be trained and prepared in supervision methods and techniques. (See F.1.f.)

Standard of Practice Thirty-Nine (SP-39)
Evaluation Information

Counselors must clearly state to students and supervisees in advance of training the levels of competency expected, appraisal methods, and timing of evaluations. Counselors must provide students and supervisees with periodic performance appraisal and evaluation feedback throughout the training program. (See F.2.c.)

Standard of Practice Forty (SP-40)
Peer Relationships in Training

Counselors must make every effort to ensure that the rights of peers are not violated when students and supervisees are assigned to lead counseling groups or provide clinical supervision. (See F.2.e.)

Standard of Practice Forty-One (SP-41)
Limitations of Students and Supervisees

Counselors must assist students and supervisees in securing remedial assistance, when needed, and must dismiss from the training program students and supervisees who are unable to provide competent service due to academic or personal limitations. (See F.3.a.)

Standard of Practice Forty-Two (SP-42)
Self-Growth Experiences

Counselors who conduct experiences for students or supervisees that include self-growth or self-disclosure must inform participants of counselors' ethical obligations to the profession and must not grade participants based on their nonacademic performance. (See F.3.b.)

Standard of Practice Forty-Three (SP-43)
Standards for Students and Supervisees

Students and supervisees preparing to become counselors must adhere to the Code of Ethics and the Standards of Practice of counselors. (See F.3.e.)

SECTION G: RESEARCH AND PUBLICATION

Standard of Practice Forty-Four (SP-44)
Precautions to Avoid Injury in Research

Counselors must avoid causing physical, social, or psychological harm or injury to subjects in research. (See G.1.c.)

Standard of Practice Forty-Five (SP-45)
Confidentiality of Research Information

Counselors must keep confidential information obtained about research participants. (See G.2.d.)

Standard of Practice Forty-Six (SP-46)
Information Affecting Research Outcome

Counselors must report all variables and conditions known to the investigator that may have affected research data or outcomes. (See G.3.a.)

Standard of Practice Forty-Seven (SP-47)
Accurate Research Results

Counselors must not distort or misrepresent research data, nor fabricate or intentionally bias research results. (See G.3.b.)

Standard of Practice Forty-Eight (SP-48)
Publication Contributors

Counselors must give appropriate credit to those who have contributed to research. (See G.4.a. and G.4.b.)

SECTION H: RESOLVING ETHICAL ISSUES

Standard of Practice Forty-Nine (SP-49)
Ethical Behavior Expected

Counselors must take appropriate action when they possess reasonable cause that raises doubts as to whether counselors or other mental health professionals are acting in an ethical manner. (See H.2.a.)

Standard of Practice Fifty (SP-50)
Unwarranted Complaints

Counselors must not initiate, participate in, or encourage the filing of ethics complaints that are unwarranted or intended to harm a mental health professional rather than to protect clients or the public. (See H.2.f.)

Standard of Practice Fifty-One (SP-51)
Cooperation With Ethics Committees

Counselors must cooperate with investigations, proceedings, and requirements of the ACA Ethics Committee or ethics committees of other duly constituted associations or boards having jurisdiction over those charged with a violation. (See H.3.)

REFERENCES

The following documents are available to counselors as resources to guide them in their practices. These resources are not a part of the Code of Ethics and the Standards of Practice.

American Association for Counseling and Development/Association for Measurement and Evaluation in Counseling and Development. (1989). *The responsibilities of users of standardized tests* (rev.). Washington, DC: Author.

American Counseling Association. (1988). *Ethical standards.* Alexandria, VA: Author.

American Psychological Association. (1985). *Standards for educational and psychological testing* (rev.). Washington, DC: Author.

American Rehabilitation Counseling Association, Commission on Rehabilitation Counselor Certification, and National Rehabilitation Counseling Association. (1995). *Code of professional ethics for rehabilitation counselors.* Chicago, IL: Author.

American School Counselor Association. (1992). *Ethical standards for school counselors.* Alexandria, VA: Author.

Joint Committee on Testing Practices. (1988). *Code of fair testing practices in education.* Washington, DC: Author.

National Board for Certified Counselors. (1989). *National Board for Certified Counselors code of ethics.* Alexandria, VA: Author.

Prediger, D.J. (Ed.). (1993, March). *Multicultural assessment standards.* Alexandria, VA: Association for Assessment in Counseling.

P~ART~ II

ACA CODE OF ETHICS WITH ILLUSTRATIVE VIGNETTES

This section of the casebook presents the revised ACA Code of Ethics, adopted by the Governing Council in April 1995, together with illustrative vignettes. Each of the individual ethical standards that comprise the code is followed by vignettes intended to clarify the meaning of the standard. Vignettes that illustrate compliance are presented first and are marked *plus* (**+**). They are followed by vignettes that illustrate violation marked *minus* (**−**). The vignettes are not intended to be comprehensive examples and do not address every aspect of each standard.

After many of the individual standards, a note in parentheses directs you to another standard or standards. In reviewing the vignettes, it is important to keep in mind that the individual standards are very much interrelated.

A series of questions (Study and Discussion Guide) is presented at the beginning of each major section of the Code of Ethics. These questions are intended to stimulate thought and discussion with fellow students or colleagues. They are designed to guide you in thinking through the applications of the standards to your own practice.

CODE OF ETHICS

PREAMBLE

The American Counseling Association is an educational, scientific, and professional organization whose members are dedicated to the enhancement of human development throughout the life-span. Association members recognize diversity in our society and embrace a cross-cultural approach in support of the worth, dignity, potential, and uniqueness of each individual.

The specification of a code of ethics enables the association to clarify to current and future members, and to those served by members, the nature of the ethical responsibilities held in common by its members. As the code of ethics of the association, this document establishes principles that define the ethical behavior of association members. All members of the American Counseling Association are required to adhere to the Code of Ethics and the Standards of Practice. The Code of Ethics will serve as the basis for processing ethical complaints initiated against members of the association.

SECTION A:
THE COUNSELING RELATIONSHIP

Study and Discussion Guide

✦ *Client Welfare: What steps can you take to ensure that the welfare of your client is the guiding principle for your practice? How can you determine what is in the best interests of your clients?*

✦ *Respecting Diversity: Are the ethical standards sufficiently comprehensive and specific to guide you in working with diverse client populations? Are you aware of any subtle biases you may have against those who are different from you? How can you guard against racial and sexual stereotyping in your counseling relationships with clients?*

✦ *Informed Consent: What procedures do you use to inform prospective clients about the nature of counseling at the beginning of the relationship? When counseling with minors, how can you protect their best interests?*

♦ **Counselor's Personal Needs and Values:** *How can you recognize when you are meeting your personal needs at the expense of a client? Do you think it is possible to continue your work as a counselor if you do not meet your own needs? Can you think of any values you hold that you might impose on certain clients? If you became aware of personal problems that were negatively impacting your work, what would you do?*

♦ **Dual Relationships:** *Do you think that all forms of dual relationships are unethical? What might you be likely to do in a situation where a dual relationship could not be avoided?*

♦ **Sexual Intimacies With Current and Former Clients:** *What do you think you might say to a client who told you that she and her previous counselor had been involved in a sexual relationship for several months before she terminated the professional relationship? What action—if any—might you take? What are your thoughts on the matter of sexual intimacies with former clients?*

♦ **Group Work:** *What do you consider to be the main ethical issues in working with groups? What are the ethical dimensions of screening, selecting, and orienting group members?*

♦ **Establishing Fees:** *Do you think that ethical practice dictates that counselors offer a sliding fee scale? How might you determine an appropriate fee structure? In what ways might you meet your ethical obligation to provide some pro bono service?*

♦ **Bartering:** *What are your thoughts about the advantages and disadvantages of bartering with clients? Can you think of any circumstances under which you would agree to barter with a client?*

♦ **Termination and Referral:** *What might you do if you thought that you could not be of help to a client, yet the client wanted to continue seeing you? What action might you take if this client refused to accept a referral? What ethical issues are involved in termination with clients?*

A.1. Client Welfare

a. *Primary Responsibility.* **The primary responsibility of counselors is to respect the dignity and to promote the welfare of clients.**

+ Mary is a 72-year-old client who has suffered a stroke that has left her with halting speech. Although she moves slowly, she has regained most of her mobility. She seeks counseling at a community agency for help in deciding whether to sell her home and move into an assisted-living facility. The counselor, after listening patiently, learns that Mary prizes her independence gained during her 20 years as a widow, takes great joy in growing flowers in her garden, and looks forward to weekends when her grandchildren come for overnight visits. She helps Mary clarify that she really wants to remain in her home, and together they explore options that would further this goal, such as having a noon hot meal delivered by a local organization and arranging for a speech therapist to make home visits.

− Mary, the client in the preceding scenario, visits the community agency and is assigned a different counselor. This counselor notes Mary's speech disability and her age, and does not devote the time or patience required to explore Mary's values in life fully. The counseling process focuses on helping her make the transition to an assisted-living facility where the counselor believes she will be better off, with others like herself who are elderly and incapacitated.

b. *Positive Growth and Development.* **Counselors encourage client growth and development in ways that foster the clients' interest and welfare; counselors avoid fostering dependent counseling relationships.**

+ A middle school counselor is seeing a seventh grader who is very insecure and frequently asks for advice. The counselor responds by helping the student to analyze problems and weigh possible consequences of various actions. Although the client continues to question herself and her ability to make good choices, she is beginning to gain confidence in making her own decisions.

− A counselor in private practice is seeing Glenn, who is going through a divorce. The client frequently expresses fears of being alone and of making bad decisions about day-to-day matters. The counselor suggests to Glenn that he call her any time for support and to talk over pending decisions.

He becomes increasingly dependent on the counselor, asks that his appointments be increased to twice weekly, and postpones even minor decisions until he can discuss them during sessions.

c. *Counseling Plans.* **Counselors and their clients work jointly in devising integrated, individualized counseling plans that offer reasonable promise of success and are consistent with abilities and circumstances of clients. Counselors and clients regularly review counseling plans to ensure their continued viability and effectiveness, respecting clients' freedom of choice. (See A.3.b.)**

+ Sara, a community agency counselor who serves a diverse client population in a large city, practices from the framework of reality therapy. She works with clients to determine what aspects of their present behavior they are willing to change. Once they identify specific thoughts and actions, she works collaboratively with them in designing an individualized action plan. She helps them develop plans that are clear, attainable, and realistic, and works to ensure that it is *their* plan. Sara teaches her clients how to monitor their plans and modify them as needed.

− Karen, who works in the same community agency with Sara, does not practice from any particular theoretical framework and does not believe in being structured with clients. She encourages clients to talk about whatever they want throughout the sessions, and rarely works on plans or suggests homework. She does not work collaboratively with clients to design specific ways they can translate what they are learning in her office to their daily lives. Karen does little to assess the effectiveness of the counseling sessions, trusting that clients must be benefiting or they would not be returning.

d. *Family Involvement.* **Counselors recognize that families are usually important in clients' lives and strive to enlist family understanding and involvement as a positive resource, when appropriate.**

+ Marlene has been seeing a counselor to deal with her depression. Through the counseling process, she has become aware that she has been so involved in meeting the needs of her husband and children that she has lost touch with her own needs. She has decided that she would like to seek employment, but she has taken no action because she fears that her family will not support her in her decision. Marlene and the counselor decide together to invite her husband and children to a family session in which Marlene can feel supported as she expresses her feelings and wishes.

— John is a 14-year-old client whose parents have brought him to a counselor in private practice because his poor impulse control is causing problems at home and at school. The counselor works with John to develop strategies for helping him think before he acts and assigns him homework so that he can practice these strategies. The counselor makes no attempt to ascertain whether John is willing to involve his parents, nor does the counselor try to include the parents in working with him to help him succeed at his homework assignments.

e. *Career and Employment Needs.* **Counselors work with their clients in considering employment in jobs and circumstances that are consistent with the clients' overall abilities, vocational limitations, physical restrictions, general temperament, interest and aptitude patterns, social skills, education, general qualifications, and other relevant characteristics and needs. Counselors neither place nor participate in placing clients in positions that will result in damaging the interest and the welfare of clients, employers, or the public.**

+ A 55-year-old geologist accepts an offer of early retirement from the company where he had worked for 25 years. He seeks counseling when he realizes he is not ready to retire fully. During the initial session, he states that he wants a change from geology and wants an interesting job, and that salary is not an issue because he is financially secure. The counselor gathers pertinent information and administers a battery of career assessment measures. The results indicate a possible interest in retail work, specifically in sporting goods. Because the client is an athletic man who has spent much leisure time hunting and fishing, this idea appeals to him. The counselor notes that his mathematical and organizational skills will also qualify him for managerial duties. The client leaves the session with plans to put together a resume and begin to look for a job in sporting goods management.

— A 42-year-old married woman comes for career counseling after 14 years of working within the home. She continues to feel a strong responsibility to her family. Her children are older but still at home. She has a business degree and did personnel work prior to the birth of her first child. She wants to find part-time work in the business world. The counselor discusses the currently depressed job market and notes that part-time work in personnel would be basically clerical. The counselor is concerned that when the client does seek full-time employment in the future, she might not be taken seriously as a prospective candidate due to her many years at home and in part-time employment. The counselor reiterates to the client the importance of getting back in the work force full-time and using her degree before her skills are obsolete. The client is discouraged at this all-or-nothing approach and does not return for further counseling.

A.2. Respecting Diversity

a. *Nondiscrimination.* **Counselors do not condone or engage in discrimination based on age, color, culture, disability, ethnic group, gender, race, religion, sexual orientation, marital status, or socioeconomic status. (See C.5.a., C.5.b., and D.1.i.)**

+ A counselor works in a high school that has an ethnically and racially diverse student population. The counselor reviews a set of teacher recommendations for students to be placed in the gifted and talented program, and notices that almost all the students who have been recommended are white and middle class. The counselor also notes that a number of minority students could qualify for the gifted program on criteria other than teacher recommendation. The counselor arranges a meeting with the teachers to discuss this discrepancy.

— A Hispanic female client seeks counseling for depression. She tells the counselor that she is miserable because her husband will not let her visit her relatives and because her prayers to God have not been answered. The counselor has difficulty understanding the client's English and feels a bias against "women who use religion as an excuse for staying in unhappy marriages." Nonetheless, the counselor continues to try to work with the client, attempting cognitive restructuring strategies to alleviate the depression.

b. *Respecting Differences.* **Counselors will actively attempt to understand the diverse cultural backgrounds of the clients with whom they work. This includes, but is not limited to, learning how the counselor's own cultural/ethnic/racial identity impacts her or his values and beliefs about the counseling process. (See E.8. and F.2.i.)**

  + A school counselor is working in a very diverse district. She makes a conscious effort to gain as much knowledge as she can about the various ethnic groups represented in her district. She works to convey to her clients respect and appreciation for each of them as individuals. She attempts to refrain from making assumptions about clients and encourages her clients to teach her about their worlds.

  − Melissa is a high school counselor who works in a culturally diverse school. She says that she is color blind and that race and culture should not be factors in counseling. However, many of the students from ethnic backgrounds different from that of the counselor feel that they are not understood. Some have expressed that they were insulted by her stereotypical views about their culture. As a result, Melissa is ineffective in working with a large portion of the student body.

A.3. Client Rights

a. *Disclosure to Clients.* **When counseling is initiated, and throughout the counseling process as necessary, counselors inform clients of the purposes, goals, techniques, procedures, limitations, potential risks, and benefits of services to be performed and other pertinent information. Counselors take steps to ensure that clients understand the implications of diagnosis, the intended use of tests and reports, fees, and billing arrangements. Clients have the right to expect confidentiality and to be provided with an explanation of its limitations, including supervision and/or treatment team professionals; to obtain clear information about their case records; to participate in** the ongoing counseling plans; and to refuse any recommended services and be advised of the consequences of such refusal. (See E.5.a. and G.2.)

+ Brad, a graduate student in counseling, is serving his supervised internship in a mental health center. During initial sessions with his clients, he informs them that he is an intern and that he meets weekly with his supervisor at the center to discuss his cases. He explains how this affects the confidentiality of the sessions and adds that in these weekly meetings he will focus on himself and his skill development as much as he will on his clients. He also discloses that he meets periodically with a professor and small group of fellow interns at the university, and that he will take care to protect clients' specific identities in his discussions with peers.

– Another graduate student, Willene, is serving her internship in an agency. Because Willene is the only intern on staff, she is concerned that her clients are likely to conclude that they are receiving second-class treatment if they know she is in training. Although the disclosure statement given to clients at the agency does list Willene as an intern, she does not mention her status during initial sessions with clients when she discusses counseling goals, procedures, confidentiality, and other pertinent information.

b. *Freedom of Choice.* **Counselors offer clients the freedom to choose whether to enter into a counseling relationship and to determine which professional(s) will provide counseling. Restrictions that limit choices of clients are fully explained. (See A.1.c.)**

+ A counseling center is run by a religious organization that has strict beliefs against abortion. The center hires only counselors who are comfortable with the center's philosophy and agree not to advise any client to have an abortion. To safeguard client integrity and to avoid initiating a relationship in which counselors may be unable to be of professional assistance, counselors inform all prospective clients concerned with unwanted pregnancies about the center's position. Clients are given the opportunity to choose whether to make an appointment at the center or seek help elsewhere.

— Laura works in the counseling center on a university campus. The university policy for the center limits to five the number of counseling sessions that can be held with any individual client. Clients with long-term counseling needs are to be referred elsewhere. Laura does not inform clients of this limitation at the outset. If it becomes evident that longer-term counseling will be needed, she informs the client at the end of the fourth session that the next session will have to be the last at the counseling center.

c. *Inability to Give Consent.* **When counseling minors or persons unable to give voluntary informed consent, counselors act in these clients' best interests. (See B.3.)**

+ Twelve-year-old Danny is brought for counseling by his mother. Even though Danny is too young to give legally valid informed consent, the counselor includes Danny along with his mother in a verbal explanation of all information on the counselor's disclosure statement, using language that Danny can understand. The counselor is careful to check to ensure that Danny comprehends the information and to ascertain his willingness to participate in counseling.

— Mark, a fifth grader, is referred to the school counselor by his teacher. The teacher tells the counselor that Mark causes constant disruptions by "acting the class clown," and that she wants to see an immediate change in his behavior because he is impeding the learning process for the other children. The counselor calls Mark into her office and, without exploring the reasons for his behavior, presents him with a behavior management plan that she likes to use with students who are disruptive.

A.4. Clients Served by Others

If a client is receiving services from another mental health professional, counselors, with client consent, inform the professional persons already involved and develop clear agreements in order to avoid confusion and conflict for the client. (See C.6.c.)

+ Joyce and Henry come to see Charles, a marriage and family counselor, for couples counseling. At the intake session they disclose the fact that each of them is currently in individual counseling with their own counselors. Charles discusses with them the pros and cons of counseling as a couple, and lets them know that he would need to contact each of their counselors to avoid potential conflicts or confusion. He asks for Joyce's and Henry's written permission to contact their counselors.

— The same couple approaches a different marriage and family counselor, Matthew, who agrees to begin seeing them as a couple. Instead of suggesting that he needs to contact their individual counselors, Matthew questions them about what they are learning in their individual sessions. He then states that he views their struggles very differently than either of the other counselors. Furthermore, he thinks they need more work as a couple, rather than continuing their individual counseling.

A.5. Personal Needs and Values

a. *Personal Needs.* **In the counseling relationship, counselors are aware of the intimacy and responsibilities inherent in the counseling relationship, maintain respect for clients, and avoid actions that seek to meet their personal needs at the expense of clients.**

+ Tom, a recovering alcoholic, works as a substance abuse counselor in a drug and alcohol rehabilitation center. Tom shares with his clients that he is in recovery. He self-discloses when he feels that doing so will be useful to his clients but takes care to keep the focus on them. Tom is aware that his work satisfies his personal needs to feel worthwhile and to make a difference in the lives of clients who are struggling to free themselves of chemical dependency, and self-monitors carefully to help ensure that his clients' needs are kept foremost.

— The son of a school superintendent comes to his junior high school counselor because he is failing in science. The counselor, who is new to the school district, wants to make a good impression on the administration. She counsels with the boy three times a week and provides him with tutoring in science. Other students who are failing are seen weekly at most.

b. *Personal Values.* **Counselors are aware of their own values, attitudes, beliefs, and behaviors and how these apply in a diverse society, and avoid imposing their values on clients. (See C.5.a.)**

+ A school counselor has strong personal beliefs against abortion. A 15-year-old girl comes to the counselor because she is pregnant and wants information about the physical and emotional effects of an abortion. The counselor responds with factual information about the emotional effects and suggests she talk with the school nurse about physical effects. The counselor asks the girl whether she has discussed this decision with her parents, and the girl asks if she could bring her parents in to talk the situation over in the counselor's presence. The counselor agrees. Throughout the discussion, the counselor remains objective and does not try to promote her antiabortion beliefs to the client or her parents.

− A Hispanic freshman student seeks counseling at a community college counseling center. She is struggling with trying to find ways to blend the Anglo and Hispanic cultures that impact her life and to fit in with new friends without losing her Hispanic heritage, which is a vital link to her family. The counselor has a number of preconceived notions about the Hispanic culture. For example, the counselor believes that bright, young Hispanic females will never succeed as career women unless they rebel against their culture's view of women as subservient. As the session progresses, the counselor allows some of her biases to enter into the counseling dialogue. The student leaves feeling more confused than when she came in.

A.6. Dual Relationships

a. *Avoid When Possible.* **Counselors are aware of their influential position with respect to clients, and they avoid exploiting the trust and dependency of clients. Counselors make every effort to avoid dual relationships with clients that could impair professional judgment or increase the risk of harm to clients. (Examples of such relationships include, but are not limited to, familial, social, financial, business, or close personal relationships with clients.) When a dual relationship cannot be avoided, counselors take appropriate professional precautions** such as informed consent, consultation, supervision, and documentation to ensure that judgment is not impaired and no exploitation occurs. (See F.1.b.)

+ Joanna, a counselor in private practice, is having lunch with Mary, who is a personal friend. Mary tells the counselor that she is very worried about her teenage son, who she suspects has begun to experiment with drugs. Mary goes on to state that she wouldn't entrust her son's care to "just any counselor" and asks Joanna if she will see him. Joanna declines and explains the risks of such a dual relationship. She does give Mary the names of several counselors she can recommend to work with the boy.

− George is a counselor in private practice. One of his clients is a real estate broker from whom he recently bought a vacation home. George believes he got a real deal on the purchase price. He regularly meets with another of his clients to play tennis, believing that this activity helps build bonds of trust. George thinks that if he is real with his clients, they will work even harder in their therapy with him. He does not see any need to consult with his colleagues about these dual relationships because he believes they couldn't possibly understand all the reasons for his actions.

b. *Superior/Subordinate Relationships.* **Counselors do not accept as clients superiors or subordinates with whom they have administrative, supervisory, or evaluative relationships.**

+ Catherine has been working as a receptionist at a family counseling center for the past year. She has been having marital difficulties and her husband has agreed to try counseling to work out solutions. Catherine asks one of the counselors at the center to provide marriage counseling for her and her husband. The counselor declines, explains the dual relationship issues involved, and suggests two other marriage counselors whose offices are nearby.

− Alan, a residence hall director who is responsible for hall discipline, has a master's degree in counseling. He is approached by a student living in his hall who says he needs to address some personal concerns and wants Alan to be his counselor. Although the university has services available through the counseling center, Alan arranges to see the student weekly for counseling.

A.7. Sexual Intimacies With Clients

a. *Current Clients.* **Counselors do not have any type of sexual intimacies with clients and do not counsel persons with whom they have had a sexual relationship.**

+ A client suggests to her counselor that they see each other socially, on a dating basis, because they have such a close relationship. She also indicates that she finds him sexually attractive. The counselor tells her that this will not be possible or ethically appropriate and that his code of ethics forbids such relationships. He explains the potential for exploitation involved.

− Sharon, a counselor in private practice, receives a phone call from a former male friend with whom she had a sexual relationship. He tells her that he is grieving the death of his father and requests counseling from her. Because Sharon specializes in grief counseling, and because she has not seen him in over a year, she agrees to see him as a client.

b. *Former Clients.* **Counselors do not engage in sexual intimacies with former clients within a minimum of 2 years after terminating the counseling relationship. Counselors who engage in such relationships after 2 years following termination have the responsibility to examine and document thoroughly that such relations did not have an exploitative nature, based on factors such as duration of counseling, amount of time since counseling, termination circumstances, client's personal history and mental status, adverse impact on the client, and actions by the counselor suggesting a plan to initiate a sexual relationship with the client after termination.**

+ Susan served as Frank's counselor for 6 months. While in counseling, Frank worked on his fears of intimacy and learned skills to be assertive in asking for what he wanted. About 2 years after counseling ended, Susan and Frank meet at a social function. Frank tells Susan that he wants to strike up a personal relationship. He feels that enough time has passed since their professional relationship ended and that he is sexually attracted to her. Susan responds that although she finds Frank to be a most interesting person, she also feels uncomfortable in pursuing a personal relationship at any time because of the nature of their former relationship. She explains the ethics of her profession and her personal beliefs about keeping her personal and professional lives separate.

- Sarah was Bob's counselor for a number of months. Sarah suggested termination because of their mutual sexual attraction, which she felt was getting in the way of the effectiveness of the counseling relationship. More than a year after termination Sarah calls Bob and suggests that they begin seeing each other socially. She assures Bob that there will be no problem in starting a new kind of relationship because so much time has elapsed since their professional relationship ended. After all, both of them have had time to cool off, and they are both adults able to make decisions for themselves. Bob is delighted to hear from Sarah and they arrange for a date.

A.8. Multiple Clients

When counselors agree to provide counseling services to two or more persons who have a relationship (such as husband and wife, or parents and children), counselors clarify at the outset which person or persons are clients and the nature of the relationships they will have with each involved person. If it becomes apparent that counselors may be called upon to perform potential conflicting roles, they clarify, adjust, or withdraw from roles appropriately. (See B.2. and B.4.d.)

- + A marriage and family counselor agrees to see Linda and Tom for marriage counseling. The counselor explains at the outset that she will begin working with them conjointly but may wish at times to see each of them individually. She secures their understanding and agreement that she will not divulge to either of them what the other has said in individual sessions. Several weeks into the counseling process Linda, during an individual session, voices her suspicion that Tom is having an affair. Linda asks the counselor to tell her whether Tom has said anything in his sessions that might confirm this. The counselor reiterates her policy regarding confidentiality of individual sessions and explores with Linda the possibility of expressing her concern directly to Tom.

— A counselor is seeing Maria as a client in individual counseling. At Maria's request, the counselor agrees also to see her husband Frank for individual counseling. During one of Frank's early sessions, he discloses that he has been involved in a gay relationship for about a year but has not told his wife and does not foresee revealing his secret to her. Several weeks later, Maria asks the counselor to see her and Frank as a couple, in the hope that the two of them can start communicating more honestly. Knowing Frank's secret, the counselor hesitates, but then decides to see them as a couple without expressing to either Maria or Frank her reservations about seeing them together.

A.9. Group Work

a. *Screening.* **Counselors screen prospective group counseling/ therapy participants. To the extent possible, counselors select members whose needs and goals are compatible with goals of the group, who will not impede the group process, and whose well-being will not be jeopardized by the group experience.**

+ Several women apply to join a group being formed at a college counseling center for women over 30 who are searching for educational, occupational, or personal alternatives to their present situations. The counselor interviews and gives a personality inventory to each applicant. Severe personality problems are revealed in the case of one woman who applied. The counselor suggests to her that her needs might be better filled by other services that are offered at the counseling center. Arrangements are made for a referral.

— An elementary school counselor wants to begin working with second graders who are exhibiting disruptive behavior. The counselor has decided to use a group approach. Because time does not allow for interviewing prospective group members, the counselor asks each of the second-grade teachers to identify two students for inclusion in the group. Groups are formed solely on the basis of teacher selection.

b. *Protecting Clients.* **In a group setting, counselors take reasonable precautions to protect clients from physical or psychological trauma.**

+ A counselor is facilitating a growth group session. At one point, a member expresses some personal concerns that indicate he may have serious emotional problems. The counselor guides the group focus away from that member. After the group session, the counselor meets privately with the member and refers him for individual counseling.

− A teacher recommends Randy, an unusually shy student, for an ongoing social skills group that is being conducted by the school counselor. This group is composed primarily of angry and acting out children. The counselor talks with Randy, who is reluctant to join the group but agrees to do so at the counselor's urging. During the first session that Randy attends, two children in the group engage in an angry conflict. Randy is so disturbed by the expressions of anger that he refuses to talk and later refuses to ever attend another group.

A.10. Fees and Bartering (See D.3.a. and D.3.b.)

a. *Advance Understanding.* **Counselors clearly explain to clients, prior to entering the counseling relationship, all financial arrangements related to professional services including the use of collection agencies or legal measures for nonpayment. (See A.11.c.)**

+ A counselor clearly spells out her policies and practices regarding fees in a written informed consent document. She encourages her clients to ask any questions after reading the material so as to minimize later misunderstandings. From the outset, she clarifies matters pertaining to financial arrangements so that these issues will be less likely to interfere with the counseling process.

− Ray tells his clients at the outset the amount of his fee and arrangements for payment. He fails to discuss any other matters regarding fees. At the end of one month he finds that he has earned insufficient income to meet his expenses. He sends all his clients a written notice that his fee will increase from $70 to $85 by next month. When one of Ray's clients tells him that she feels ripped off by this unplanned increase, Ray becomes defensive.

b. *Establishing Fees.* **In establishing fees for professional counseling services, counselors consider the financial status of clients and locality. In the event that the established fee structure is inappropriate for a client, assistance is provided in attempting to find comparable services of acceptable cost. (See A.10.d., D.3.a., and D.3.b.)**

+ A counselor who has been in private practice in Los Angeles moves to a small midwestern town. He goes to the department chair of the counselor education program at the local university, introduces himself, and indicates he is interested in opening his own practice. He asks the department chair to recommend four professionals who are established in private practice in the town. After speaking with these four people, he decides to establish a fee that is in keeping with local practice and is considerably lower than what he had been charging in Los Angeles.

− A counselor has a private practice located in a wealthy suburban area. She feels that a sliding fee scale is unnecessary for this locality. When a prospective client who is one of the few residents in the area not financially comfortable calls for an appointment and indicates that he cannot afford the fee, the counselor simply says she will not be able to see him. She makes no attempt to refer him to an agency that he might be able to afford.

c. *Bartering Discouraged.* **Counselors ordinarily refrain from accepting goods or services from clients in return for counseling services because such arrangements create inherent potential for conflicts, exploitation, and distortion of the professional relationship. Counselors may participate in bartering only if the relationship is not exploitive, if the client requests it, if a clear written contract is established, and if such arrangements are an accepted practice among professionals in the community. (See A.6.a.)**

+ A client is undergoing an expensive divorce and tells his counselor that he will have to terminate his weekly counseling sessions unless they can make other financial arrangements. The client has noticed that the counselor's office is furnished with period furniture and some inexpensive antiques. Because he owns an antiques and collectibles shop, he asks if she might be willing to exchange counseling services for some furniture she could select at the shop. The counselor explains the potential problems she sees with his proposal. However, she does agree to reduce her fee and suggests that he come for counseling every other week for the time being.

— Barbara is providing counseling to Rodney, who suddenly finds himself among the ranks of the unemployed. Because Barbara knows that Rodney had worked as a mechanic, and because Barbara's car needs an engine tune-up, the counselor suggests that Rodney might service her car in lieu of paying the fee. Rodney is hesitant to work on his counselor's car, but Barbara assures him that she has confidence in him. The client reluctantly agrees to the bartering arrangement.

d. *Pro Bono Service.* **Couselors contribute to society by devoting a portion of their professional activity to services for which there is little or no financial return (pro bono).**

+ Betty has earned her doctorate in counseling psychology and works as a counselor in private practice. She provides an hour of weekly supervision at a United-Way-funded agency, at no charge, for a counselor who has just completed his master's degree and is working toward state professional counselor licensure.

— Cindy has a solo private practice. She refuses to devote any of her professional time to activities that provide little or no financial gain. She believes that professionals who are not in private practice just don't realize the struggle involved in maintaining financial stability, and that she simply cannot afford to give away any of her time.

A.11. Termination and Referral

a. *Abandonment Prohibited.* **Counselors do not abandon or neglect clients in counseling. Counselors assist in making appropriate arrangements for the continuation of treatment, when**

necessary, during interruptions such as vacations, and following termination.

+ Mary Lou knows that she is going to spend 4 weeks in Europe during the summer. She informs her clients in February and lets them know that it is possible for them to see one of her colleagues should they feel a need to do so during her absence. Early in the spring, she informs prospective clients who call her that she will not be accepting any new clients until she returns from her trip, and gives them the names and telephone numbers of several well-qualified counselors.

— Beverly is a counselor in a community agency. She knows that she will be leaving her position at the agency within 4 months to accept a position in another state. She does not inform the agency director until 3 weeks in advance because she is concerned that he might fire her when he learns of her intended termination. She figures that 3 weeks is enough time for her clients to adjust to her departure and for the director to find a suitable replacement for her.

b. *Inability to Assist Clients.* **If counselors determine an inability to be of professional assistance to clients, they avoid entering or immediately terminate a counseling relationship. Counselors are knowledgeable about referral resources and suggest appropriate alternatives. If clients decline the suggested referral, counselors should discontinue the relationship.**

+ A counselor for the juvenile court is assigned to work with a young man who has serious problems relating to authority figures. This client constantly ridicules and insults police, administrators, and other authority figures with whom he interacts. The counselor is unable to develop rapport with the client and finds it difficult to work with this attitude. With the client's permission, he refers the young man to another counselor who has a record of success in working with rebellious young people.

— A school counselor is working with a student who is distressed about her family situation. The student's mother and the mother's live-in male friend are steady cocaine users, and the student feels pressured by the male friend to try the drug. The counselor has no training in chemical dependency counseling but feels confident that she can work with the student. She continues to counsel with the student, unaware that a local family service center has an excellent program for teen-agers from substance abusive homes that is available at no charge.

c. *Appropriate Termination.* **Counselors terminate a counseling relationship, securing client agreement when possible, when it is reasonably clear that the client is no longer benefiting, when services are no longer required, when counseling no longer serves the client's needs or interests, when clients do not pay fees charged, or when agency or institution limits do not allow provision of further counseling services. (See A.10.b. and C.2.g.)**

+ Gary has been in individual counseling for almost 7 months. For the first few months, he was making steady gains toward meeting his goals. However, for the past couple of months the counselor has felt that Gary has been doing very little, either in the sessions or outside them. The counselor has shared her reactions with Gary, but he has been reluctant to consider terminating the counseling relationship. Finally, Gary acknowl-edges that he is not really interested in making more changes and that he is satisfied, but that he likes coming to see her anyway. After further discussion, they agree to have two more sessions devoted to preparing for termination.

− A college counselor reviews her records of 4 months' work with a client named Marcy. The counselor decides that very little progress has been made, and she feels increasingly frus-trated with the client. Because the end of the semester is only 3 weeks away, the counselor continues to meet with Marcy and just talk rather than confronting the issue of lack of progress toward goals. After the semester ends, Marcy tells a friend that she was dissatisfied with counseling and will not return next year.

A.12. Computer Technology

a. *Use of Computers.* **When computer applications are used in coun-seling services, counselors ensure that (1) the client is intel-lectually, emotionally, and physically capable of using the** computer application; (2) the computer application is appropriate for the needs of the client; (3) the client understands the purpose and operation of the computer applications; and (4) a follow-up of client use of a computer application is provided to correct possible misconceptions, discover inappropriate use, and assess subsequent needs.

+ A high school counselor encourages students to use a computerized guidance information system to investigate various colleges. He meets with students individually to assess their capability to use computer applications and shows them how to operate the system. When the students complete their work on the computer, he meets with them again to discuss their findings and help them determine what steps to take next.

− A counselor and his client agree that the client will conduct a self-directed search on a computer as part of the career counseling process. The counselor gives the materials to the client and helps her get started at a computer terminal located in a workroom. About 15 minutes later, the client has difficulty following the instructions on the computer screen. She goes to the counselor's office to ask for assistance, but the counselor is not in. She leaves in frustration and does not return for further counseling.

b. *Explanation of Limitations.* **Counselors ensure that clients are provided information as a part of the counseling relationship that adequately explains the limitations of computer technology.**

+ A counselor is preparing to interpret a career interest inventory to a client. When the client sees the computer-generated scores and narrative report he remarks, "This is really impressive! Now I can find out what career I should choose." The counselor carefully explains that the inventory cannot tell the client what he should do and that the results are only one tool for helping him to make his own decision.

− An employee assistance counselor receives the computer-generated results of a test that purports to indicate management potential. Susan, who is a management trainee with the company, does not score well on the test although her supervisor's ratings of her work have been extremely positive. Susan tells the counselor that the test results have caused her to cancel her plans to return to school for her MBA. The counselor does not discuss the test's limitations with Susan nor does he explore with her other data that indicate she may have good management potential.

c. *Access to Computer Applications.* **Counselors provide for equal access to computer applications in counseling services. (See A.2.a.)**

+ A counselor at a community college has received funding to purchase some state-of-the-art computer hardware and software for the counseling center. The counselor is aware that a few students who attend the college are visually impaired. He orders equipment needed to enhance visually the material that appears on computer screens in the counseling center and arranges for a reader to be available to assist students who cannot read the enhanced screens.

− John, the head counselor in a high school, receives a grant to purchase computer software. Because the counselors each have heavy caseloads of over 500 students, John purchases a set of career and educational guidance materials on diskettes that are designed for stand-alone, self-help use. He intends to set up a sign-out system so that students may use the materials at home. He fails to consider that some students' families have limited financial means and that these students do not have computers at home.

SECTION B:
CONFIDENTIALITY

Study and Discussion Guide

+ *Explaining Confidentiality: What information do you give clients about the nature and purpose of confidentiality, and how do you present it? Does what you tell your client depend on such factors as the client's age or whether counseling is voluntary or involuntary?*

◆ *Exceptions to Confidentiality:* What might you want to tell clients about the exceptions to confidentiality? Do you think that informing clients about the limits to confidentiality increases or decreases trust? What are your thoughts about confidentiality as it pertains to contagious, fatal diseases? As it pertains to minor clients?

◆ *Confidentiality With Groups and Families:* Do confidentiality requirements need to be tailored to individual, group, and family counseling? What are the limitations of confidentiality in groups? In working with families?

◆ *Counseling With Couples and Families:* What special ethical issues are involved in counseling couples and families? What do you need to tell couples (or families) at the first meeting about your policies pertaining to confidentiality?

◆ *Records:* What guidelines do you have for maintaining adequate records on your clients? Under what conditions do you disclose client records to another party, or to the client?

B.1. Right to Privacy

a. *Respect for Privacy.* **Counselors respect their clients' right to privacy and avoid illegal and unwarranted disclosures of confidential information. (See A.3.a. and B.6.a.)**

✦ Ron works as a counselor in an elementary school. As part of his job, he conducts several short-term groups with children. The principal calls Ron in for a conference and says that due to a district push for accountability, he needs to know what progress each child in each of his groups is making. Ron explains to the principal that he believes it would be unprofessional and unethical to comply with this request. However, he is willing to summarize some key themes and general concerns of children in the groups and to give this information to the principal. In doing so, Ron takes care to ensure that no individual child can be identified based on this information.

— Joe, an 18-year-old high school senior, was arrested for possession of a controlled substance, was given deferred adjudication, and is now on probation. Joe has been seeing the school counselor about his post-high-school plans. Joe's probation officer contacts the counselor and requests a report on the counselor's sessions with Joe. Although Joe has not signed a release of information, the counselor complies, fearing that a refusal might cause the probation officer to file an adverse report on Joe.

b. *Client Waiver.* **The right to privacy may be waived by the client or his or her legally recognized representative.**

+ Andrew, a counselor in private practice, is contacted by one of his former clients. The client tells Andrew that she wants her counseling records released to her attorney. Andrew reviews with her the nature of the information that is contained in her records to ensure that she understands the ramifications of her request. He sends the client a written release form, and when he receives it with her signature, he sends a copy of the records to the attorney.

− A counselor is seeing a client who reports that she suffers from numerous physical ailments as well as the anxiety for which she has sought counseling. The counselor, believing that her chronic anxiety is exacerbating her physical symptoms, asks for permission to talk with her physician. The client refuses. The counselor, without the client's permission or knowledge, sends the physician a letter summarizing and including confidential information about the counseling process.

c. *Exceptions.* **The general requirement that counselors keep information confidential does not apply when disclosure is required to prevent clear and imminent danger to the client or others or when legal requirements demand that confidential information be revealed. Counselors consult with other professionals when in doubt as to the validity of an exception.**

+ A student comes to the university counseling center and in his first session discloses that he is feeling despondent over breaking up with his girl friend. He reveals that the previous evening he attempted to slash his wrists but stopped when he began to draw blood. After exploring his current emotional state, the counselor suggests that he consider admission to the student health servie. The student refuses, although he admits that he cannot be sure that he will not attempt self-destructive behavior agan. The counselor, having assessed the student as being at cotinuing high risk to himself, contacts the psychiatrist at the sudent health center after informing the client of his intent to do so.

— A high school counselor is contacted by a teacher who reports that Diane, a student in the teacher's English class, has written a poem about death. When the teacher talked with Diane, the student threatened to kill herself. The counselor calls Diane into her office, and Diane admits to being deeply despondent and wanting to end her life. Diane refuses to make a commitment to a no-suicide agreement but begs the counselor not to tell her parents or anyone else. The counselor is concerned for Diane's safety but agrees to keep Diane's disclosures confidential.

d. *Contagious, Fatal Diseases.* **A counselor who receives information confirming that a client has a disease commonly known to be both communicable and fatal is justified in disclosing information to an identifiable third party, who by his or her relationship with the client is at a high risk of contracting the disease. Prior to making a disclosure the counselor should ascertain that the client has not already informed the third party about his or her disease and that the client is not intending to inform the third party in the immediate future. (See B.1.c. and B.1.f.)**

+ Walt discloses to his counselor that he has recently learned that he is HIV positive. He is agitated, angry, and wanting revenge. From his perspective, he is a victim and doesn't see why he should be concerned about anybody but himself. Knowing that Walt has recently married, the counselor asks him about his intentions to inform his wife of his HIV status. Walt adamantly states that he has no intention, now or in the future, of telling her. He is sure she would divorce him. The counselor informs him that if he steadfastly holds to this decision, she will feel ethically compelled to inform his wife. (The state in which the counselor practices has a partner notification statute that would permit this.) During the remainder of the session, the counselor continues to explore with Walt the ramifications of his decision to keep his HIV status from his wife.

▬ A counselor learns that one of his new clients, Dave, has tested HIV positive. Without exploring the issue with Dave, and without finding out whether Dave intends to tell his woman friend, the counselor calls the woman friend and informs her about Dave's condition. The counselor's rationale for taking this action is his concern for the woman friend. He tells himself that in matters such as this, time is of the essence, and he dares not put someone's life in jeopardy. If Dave is angry about the disclosure, the counselor believes that this can be worked through in later sessions.

e. *Court-Ordered Disclosure.* **When court ordered to release confidential information without a client's permission, counselors request to the court that the disclosure not be required due to potential harm to the client or counseling relationship. (See B.1.c.)**

✛ The court orders a counselor to release the records of a minor client who is the subject of a custody suit. Because the child is highly anxious about being placed in the middle of his parents' conflict in court, the counselor believes that it will not be in the child's best interest to disclose the specific content of the counseling sessions. The counselor requests to the court that the child's records not be released and explains the importance of preserving the child's confidentiality and the counseling relationship.

▬ Fred is a counselor who, like the counselor in the preceding scenario, receives a subpoena for the records of a minor client who is the subject of a custody suit. Fred believes that it will not be in the child's best interest to disclose the specific content of the counseling sessions. However, Fred is intimidated by the idea of testifying in court and rationalizes that he has to obey a court order in any event. He sends the records without discussing his decision with the client or the custodial parent.

f. *Minimal Disclosure.* **When circumstances require the disclosure of confidential information, only essential informati** is revealed. To the extent possible, clients are informed fore confidential information is disclosed.

+ A woman begins seeing a counselor at a mental health center soon after she completes an inpatient treatment program for addiction to alcohol. The woman has a history of violent behavior when intoxicated. She maintains her sobriety for several months. Then one evening, obviously intoxicated, she calls the counselor. She threatens to kill her mother. Although the client is incoherent, the counselor discerns that she has a gun. The counselor attempts to explain his obligation to breach confidentiality in order to warn and protect someone in danger, but the client is not receptive. The counselor calls the mother but is unable to reach her. He then calls the police, telling them only the specific nature of the threat and names and addresses of the client and her mother.

– Ayeesha, a 13-year-old student, comes at the urging of her friends to see her school counselor. Through the course of an extended interview, the counselor ascertains that the girl is considering suicide and that she has a plan. Ayeesha declines to consider making a commitment to a no-suicide agreement and remains evasive about her intentions. Without discussing her intentions with Ayeesha, the counselor calls the parents. The father, who answers the phone, seems concerned, so the counselor reviews with him what Ayeesha has said. The next day, the counselor learns that the family has moved out of town. Further inquiries reveal that the father has previously been investigated on charges of sexual abuse of his daughters.

g. *Explanation of Limitations.* **When counseling is initiated and throughout the counseling process as necessary, counselors inform clients of the limitations of confidentiality and identify foreseeable situations in which confidentiality must be breached. (See G.2.a.)**

+ A counselor in private practice has entered into a contractual agreement with a managed care company. During his initial sessions with new clients who have been referred by the company, he devotes considerable time to discussing the specific limits that are placed on confidentiality by company policies and procedures. He also explains the exceptions to confidentiality that are legally and ethically required, such as danger to self or others, child abuse, and court order. He gives clients an informed consent document to take home and read, and routinely begins the second session by inviting them to ask questions about the document.

— A middle school counselor has a very large number of student clients assigned to him. Although the Student Handbook sent to each student's home does include an explanation of confidentiality and its limits in counseling, the counselor does not make it a routine practice to discuss these matters with every student who comes for counseling. Bobby, a sixth grader, has been referred to the counselor because of his angry outbursts in class. During their third session, Bobby begins talking about his father. The boy discloses that his father sometimes becomes inebriated and beats him. When the counselor informs Bobby that he must report this to Children's Protective Services, the boy is furious and says, "But I thought counseling was confidential!"

h. *Subordinates*. **Counselors make every effort to ensure that privacy and confidentiality of clients are maintained by subordinates including employees, supervisees, clerical assistants, and volunteers. (See B.1.a.)**

+ New clerical staff members are hired to work in a counseling agency. The agency director presents a training program for them that includes discussion of the importance of confidentiality in counseling. Appropriate management of case files to protect the clients is emphasized. The staff members are instructed not to reveal information about clients in response to inquiries made by phone, letter, or in person but to channel such inquiries to the director of the agency.

— Jill, a secretary in a community counseling center, is careless about leaving clients' folders on her desk. Other clients can see these open files as they pass by her desk. The head counselor, who is Jill's supervisor, knows of this situation and has cautioned her to take more care with the files, yet the situation has not changed. The supervisor decides not to say anything more to Jill because she is a pleasant person to work with and does much to make the office area a warm and inviting place for clients.

i. ***Treatment Teams.*** **If client treatment will involve a continued review by a treatment team, the client will be informed of the team's existence and composition.**

+ Mahmoud, who works in an inpatient facility, informs his clients that certain members of the treatment staff will have access to his records. He also tells them that case conferences take place on a regular basis and assures them that the team approach is designed to include a variety of perspectives in providing services to clients. He encourages them to ask questions throughout their stay at the facility.

− Regina is a member of a treatment team at a psychiatric hospital. She tells her clients very little about who is on this team or what functions the team members perform. Regina is concerned that if her clients know that their progress will be reviewed by a treatment team, it will inhibit their self-disclosures.

B.2. Groups and Families

a. ***Group Work.*** **In group work, counselors clearly define confidentiality and the parameters for the specific group being entered, explain its importance, and discuss the difficulties related to confidentiality involved in group work. The fact that confidentiality cannot be guaranteed is clearly communicated to group members.**

+ A high school counselor regularly conducts groups. He informs students from the outset that confidentiality cannot be guaranteed and discusses the exceptions to confidentiality. He emphasizes the importance of respecting one another's confidences and explains that trust will not develop in the group unless confidentiality is maintained. From time to time, he reminds the members of how easy it would be to breach confidentiality unintentionally, and clarifies by using examples that are realistic for the students.

− Rosa facilitates a women's support group at the United-Way-funded agency where she is employed. Because this is an open group, she briefly discusses the importance of confidentiality whenever a new member enters the group. She trusts that the more experienced members will discuss the topic if it becomes an issue for the group. Rosa is concerned that if she overemphasizes the difficulties in enforcing confidentiality, members will be afraid to share.

b. *Family Counseling.* **In family counseling, information about one family member cannot be disclosed to another member without permission. Counselors protect the privacy rights of each family member. (See A.8., B.3., and B.4.d.)**

+ A marriage and family counselor tells all couples at the outset of the counseling relationship that he will not disclose information that either of them may share during an individual session, but that it is important that they do not keep secrets from one another. He explains the rationale: such triangles work against the purposes of relationship counseling. In addition to discussing this, the counselor provides written informed consent materials that include examples of how secrets often sabotage the goals of couples counseling.

− Mary, a marriage and family counselor, is counseling conjointly with a couple. The husband comes alone to one of the sessions because his wife is ill. During the session he discloses to Mary that he has been having an affair. He feels guilty about withholding this from his wife but states that he is not ready to talk about this in a session with her. At this juncture, Mary informs him that she doesn't know how she can continue working with them as a couple unless he admits to the truth. She encourages him to tell his wife, stating that the eventual outcome will be better than living a lie. Mary says that if he is not willing to do this, then she has no alternative but to share this information with his wife.

B.3. Minor or Incompetent Clients

When counseling clients who are minors or individuals who are unable to give voluntary, informed consent, parents or guardians may be included in the counseling process as appropriate. Counselors act in the best interests of clients and take measures to safeguard confidentiality. (See A.3.c.)

+ Roger is an elementary school counselor. Part of his job is to provide individual counseling to first- and second-grade children who have been identified by their teachers as having adjustment problems. Typically, after Roger meets with a child and gains the child's consent, he invites the parent and teacher to a conference so that he can talk to them about the best ways to proceed with the child. He realizes that his work with young children will be enhanced if the parents provide informed consent and are cooperative. Roger explains the importance of confidentiality to both the parents and the teacher as a way to avoid future misunderstandings.

- Carol, a private practitioner, is counseling a child named Jonathan. When Jonathan's father comes to pick him up after a session, the father wants to know how his son is progressing. Carol replies that generally she does not talk in detail to the parents, but she does give him a general idea about Jonathan's progress. The father demands more specific examples, and Carol provides some detailed disclosures about Jonathan's sessions. After the father leaves, the counselor realizes that she felt intimidated by the father's tone, and she hopes that the father won't tell Jonathan what she disclosed.

B.4. Records

a. *Requirement of Records.* **Counselors maintain records necessary for rendering professional services to their clients and as required by laws, regulations, or agency or institution procedures.**

+ A licensed counselor in private practice keeps careful records pertaining to each of his clients, including dates and lengths of sessions, types of services, progress notes, and billing information. As is required by the licensure law in his state, he keeps the records of adult clients for 7 years.

- Although an agency counselor is aware that he is expected to maintain treatment notes and records on all his clients, he is reluctant to make extensive case notes because his schedule is so busy. He believes that he has an excellent memory for his sessions despite his heavy caseload, and that even if he forgets something important the client will bring it up in the next session. To satisfy the demands of the agency, he quickly enters the minimal required data at the end of each day.

b. *Confidentiality of Records.* **Counselors are responsible for securing the safety and confidentiality of any counseling records they create, maintain, transfer, or destroy whether the records are written, taped, computerized, or stored in any other medium. (See B.1.a.)**

+ So that a school counselor may have control over his counseling session notes, a separate locking file is provided for the counselor's office. This permits the counseling notes to be kept confidential and separate from students' educational records that are accessible to parents under provisions of the Family Educational Rights to Privacy Act (FERPA).

− After completing a session with a client, a counselor makes a few personal notes that he leaves on his desk in an open notebook. He then leaves his office for a moment and goes down the hall to get a cup of coffee. His next client arrives early for her appointment, notices that the door to the counselor's office is open, and walks in and casually reads the remarks from the open notebook on the desk.

c. *Permission to Record or Observe.* **Counselors obtain permission from clients prior to electronically recording or observing sessions. (See A.3.a.)**

+ A counselor intern explains to each of her clients at the first session that she is a trainee and is working under supervision. She asks for permission to audiotape the sessions, explaining that she will be reviewing the tapes to assess her work and that her supervisor will also listen to portions of the tapes and provide her with feedback.

− Ellen has earned her master's degree and is working toward her licensure as a professional counselor. She works in an agency that has an observation facility, and her supervisor periodically observes from behind the one-way mirror. Ellen does inform clients that she is working toward her license and that she is being supervised. However, she does not tell her clients about the one-way mirror.

d. *Client Access.* **Counselors recognize that counseling records are kept for the benefit of clients, and therefore provide access to records and copies of records when requested by competent** clients, unless the records contain information that may be misleading and detrimental to the client. In situations involving multiple clients, access to records is limited to those parts of records that do not include confidential information related to another client. (See A.8., B.1.a., and B.2.b.)

+ Fred receives a call from Marcia, a former client whom he saw individually for 3 months. Marcia's husband also attended several conjoint counseling sessions and came to see Fred twice for individual sessions. Marcia now tells Fred that she and her husband are divorced, she is moving to another state, and she wants a copy of her records. Fred agrees to send her a copy of the records of her individual sessions and explains that he cannot release those portions of the records that include confidential information about her former husband without the husband's consent.

− Margaret is a 40-year-old client who has been seeing a counselor in private practice. Margaret asks to look at the records the counselor is keeping of their sessions. When the counselor asks why she wants to examine the records, Margaret explains that she had a bad experience with a former boss who wrote negative comments about her and placed them in her file. Since that incident, she tends not to be very trusting about what is recorded about her. The counselor responds that his records are meant for his own use, although he will allow her to see them if she insists. He also suggests that if she can't trust him, then perhaps they should talk about referring her to another counselor.

e. *Disclosure or Transfer.* Counselors obtain written permission from clients to disclose or transfer records to legitimate third parties unless exceptions to confidentiality exist as listed in Section B.1. Steps are taken to ensure that receivers of counseling records are sensitive to their confidential nature.

+ A counselor receives a telephone call from Dave, a former client. Dave tells the counselor that he has moved to another state and asks that his records be sent to the clinic where he plans to resume his counseling. The counselor explains that his policy is to secure written permission before releasing records and offers to send Dave a written form that would grant authorization to have his records transferred. Dave agrees to this procedure and returns the form with his signature. The counselor includes with the records a cover letter that explains their confidential nature.

— A counselor receives a request from a psychiatrist requesting the records of a former client. Although the psychiatrist's written request does not include a written authorization from the client, the counselor sends the records in the assumption that there will be no problem in sending records to a physician.

B.5. Research and Training

a. *Data Disguise Required.* **Use of data derived from counseling relationships for purposes of training, research, or publication is confined to content that is disguised to ensure the anonymity of the individuals involved. (See B.1.g. and G.3.d.)**

+ A researcher asks several college counseling centers for reports of cases involving eating disorders. The researcher specifies that the case reports must omit any identifying information. When one report is received with identifying information inadvertently included, the researcher returns it to the sender.

— A family counselor uses one of his cases as the basis for a presentation on family therapy techniques at a local conference. Although he does not name any of the family members, he provides detailed information and only thinly disguises events and situations. After his presentation, a member of the audience approaches him and lets him know that she felt very uncomfortable because she has a pretty good idea who this family might be.

b. *Agreement for Identification.* **Identification of a client in a presentation or publication is permissible only when the client has reviewed the material and has agreed to its presentation or publication. (See G.3.d.)**

+ A counselor has submitted an article for publication that describes an innovative, experiential group process. She includes actual photographs of participants to illustrate the procedures. The counselor obtained the written permission of each of the participants before submitting the materials to the journal.

▬ Alicia, an assistant professor, is pleased to be contacted by a doctoral student who wants to replicate and extend Alicia's dissertation study. Alicia sends the complete data that include a list of student subjects by names and their scores on various tests used in the original study. These students had not given permission to disclose their identities.

B.6. Consultation

a. *Respect for Privacy.* **Information obtained in a consulting relationship is discussed for professional purposes only with persons clearly concerned with the case. Written and oral reports present data germane to the purposes of the consultation, and every effort is made to protect client identity and avoid undue invasion of privacy.**

✦ A consultant conducts a stress management workshop for all the teachers in a particular elementary school. When she meets with the principal and is asked for information that might help him reduce teacher stress, she provides only general information about sources of stress for the teachers, taking care to avoid identifying any particular teacher.

▬ A counselor accepts an opportunity to serve as a consultant at a psychiatric hospital. He is hired to conduct a training workshop for the staff in techniques for managing difficult clients. The director of the hospital asks for feedback on the effectiveness of the workshop. The counselor informs the director that he had only limited success with the small-group exercises that were included in the training as a means for staff to practice the techniques. He goes on to suggest that several staff members appear to be contributing to a great deal of conflict on the ward. Although he does not name these staff members, the director is able to ascertain their identities from the description the counselor has given.

b. *Cooperating Agencies.* **Before sharing information, counselors make efforts to ensure that there are defined policies in other agencies serving the counselor's clients that effectively protect the confidentiality of information.**

+ Before sending a written report based on a training workshop for staff members, the consultant checks the agency's policies to ensure that the confidentiality of the participants in the workshop will be safeguarded.

− A counselor in one agency sends some detailed information on his cases to another agency that will receive the clients for follow-up treatment. She does not make any effort to find out about the receiving agency's policies, nor does she inquire about the possible uses of the information they will receive.

SECTION C:
PROFESSIONAL RESPONSIBILITY

Study and Discussion Guide

+ **Boundaries of Competence:** *Assume that your employer asks you to perform services for which you do not have the needed training or experience. What might you say to your employer? If you wanted to develop and practice in a new area of specialty, how might you obtain the appropriate education, training, and supervised experience?*

+ **Maintaining Expertise:** *What steps do you need to take to maintain competence in the skills you use and to keep current with new developments? To what extent do you need to participate in continuing education activities to believe that you are being ethical?*

+ **Seeking Consultation:** *Under what circumstances might you consult with another professional regarding your ethical obligations to a client? How can you determine when a client's condition represents a clear and imminent danger to the client or others? How can you assess the degree of danger?*

+ **Impairment:** *What are your opinions about impaired counselors who continue to practice? How might you recognize early signs of burnout or impairment in yourself? What might you do if you became aware that an impaired condition was beginning to negatively impact your work?*

✦ **Sexual Harassment:** *Can you think of ways that you can prevent sexual harassment from occurring in your workplace? How might you deal with a sexual attraction to a client? How might you react toward a client who was sexually attracted to you? How willing do you think you are to seek consultation regarding any of your concerns in this area?*

✦ **Clients Served by Others:** *If you were to discover that one of your clients was also seeing another therapist, and the client did not want to terminate with the other therapist or with you, what might you do?*

C.1. Standards Knowledge

Counselors have a responsibility to read, understand, and follow the Code of Ethics and the Standards of Practice.

+ Connie is a counselor who works in a group private practice with four other counselors. When the 1995 Code of Ethics and Standards of Practice are published, she reads them carefully. She asks her partners in the practice to also read the documents and requests that the five of them meet to discuss their understanding of the standards and how they apply to their practice.

− A licensed counselor reads the 1995 Standards of Practice but takes the time for only a cursory reading of the Code of Ethics. She reasons that because the Code of Ethics contains aspirational standards it is too lofty to be of any practical value in guiding her practice.

C.2. Professional Competence

a. *Boundaries of Competence.* **Counselors practice only within the boundaries of their competence, based on their education, training, supervised experience, state and national professional credentials, and appropriate professional experience. Counselors will demonstrate a commitment to gain knowledge, personal awareness, sensitivity, and skills pertinent to working with a diverse client population.**

+ Daniel is working in a community agency that serves a culturally diverse client population. Realizing that he has limited knowledge of some of the cultural groups with whom he works, he attends several workshops dealing with specific needs of these client groups. Daniel is aware that his graduate training did not equip him to meet effectively all the challenges that he is now facing, and he is committed to continuing his education as a means to fill this gap.

— A counselor is approached by a local church to give a week-end marriage enrichment seminar. The counselor has no training in this area, but because she is a member of the church and is familiar with the church's views on marriage, she agrees to conduct the seminar.

b. *New Specialty Areas of Practice.* **Counselors practice in specialty areas new to them only after appropriate education, training, and supervised experience. While developing skills in new specialty areas, counselors take steps to ensure the competence of their work and to protect others from possible harm.**

+ Will is asked to facilitate a support group for AIDS patients. Although he has attended several workshops on AIDS-related issues and counseling and has done extensive reading in journals and books on the subject, he has limited experience in working directly with persons with AIDS. He arranges to cofacilitate the group for the first 3 months with a colleague who has considerable experience in working with AIDS patients. He also seeks ongoing supervision of his work.

— John, a counselor just beginning his private practice, has had limited exposure to the field of addictions counseling. When he discovers that treatment of substance abuse will be reimbursed by many insurance companies, he attends a 2-day workshop on substance abuse treatment and begins to advertise that one of his areas of expertise is in substance abuse.

c. *Qualified for Employment.* **Counselors accept employment only for positions for which they are qualified by education, training, supervised experience, state and national professional credentials, and appropriate professional experience. Counselors hire for professional counseling positions only individuals who are qualified and competent.**

+ The director of a community counseling agency has placed an advertisement seeking a counselor to staff its satellite center in a small community about 2 hours' drive from the main office where the director works. The person hired to staff the satellite center will need to work independently, with only minimal supervision from the director. She interviews a man who recently completed his master's degree. Although the director is favorably impressed with the applicant, she does not hire him because she realizes that this recent graduate lacks sufficient experience to work without closer supervision.

– A recent graduate of a master's program with an emphasis in career counseling sees an advertisement that a community college counseling center is seeking a counselor to conduct vocational counseling and career information workshops. She applies for the position. When she is interviewed, she learns that recent staff reassignments have caused the job description to be changed. It now involves primarily clinical assessment and psychological testing. Although she has completed coursework in these areas, she has had no supervised experience in testing and assessment. Nonetheless, she accepts the position when it is offered to her.

d. *Monitor Effectiveness.* **Counselors continually monitor their effectiveness as professionals and take steps to improve when necessary. Counselors in private practice take reasonable steps to seek out peer supervision to evaluate their efficacy as counselors.**

+ A counselor practices in a city whose population has expanded dramatically due to an influx of immigrants from Central American countries. The counselor's parents immigrated from Mexico, and he is fluent in Spanish, but he grew up in the United States and has little knowledge of Central American cultures. As he begins to receive more clients who are recent immigrants, he seeks supervision regarding his work with these clients.

– A counselor in private practice has been in business for more than 10 years. Her practice is thriving. In recent months, she has encountered an increasing number of culturally diverse clients. She has not had specific course work or training in working with these client groups. Although she realizes that her effectiveness is limited in working with several clients, she ascribes the problem to having "some exceptionally difficult clients lately." She does not see any need to seek supervision of her work.

e. *Ethical Issues Consultation.* **Counselors take reasonable steps to consult with other counselors or related professionals when they have questions regarding their ethical obligations or professional practice. (See H.1.)**

+ Mustafa, a counselor who works on an army base, encounters an ethical dilemma in working with a servicewoman and her family. He consults with two different professionals who have expertise in family counseling to explore his options for dealing with the dilemma. Both consultants offer similar suggestions, and he follows their advice. He documents the consultations in his case notes.

− A counselor is working under supervision toward her license. She is uncertain what to do after a client admits to having committed a crime. The counselor, afraid that admitting her ignorance will affect her supervisor's evaluation of her, fails to consult with the supervisor or take any other action.

f. *Continuing Education.* **Counselors recognize the need for continuing education to maintain a reasonable level of awareness of current scientific and professional information in their fields of activity. They take steps to maintain competence in the skills they use, are open to new procedures, and keep current with the diverse and/or special populations with whom they work.**

+ A counselor has not had any specialized training or course work in counseling gay and lesbian clients. He does not want to deny counseling services to this population, but he is concerned that some of his attitudes and his limited knowledge will hamper his effectiveness. He attends a professional development institute on counseling gay and lesbian clients, and attends several meetings of a local organization of gay and lesbian mental health professionals. He realizes that he needs to be open to learning and that he will have to challenge some of his assumptions.

- ━ Brian graduated with his master's degree in counseling 15 years ago and now practices in a community clinic. In the past 15 years, he has acquired only the minimal continuing education credits required by his employer, has not attended any professional conferences, and has not done much reading in the field. He argues that he is too busy with the demands the agency places on him to deal with the luxury of continuing education.

g. *Impairment.* **Counselors refrain from offering or accepting professional services when their physical, mental, or emotional problems are likely to harm a client or others. They are alert to the signs of impairment, seek assistance for problems, and, if necessary, limit, suspend, or terminate their professional responsibilities. (See A.11.c.)**

- ✦ A counselor in private practice facilitates grief groups two evenings a week. The counselor suffers the unexpected loss of both of her parents in an auto accident. As a result, she does not feel that she can provide competent counseling services for the group members. She informs them of the situation and, with their approval, makes arrangements for another qualified professional to conduct the sessions.

- ━ A private practitioner works with individuals and couples. The counselor becomes involved in a bitter custody battle during her own divorce proceedings. During an intense session with a couple, she finds herself siding with the wife and feeling critical of the husband for his lack of sensitivity. She makes no attempt to seek consultation about this event nor does she seek any type of assistance.

C.3. Advertising and Soliciting Clients

a. *Accurate Advertising.* **There are no restrictions on advertising by counselors except those that can be specifically justified to protect the public from deceptive practices. Counselors advertise or represent their services to the public by identifying their credentials in an accurate manner that is not false,**

misleading, deceptive, or fraudulent. Counselors may only advertise the highest degree earned which is in counseling or a closely related field from a college or university that was accredited when the degree was awarded by one of the regional accrediting bodies recognized by the Council on Postsecondary Accreditation.

+ In establishing a private practice, a counselor places advertisements in the yellow pages and the newspaper, and mails announcements to local professionals. The advertisements give the counselor's name, address, and telephone number, and accurately state that she has a master's degree in counseling (which she received from a state university that is fully accredited) and is licensed as a professional counselor in the state.

– Max Moore is a school counselor who has a master's degree in counseling. He recently earned a doctorate in educational administration. He wants to develop a part-time private practice in counseling and consulting. He has a set of business cards printed that read, "Max Moore, Ph.D. - Counseling and Psychological Consulting Services."

b. *Testimonials*. **Counselors who use testimonials do not solicit them from clients or other persons who, because of their particular circumstances, may be vulnerable to undue influence.**

+ A consultant conducts a workshop for teachers and asks participants to evaluate the content and presentation style. Feedback is positive, and she decides to create a promotional flyer and market the workshop to other school districts. She secures the permission of some of the teachers to include a few of their comments from the evaluation form in her flyer. The comments are included in an appropriate way to give potential consumers an idea of the focus and format of the workshop.

– A supervisor in a community counseling agency conducts a workshop on burnout prevention techniques. She decides she wants to offer the workshop to counselors at other agencies. She approaches some of the counselors in the agency where she works and asks them to write statements describing their reactions to the workshop. The counselors are reluc-

tant to refuse or to write anything less than glowing en-
dorsements because of her supervisory position in the
agency.

c. *Statements by Others.* **Counselors make reasonable efforts to
ensure that statements made by others about them or the profession of counseling are accurate.**

+ A licensed professional counselor in private practice is sometimes mistakenly labeled as a psychologist by prospective clients and members of the community. Whenever this occurs,
the counselor carefully explains her credentials to clarify
the distinction.

− A counselor educator is scheduled as a keynote speaker for a
state conference. The group that has hired her designs a promotional flyer in which they exaggerate her experience and
areas of expertise. The counselor has an opportunity to review this flyer before it goes to press but does not correct
the inaccuracies.

d. *Recruiting Through Employment.* **Counselors do not use their
places of employment or institutional affiliation to recruit or
gain clients, supervisees, or consultees for their private practices. (See C.5.e.)**

+ An elementary school counselor has specialized training in
family therapy and maintains a part-time private practice in
marriage and family counseling. As she works with various
children in the school, she sometimes determines that family
counseling might be helpful. Whenever she suggests this to
the parents of her child clients, she gives them a list of other
qualified counselors as referrals.

− A counselor is employed on a part-time basis by a rape crisis
center to train and supervise volunteers as telephone hot line
support staff. During training sessions, the counselor invites
trainees to see her in her private practice if they feel a need
for personal counseling.

e. *Products and Training Advertisements.* **Counselors who
develop products related to their profession or conduct
workshops or training events ensure that the advertise-**

ments concerning these products or events are accurate and disclose adequate information for consumers to make informed choices.

+ A counselor conducts parent effectiveness training workshops, using training materials that he has developed. In his promotional material, he includes the purpose, content, and format of the training, along with a description of the materials that are required reading for the participants. He is careful to clarify that the cost of all required materials is included in the workshop fee.

− A counselor advertises an upcoming weekend training workshop for practicing counselors who want to learn how to incorporate family-of-origin work into their practices. The advertisements do not inform potential participants that the workshop is highly experiential and that they will be expected to do some of their own family-of-origin work as part of the training.

f. *Promoting to Those Served.* **Counselors do not use counseling, teaching, training, or supervisory relationships to promote their products or training events in a manner that is deceptive or would exert undue influence on individuals who may be vulnerable. Counselors may adopt textbooks they have authored for instruction purposes.**

+ A counselor educator teaches a multicultural counseling course. The required textbook is one that she has authored. She provides students with articles written by others and presents a variety of viewpoints so that students receive a balanced perspective.

− A part-time faculty member teaches one counseling course and serves as an intern supervisor. He also has a private practice in which he conducts therapy groups. During the semester, he makes several announcements in his class about his groups and encourages students to consider joining one of the groups after the semester ends. In his work with supervisees, he occasionally asks a supervisee if he or she might be interested in attending one of the groups.

g. *Professional Association Involvement.* **Counselors actively participate in local, state, and national associations that foster the development and improvement of counseling.**

+ Sally joined ACA as a student member while she was pursuing her master's degree in rehabilitation counseling. After graduation, she becomes a professional member and also joins the American Rehabilitation Counseling Association (ARCA). She joins her state association of rehabilitation counselors and attends their annual conferences. After several years of working in the field, she submits a proposal that is accepted and gives a presentation at this state association's convention. She is active in her local rehabilitation counseling organization and has recently been elected to an officer position in it.

− Carl, a licensed counselor, does not belong to any professional organizations and states that he does not have time to attend conferences. He tells colleagues that these conferences never offer anything new and he is unlikely to get anything practical to help him in his work if he were to attend them. He believes that he could not get much out of belonging to a professional association.

C.4. Credentials

a. *Credentials Claimed.* **Counselors claim or imply only professional credentials possessed and are responsible for correcting any known misrepresentations of their credentials by others. Professional credentials include graduate degrees in counseling or closely related mental health fields, accreditation of graduate programs, national voluntary certifications, government-issued certifications or licenses, ACA professional membership, or any other credential that might indicate to the public specialized knowledge or expertise in counseling.**

+ A school counselor enters into a part-time private practice. Because she works in a small town, many of her private practice clients are aware that she is a school counselor. She explains to them the meaning of her various credentials. She helps clients understand the distinction between the school counselor certificate she holds, which allows her to provide services to student clients, and her license to practice outside the school setting.

— A counselor relocates from another state and joins a private practice partnership with two licensed counselors. State regulations for counselor licensure require a review of credentials by the state board of examiners and completion of a written licensure examination. The counselor, before she completes the board review or the examination, allows her partners to send out announcements that do not distinguish her credentials from those of her partners.

b. *ACA Professional Membership.* **ACA professional members may announce to the public their membership status. Regular members may not announce their ACA membership in a manner that might imply they are credentialed counselors.**

+ Paula is a special education teacher. She earned her master's degree in counseling several years ago, maintains her professional membership in ACA, but has decided that she would rather remain in the classroom. She does some occasional consulting and decides to have some business cards printed. On her cards, she describes herself as a "Teacher and Consultant." She does not include mention of her ACA membership to avoid any possibility of giving readers the impression that she is a practicing counselor.

— Pete has a bachelor's degree and has completed all requirements to become a certified drug and alcohol counselor. He joins ACA as a regular member. He has a set of business cards printed that give his name, followed by this information: "Certified Drug and Alcohol Counselor, member of the American Counseling Association."

c. *Credential Guidelines.* **Counselors follow the guidelines for use of credentials that have been established by the entities that issue the credentials.**

+ Alan is a licensed professional counselor in the state where he practices. As required by state licensing board regulations, he displays his license in a prominent location in his office where clients can readily see it. As is also required by the board, he posts the toll-free complaints hot line telephone number of the licensure office.

- David is licensed as a counselor in a state that has a separate license for hypnotherapists. He takes a training course in hypnosis but does not complete his supervised experience nor does he qualify for licensure as a hypnotherapist. Contrary to board regulations, he begins to advertise himself as a "Licensed Counselor and Hypnotherapist."

d. *Misrepresentation of Credentials.* **Counselors do not attribute more to their credentials than the credentials represent, and do not imply that other counselors are not qualified because they do not possess certain credentials.**

- ✛ Tanya is a counselor who holds a master's degree. She acquires licensure in her state and also becomes a National Board Certified Counselor. She seeks specialized additional training and receives her certification as a chemical dependency counselor. A prospective client calls to inquire about her services. The client tells her that he has attended one session with another counselor who is also state licensed. He says that he liked this counselor but fears the other counselor is not qualified because he does not possess all the other credentials that Tanya has listed in her ad in the yellow pages. Tanya is careful to explain that this other counselor's license makes him qualified to provide the services this client is seeking.

- Three private practitioners—a counselor and two psychologists—decide to incorporate into a single mental health counseling center. They develop a brochure that indicates that all three are providing psychological services. The state licensure regulations for psychologists in the state specifically prohibit any professionals except psychologists from presenting themselves to the public by any description incorporating the term *psychologist* or *psychological.*

e. *Doctoral Degrees From Other Fields.* **Counselors who hold a master's degree in counseling or a closely related mental health field, but hold a doctoral degree from other than counseling or a closely related field, do not use the title "Dr." in their practices and do not announce to the public in rela-**

tion to their practice or status as a counselor that they hold a doctorate.

+ Jim is a practicing dentist who is also licensed as a counselor. He has had specialized training in hypnosis. Jim has two sets of business cards, one for his counseling practice and one for his dental practice. His business card for counseling announces only his master's degree in counseling and his licensed status as a counselor.

− Larry Adams has a PhD in history and is a university professor. He recently earned a master's degree in counseling and now wants to begin a part-time private practice. He rents a small office and orders a set of business cards that read "Dr. Larry Adams—Counseling Services for Individuals and Couples."

C.5. Public Responsibility

a. *Nondiscrimination.* **Counselors do not discriminate against clients, students, or supervisees in a manner that has a negative impact based on their age, color, culture, disability, ethnic group, gender, race, religion, sexual orientation, or socioeconomic status, or for any other reason. (See A.2.a.)**

+ A counselor educator teaches a course on counseling women and girls. She welcomes male students in her classes. She makes sincere efforts to create a climate of openness and respect for differences as the students explore gender and other issues.

− A counselor in a community agency does what he can to refer gay men and lesbians to other counselors on the staff. He admits that he has tried to avoid contact with gay men and lesbians, and he feels it might be difficult for him to be objective in counseling. He does not take any steps to discuss his concerns with colleagues, nor is he interested in learning how to work with these clients.

b. *Sexual Harassment.* **Counselors do not engage in sexual harassment. Sexual harassment is defined as sexual solicitation, physical advances, or verbal or nonverbal conduct that is sexual in nature, that occurs in connection with professional activities or roles, and that either (1) is unwelcome, is offensive, or** creates a hostile workplace environment, and counselors know or are told this; or (2) is sufficiently severe or intense to be perceived as harassment to a reasonable person in the context. Sexual harassment can consist of a single intense or severe act or multiple persistent or pervasive acts.

+ A counselor is cofacilitating a daylong personal growth group for young adults. As the group progresses through its morning session, the counselor notices that his female cofacilitator is flirting with a male group member and hugs him inappropriately during breaks. At the first opportunity, the counselor confronts the cofacilitator and explains his objections to her behavior. The cofacilitator ceases her sexual harassment of the group member.

− A counselor in a community mental health clinic is counseling a young woman regarding her mild depression and sexual dysfunction that are related to some incidents with her father during her adolescence. After a few sessions, the counselor begins using experiential, role-playing techniques with the client in which he plays the role of her father. The counselor begins to flirt and try to persuade her to have an affair with him, saying that he is doing this to desensitize her to some of her sexual hang-ups.

c. *Reports to Third Parties.* Counselors are accurate, honest, and unbiased in reporting their professional activities and judgments to appropriate third parties including courts, health insurance companies, those who are the recipients of evaluation reports, and others. (See B.1.g.)

+ Steve receives a court-ordered subpoena for all his records concerning a client. His case notes of early sessions reveal that his initial diagnosis was inaccurate. The notes also show that both the diagnosis and treatment plan were later revised to address more accurately the client's concerns and needs. Although Steve is somewhat embarassed that officers of the court will be reading his records and will see his early error, he submits the records to the court in their entirety as required.

− Dylan is required to assign a *DSM-IV* diagnosis for all clients who want to receive reimbursement from their insurance carriers. Because most health insurance companies do not cover marital counseling, when he counsels a couple he gives each person a diagnosis that will be acceptable to the third-party payer and bills them for individual sessions.

d. *Media Presentations.* **When counselors provide advice or comment by means of public lectures, demonstrations, radio or television programs, prerecorded tapes, printed articles, mailed material, or other media, they take reasonable precautions to ensure that (1) the statements are based on appropriate professional counseling literature and practice; (2) the statements are otherwise consistent with the Code of Ethics and the Standards of Practice; and (3) the recipients of the information are not encouraged to infer that a professional counseling relationship has been established. (See C.6.b.)**

+ Vicky, a counselor in private practice, has accepted an invitation from a radio station to talk about one of her popular self-help books on combating depression. During her talk, she emphasizes that her general suggestions are not to be taken as a substitute for counseling. She avoids giving pat solutions for people suffering from depression.

– A counselor creates and markets an educational videotape that gives advice on how to get out of a destructive relationship. In the taped presentation, she is extremely prescriptive and clearly implies to viewers that if they follow her suggestions, they can turn their lives around.

e. *Unjustified Gains.* **Counselors do not use their professional positions to seek or receive unjustified personal gains, sexual favors, unfair advantage, or unearned goods or services. (See C.3.d.)**

+ Sharon, a mental health counselor, receives a telephone call from the parent of a child client with whom she had worked for several months. The parent, who is quite wealthy, reports that the child continues to do very well and offers to give Sharon an expensive gift as a means of showing her gratitude. Sharon explains that she cannot accept the gift.

– The director of an employment counseling and job placement center approaches one of the staff counselors. The director's son, Tom, is about to complete his freshman year at college and is looking for a summer job. The director asks the counselor to find Tom the best summer job available from their current listings.

C.6. Responsibility to Other Professionals

a. *Different Approaches.* **Counselors are respectful of approaches to professional counseling that differ from their own. Counselors know and take into account the traditions and practices of other professional groups with which they work.**

+ Gayle is a counseling psychologist who teaches in an interdisciplinary human services program at a university. She teaches an introductory course for undergraduate students who may eventually choose careers as counselors, social workers, school psychologists, or marriage and family therapists. In her classes she includes perspectives from all these disciplines and demonstrates a respectful attitude toward a variety of helping professions.

– Dolores is a reality therapist in private practice. She is also a part-time adjunct professor who teaches one section of the counseling theories course at a university. The full-time professor who teaches the other section of the course has a psychoanalytic orientation. Dolores frequently makes critical comments about the limited value of psychoanalysis, stating that it is a luxury for the rich.

b. *Personal Public Statements.* **When making personal statements in a public context, counselors clarify that they are speaking from their personal perspectives and that they are not speaking on behalf of all counselors or the profession. (See C.5.d.)**

+ A public offender counselor attends a community meeting designed to deal with the problem of gang violence on the streets. The counselor is a well-known and respected member of the community. When he gives his input on the issues being discussed, he emphasizes that these are his own personal views and that he is not representing the counseling profession.

— Peggy is a family counselor in a small community. She regularly attends school board meetings that are open to the public and makes dogmatic statements regarding what is in the best interests of children. She frequently uses the phrase *the counseling profession* as blanket support for her personal views.

c. ***Clients Served by Others.*** **When counselors learn that their clients are in a professional relationship with another mental health professional, they request release from clients to inform the other professionals and strive to establish positive and collaborative professional relationships. (See A.4.)**

+ Elizabeth offers a group counseling experience through a community mental health agency. A woman requests to join the group and says during her screening interview that she is currently seeing a counselor at another agency for individual counseling. Elizabeth requests permission to contact the other counselor, and the woman agrees. Elizabeth and the individual counselor agree that concurrent group and individual counseling would be advisable for this client. They also agree that with the client's permission they will communicate with each other as needed to help ensure that the best possible services are provided.

— Robert requests counseling from a counselor in private practice. He indicates that he and his wife are currently in marriage counseling through an agency in town. Robert says he is undecided about continuing in the marriage and wants to sort out his feelings and reach a decision. He intends to continue in marriage counseling in the interim. The counselor agrees to provide counseling to Robert without requesting permission to contact the other counselor.

SECTION D:
RELATIONSHIPS WITH OTHER PROFESSIONALS

Study and Discussion Guide

+ ***Defining Roles:*** *What problems have you encountered, or do you anticipate that you might encounter, in defining your professional role to* *your employer? What might you do if your employer expected you to perform functions that you viewed as incompatible with your role?*

✦ **Discrimination:** *If you became aware that another professional in your work setting was discriminating against individuals based on their religion, what might you say or do? What if it were discrimination based on sexual orientation?*

✦ **Exploitive Relationships:** *If you became aware that a colleague was engaging in exploitive behavior toward his or her supervisees, what might you do?*

✦ **Consultation:** *What do you tell clients about the possibility that you will seek consultation with other professionals to discuss their case? What kind of understanding might you want to have with your clients?*

✦ **Fees for Referral:** *If one of your colleagues asked for a fee to refer clients to you, what might you say and do?*

D.1. Relationships with Employers and Employees

a. *Role Definition.* **Counselors define and describe for their employers and employees the parameters and levels of their professional roles.**

➕ A counselor works in an employee assistance program in a corporation. She has clearly defined her goal of meeting the psychological needs of employees, and her role and functions in meeting this goal. In consultation with the employees and her employer, she has established that assisting employees to cope with job-related stress is a high priority.

➖ Clark, a school counselor, believes that his principal does not understand the nature of his professional role. The administrator expects Clark to take an active part in enforcing discipline and attending to many tasks that Clark sees as non-counseling functions. Although the counselor is disgruntled, he says nothing for fear of getting a negative evaluation.

b. *Agreements.* **Counselors establish working agreements with supervisors, colleagues, and subordinates regarding counseling or clinical relationships, confidentiality, adherence to professional standards, distinction between public and private material, maintenance and dissemination of recorded information, work load, and accountability. Working agreements in each instance are specified and made known to those concerned.**

+ The counselors in a community mental health agency complete a weekly report form that identifies the number and types of counseling contacts, meetings attended, training activities, and supervision received and provided. Client identities are not included nor can they be ascertained from the information provided. The report is used to document counselor activities and to adjust the work load among staff equitably.

- An agency that provides counseling and psychological services has never circulated its personnel policies or the codes of ethics of the various professional organizations to which its employees belong. The administration assumes that the staff members understand organization policies and know their ethical standards. Actually, breaches of the standards occasionally occur because of ignorance and misinterpretation.

c. *Negative Conditions.* **Counselors alert their employers to conditions that may be potentially disruptive or damaging to the counselor's professional responsibilities or that may limit their effectiveness.**

+ An employment counselor finds that so much of her time is needed to contact prospective employers and get information about job openings that she doesn't have enough time to update the files on the qualifications and interests of clients. The counselor informs her supervisor of this concern, and the supervisor agrees to hire an additional clerical staff person.

- A counselor is in the midst of divorce proceedings and finds that she can't attend to clients during counseling sessions. She fears that her supervisor might perceive her in a negative light if the supervisor knew her situation. Thus when she has to take time off from work to go to court, she calls in sick.

d. *Evaluation*. **Counselors submit regularly to professional review and evaluation by their supervisor or the appropriate representative of the employer.**

+ The director of the Office of Residence Life meets twice yearly with the counselors on his staff who reside in the campus dormitories. Prior to each meeting, both the director and the counselor complete an evaluation form appraising the counselor's performance. Open discussion is encouraged during the meeting. Both parties are given the opportunity to enter comments on the copy of the form that is included in the counselor's personnel record.

— A counselor considers himself in the vanguard of new practices in counseling with the elderly. He does not expect his supervisor to understand, much less be capable of evaluating, his work. In meetings with the supervisor, he describes his work in ambiguous terms and responds curtly when asked for specifics. He considers evaluation to be personally demeaning and complies only minimally with the process.

e. *In-Service*. **Counselors are responsible for in-service development of self and staff.**

+ During the month of May, a licensed professional counselor with many years' experience as a school counselor applies for and is awarded a position as director of guidance in a school system. Her duties, which are to begin in the fall, include supervision of the district's elementary and secondary school counselors. Over the summer, she completes course work in counselor supervision and receives certification as a qualified supervisor from her state licensing board. During the school year, she helps the counselors improve their counseling skills through ongoing clinical supervision.

— The state licensure law requires counselors to obtain 75 hours of continuing education every 3 years. The director of a counseling agency believes that this requirement will be a strong incentive for staff to look after their own professional development. Therefore, the director does not provide in-service training opportunities.

f. *Goals.* Counselors inform their staff of goals and programs.

+ The director of a pastoral counseling center is required to submit an annual report. As part of this process, each staff member is asked to give input into departmental goals, concerns, and programs. This input is used in establishing plans for the coming year. All staff members receive copies of the completed report and of the center's annual budget.

– The director of a counseling agency has become discouraged about the monthly staff meetings held to discuss programs and goals. Two vocal staff members dominate the meetings, and staff morale is low. Additionally, several staff members have complained that the director is too autocratic in running the meetings. To solve the problem, the director decides not to call any more meetings. He decides that if staff members need information, they will have to ask him on an individual basis.

g. *Practices.* Counselors provide personnel and agency practices that respect and enhance the rights and welfare of each employee and recipient of agency services. Counselors strive to maintain the highest levels of professional services.

+ The director of a college counseling center wants the center's policies on confidentiality to conform to the best ethical practices. He distributes copies of the 1995 ACA Code of Ethics to each counselor and staff member, and holds a meeting to review and revise the center's confidentiality statement. When the revised policy is completed, he reviews with each counselor and staff member the procedures that will be used to inform clients fully about the policy.

– The director of volunteer services at a telephone crisis hot line believes that individuals who volunteer as counselors are likely to be highly dedicated and reliable. An extensive training program is provided to new volunteers before they begin working. Therefore, the director feels no need to provide ongoing supervision to the counselors.

h. *Personnel Selection and Assignment.* Counselors select competent staff and assign responsibilities compatible with their skills and experiences.

+ Martha opened her private practice office a year ago. Her practice has grown to the point where she feels a need to hire a full-time receptionist/clerical assistant. She advertises the position and interviews an applicant who has had considerable experience working as a receptionist for a group of medical doctors. This applicant has a good grasp of office procedures and understands the importance of maintaining patient confidentiality. Her references are excellent, and she is very amenable to further training and supervision. Marsha hires the applicant.

− The director of a hospital-based substance abuse treatment center hires a chemical dependency counselor solely on the basis of a cursory interview and perusal of the applicant's vita. Because the director was favorably impressed with the counselor during the interview, he does not bother to check references. Had he checked with the state board that licenses chemical dependency counselors, he could have learned that this counselor is serving a term of probation for violations of the code of ethics.

i. *Discrimination.* **Counselors, as either employers or employees, do not engage in or condone practices that are inhumane, illegal, or unjustifiable (such as considerations based on age, color, culture, disability, ethnic group, gender, race, religion, sexual orientation, or socioeconomic status) in hiring, promotion, or training. (See A.2.a. and C.5.b.)**

+ Lori is a 29-year-old counselor who has worked for 3 years on an inpatient unit of a psychiatric hospital. She has received very positive annual evaluations from the unit director, a fact she attributes largely to the positive mentoring she has received from Marie. Marie, who is in her early sixties, has been a counselor on the same unit for over a decade. When the unit director is promoted, he recommends the 29-year-old Lori to succeed him in that position. Lori believes that Marie is better qualified to become unit director, and that the only reason Marie was not recommended was her age. Lori explains her concern to the hospital administrator, who agrees to reopen the search to fill the position and to interview Marie along with other qualified candidates.

- The director of a university residence hall is interviewing candidates for a resident adviser position. One of his top candidates, Lisa, discloses during her interview that she is a lesbian. Although she believes that her sexual orientation won't affect her job performance, she doesn't want to keep it a secret from the director or co-workers. The director had been favorably impressed with Lisa and finds himself wishing that she hadn't been so honest. He decides not to hire her in order to "protect" the student residents.

j. *Professional Conduct.* **Counselors have a responsibility both to clients and to the agency or institution within which services are performed to maintain high standards of professional conduct.**

+ Rabbi Greenberg offers pastoral counseling to members of his congregation. He has trained his office staff in methods of protecting confidentiality and regularly reinforces this training. Because he realizes that confidentiality can easily be breached through carelessness or idle gossip in a small, close-knit congregation, he takes particular care to ensure that the privacy of his clients is maintained.

- A contract between the university and the agency requires a weekly supervision session between the student intern and the field supervisor. Several weeks into the semester, the field supervisor cancels and reschedules the supervision session, and then postpones the session several times again. The intern complains to her university supervisor, who is too busy to deal with the situation for another month. Thus the intern goes without supervision for a large portion of the semester.

k. *Exploitive Relationships.* **Counselors do not engage in exploitive relationships with individuals over whom they have supervisory, evaluative, or instructional control or authority.**

+ A master's level student completes a research paper that is exceptionally well written and well conceptualized. Her professor praises her work and suggests that the paper is of publishable quality. The student, intimidated by the idea of submitting a paper for publication, asks the professor to put his name on it as co-author and submit it for her. The professor explains that it is not ethical for him to claim co-authorship but offers to guide her through the process of submitting the paper to a professional journal's editorial board.

– A counselor educator frequently invites his doctoral students to copresent with him at professional conferences. On one of these occasions, he invites one of his students to dinner, saying that he'd enjoy talking with her about her dissertation. During dinner he confesses his attraction to her and suggests that they go to his hotel room for drinks.

l. *Employer Policies.* **The acceptance of employment in an agency or institution implies that counselors are in agreement with its general policies and principles. Counselors strive to reach agreement with employers as to acceptable standards of conduct that allow for changes in institutional policy conducive to the growth and development of clients.**

+ Vaughn is employed as a counselor in a residential facility for juvenile offenders. The new director of the facility institutes a policy that involves administering what Vaughn sees as harsh punishments to residents who break the rules. Vaughn consults with the director about his ethical opposition to such methods. The director agrees to call a meeting of all staff counselors to discuss the policy.

– Arnold feels stuck in a counseling agency that has rigid policies. He believes that the agency is more concerned with keeping up its image than in really helping clients. He complains to fellow counselors about what he perceives to be unfair institutional policies, but he refuses to express his concerns to his supervisor. Arnold tells his colleagues that it might be dangerous for him to express his lack of agreement with agency policies because his supervisor might treat him as a troublemaker and his job would be in jeopardy.

D.2. Consultation (See B.6.)

a. *Consultation as an Option.* **Counselors may choose to consult with any other professionally competent persons about their**

clients. In choosing consultants, counselors avoid placing the consultant in a conflict of interest situation that would preclude the consultant being a proper party to the counselor's efforts to help the client. Should counselors be engaged in a work setting that compromises this consultation standard, they consult with other professionals whenever possible to consider justifiable alternatives.

+ Lauren, a fourth grader, describes to the counselor her conflicts with her stepfather. She says that they always seem to be fighting. Little progress seems to occur during five counseling sessions. The counselor asks for a case consultation at the next meeting with other elementary school counselors in the district. The consultation produces several suggestions and new perspectives, and alternative counseling strategies are generated.

− A counselor at a small college is perplexed about a hostile male client. She seeks consultation with the dean of students, who is also the chief discipline officer of the college. During the consultation, the counselor reveals information that allows the dean to discern that this client is one of the students who broke into a professor's office and stole some examinations.

b. *Consultant Competency.* **Counselors are reasonably certain that they have or the organization represented has the necessary competencies and resources for giving the kind of consulting services needed and that appropriate referral resources are available.**

+ A professor is offered a position as a consultant to a research project. She is told that her role will be to help with the statistical part of the study. She asks to meet with the researchers to define further the parameters of her role. During this meeting, it becomes clear that she will be expected to provide technical help with a particular computerized statistical package in which she does not have expertise. She declines the consultant position and suggests the names of other well-qualified consultants.

− A counselor eagerly accepts a well-paying opportunity to consult with a psychiatric hospital in establishing an adult substance abuse unit. The counselor has considerable experience in organizational consulting but has no specific training or experience in treating clients with substance abuse problems.

c. *Understanding With Clients.* **When providing consultation, counselors attempt to develop with their clients a clear understanding of problem definition, goals for change, and predicted consequences of interventions selected.**

+ Nicole, a school district guidance coordinator, is hired by a neighboring school district to mediate a conflict between counselors and faculty. Faculty representatives tell Nicole that they want the counselors to "get out of their offices and do something other than generate paperwork." Counselors tell her that the faculty needs to be educated about the counselor's role. Nicole goes back to the principal to be certain that she has a clear idea of her task and the principal's full support. Receiving affirmation, she calls a meeting of the principal, the faculty representatives, and the counselors to outline goals and define the problems they will be working to solve.

− A consultant is asked to recommend improvements in the operation of a psychiatric unit of a hospital. The consultant learns that the unit fails to meet several of the minimal standards of care for such facilities. He recommends strategies that will enable the hospital to come into compliance. The hospital administrator tells the consultant to delete all references to the deficiencies from his formal report. The consultant complies with this request.

d. *Consultant Goals.* **The consulting relationship is one in which client adaptability and growth toward self-direction are consistently encouraged and cultivated. (See A.1.b.)**

+ A consultant to a mental health agency is charged with helping set up an outreach center. She offers illustrations of approaches taken by other agencies and encourages the staff to assume responsibility for designing and implementing the new center.

− A consultant is retained by an employment service to help staff with their professional development in the area of interviewing skills. The consultant agrees to the goals and a fee of $500 per day of service. The entire process could be completed in five sessions; however, the consultant purposefully extends the sessions to eight by focusing on staff members' minor deficiencies.

D.3. Fees for Referral

a. *Accepting Fees From Agency Clients.* **Counselors refuse a private fee or other remuneration for rendering services to persons who are entitled to such services through the counselor's employing agency or institution. The policies of a particular agency may make explicit provisions for agency clients to receive counseling services from members of its staff in private practice. In such instances, the clients must be informed of other options open to them should they seek private counseling services. (See A.10.a., A.11.b., and C.3.d.)**

+ A campus fraternity is hosting a regional leadership conference for all the chapters in a seven-state area. The fraternity president asks the director of student development, an exciting public speaker, if she will give the keynote address. He offers to pay an honorarium. Because fraternity advisement and support are part of the responsibilities of the director's office, she declines the honorarium.

– The policy of a university counseling center is to provide only short-term counseling aimed at remediation of a specific problem. Clients are limited to six visits. A list of referral sources in the community is available, and it is the center's policy that clients may be seen by staff counselors in their private practices only in unusual circumstances and with the director's approval. Felicia, who is a staff counselor, disagrees with the policy. She regularly recommends that many of her clients continue seeing her in her private practice because it makes little sense to begin with a new counselor.

b. *Referral Fees.* **Counselors do not accept a referral fee from other professionals.**

+ Paula is a counselor in private practice. Recently, she has received several telephone inquiries from prospective clients seeking help with childhood sexual abuse issues. Because Paula does not have specific training in this area, she provides the names and phone numbers of two other professionals who have the needed expertise. One of these other professionals calls her, thanks her for the referrals, and offers to pay her a referral fee. Paula declines the offer and explains that it would not be ethical for her to accept it.

— Ted, an employee assistance counselor, refers clients who could benefit from medication for depression and some other conditions. He approaches a psychiatrist to whom he refers many clients and asks the psychiatrist to enter into an arrangement that includes giving Ted a referral fee for sending the psychiatrist so many clients.

D.4. Subcontractor Arrangements

When counselors work as subcontractors for counseling services for a third party, they have a duty to inform clients of the limitations of confidentiality that the organization may place on counselors in providing counseling services to clients. The limits of such confidentiality ordinarily are discussed as part of the intake session. (See B.1.e. and B.1.f.)

+ Deanna is hired by a private psychiatric hospital to provide stress-management training for the staff who work there. She informs the staff that she will be expected to provide the director of the hospital with feedback about what they find stressful about working in the facility. She lets the staff know that, although she will provide the director with information about sources of stress, she will take care to protect the identities of specific individuals.

— The psychiatric hospital in the preceding scenario hires Edna to provide the stress management training. Edna says nothing to the staff out of concern that they will feel inhibited if they know that any information will be shared with the director. She feels she is capable of using good judgment in deciding how much she will reveal about specific staff members in her discussions with the director.

SECTION E:
EVALUATION, ASSESSMENT, AND INTERPRETATION

Study and Discussion Guide

✦ **Informed Consent:** *Prior to using assessment with clients, how might you explain its nature and purposes in clear and specific language? In what ways do you attempt to involve your clients in the assessment process?*

✦ **Diagnosis:** *What ethical issues are involved in making a diagnosis? What are your own views about the role of diagnosis in counseling? What cultural factors do you need to take into account in making diagnoses?*

✦ **Cultural Sensitivity:** *In making a diagnosis, what attention will you give to the cultural and environmental variables that might pertain to a client's concerns? What role do you think that clients' socioeconomic and cultural experiences have in helping you to understand their problems?*

✦ **Testing:** *When might you make use of tests as a part of the counseling process? What factors do you need to take into account in selecting, administering, scoring, and interpreting tests? What are the ethical considerations in testing diverse client populations?*

E.1. General

a. *Appraisal Techniques.* **The primary purpose of educational and psychological assessment is to provide measures that are objective and interpretable in either comparative or absolute terms. Counselors recognize the need to interpret the statements in this section as applying to the whole range of appraisal techniques, including test and nontest data.**

   ✛ A private practitioner administers a personality test to his clients. He carefully explains the purpose of the test and how the results will be used in the therapeutic process.

   ━ Melody is a counselor in private practice. She limits her practice to personal counseling and rarely administers or interprets tests in her work. She usually refers to other professionals those clients who could benefit from specific types of psychological testing. She does utilize the *DSM-IV* in assigning diagnoses and designing treatment plans. Melody does not bother to read Section E (Evaluation, Assessment, and Interpretation) of the Code of Ethics. She believes she does not need to be familiar with this section because she doesn't do testing.

b. *Client Welfare.* **Counselors promote the welfare and best interests of the client in the development, publication, and utilization of educational and psychological assessment techniques. They do not misuse assessment results and interpretations and take reasonable steps to prevent others from misusing the information these techniques provide. They respect the client's right to know the results, the interpretations made, and the bases for their conclusions and recommendations.**

+ Nancy is a high school counselor. A week before the administration of achievement tests to the sophomore class, she visits classrooms in order to explain the purpose of this test series. After the results become available, she meets with each sophomore to interpret the results. She sends a letter to the parents that provides information about how test scores should be interpreted and puts a copy of this letter in the mailbox of each sophomore teacher.

− A business administrator asks the personnel counselor to administer a battery of tests to five employees who are being considered for promotion. The counselor assumes that the employees have been informed of their promotion possibilities and the purpose of the testing. She administers the tests and later learns that two employees were fired shortly after the testing and that they had not been told the purpose of the tests.

E.2. Competence to Use and Interpret Tests

a. *Limits of Competence.* **Counselors recognize the limits of their competence and perform only those testing and assessment services for which they have been trained. They are familiar with reliability, validity, related standardization, error of measurement, and proper application of any technique utilized.**

Counselors using computer-based test interpretations are trained in the construct being measured and the specific instrument being used prior to using this type of computer application. Counselors take reasonable measures to ensure the proper use of psychological assessment techniques by persons under their supervision.

+ The director of a mental health agency asks a counselor to administer a projective personality test to a client. The counselor is not trained in the administration and interpretation of this test. She explains this to the director, and they agree that a staff psychologist will administer the test.

− A counselor who works with residents in the county jail is asked to do a personality assessment of a newly incarcerated inmate. Because this counselor has little knowledge of personality tests, she administers a test that can be computer-scored and interpreted. She bases her personality assessment on the computer printout.

b. *Appropriate Use.* Counselors are responsible for the appropriate application, scoring, interpretation, and use of assessment instruments, whether they score and interpret such tests themselves or use computerized or other services.

+ A male client wants to become a nurse. He has some doubt, however, about whether this is really the right field for him. The counselor administers a vocational interest test. The results do not support his interest in the nursing field. The counselor explains that although the test shouldn't be the only factor in his decision, the results do mean that his interests are different from those of a recent sample of men who are in the nursing profession.

− All third graders are administered a test of basic skills that requires the children to bubble in their answers on a computer-scanned form. The school counselor is assigned to make sure that each form is properly bubbled in. The counselor is annoyed at being required to do this tedious clerical task and decides to just 'spot check' the answer sheets.

c. *Decisions Based on Results.* Counselors responsible for decisions involving individuals or policies that are based on as-

sessment results have a thorough understanding of educational and psychological measurement, including validation criteria, test research, and guidelines for test development and use.

+ A school counselor frequently serves on admission, review, and dismissal (ARD) committees. An ARD committee evaluates a wide range of information, including test data, and then decides if a child qualifies for special education services. The counselor has a thorough understanding of testing and measurement. She is able to help other committee members see the test results in proper perspective and use them in making wise decisions.

− A school counselor tells the parents of a third grader that their child's high achievement in the classroom coupled with superior scores on the Weschler Intelligence Scale for Children-Revised (WISC-R) predicts success should the child be advanced a grade above his age level. However, the counselor really does not understand how WISC-R scores are derived or what abilities they represent.

d. *Accurate Information.* **Counselors provide accurate information and avoid false claims or misconceptions when making statements about assessment instruments or techniques. Special efforts are made to avoid unwarranted connotations of such terms as** *IQ* **and** *grade equivalent scores.* **(See C.5.c.)**

+ After achievement test results for the sixth-grade class have been received, the school counselor sends the scores to the parents. She includes a cover letter that explains the meaning of the test scores in lay rather than psychometric terminology. She also invites parents to come to the school and discuss the results.

− A test publisher has changed the norm group in revising a standardized achievement test battery. This change results in more difficult norms and is carefully described in the test manual. The counselor, after reading the manual, decides this information is too technical for teachers to understand or appreciate. When several students score significantly lower on the test than they had scored in previous years, their teachers recommend that they be placed in a different, less advanced reading group.

E.3. Informed Consent

a. *Explanation to Clients.* **Prior to assessment, counselors explain the nature and purposes of assessment and the specific use of results in language the client (or other legally authorized person on behalf of the client) can understand, unless an explicit exception to this right has been agreed upon in advance. Regardless of whether scoring and interpretation are completed by counselors, by assistants, or by computer or other outside services, counselors take reasonable steps to ensure that appropriate explanations are given to the client.**

+ Two college counselors work to develop a computer program to assist entering students choose the most appropriate freshman English course. They want to design the software so that students can complete the program without assistance. Over a period of 2 years, the program is pilot tested, and validation studies are conducted. When the program is completed, the manual carefully describes how to interpret and use the results in language that the students can understand.

− A school system purchases a computerized software package for 4-year course planning that is designed for students to complete with counselor assistance. To save time, the counselor writes an instruction manual to accompany the software and instructs students to complete the process independently in the school's computer lab.

b. *Recipients of Results.* **The examinee's welfare, explicit understanding, and prior agreement determine the recipients of test results. Counselors include accurate and appropriate interpretations with any release of individual or group test results. (See B.1.a. and C.5.c.)**

+ A counselor develops a computer application designed to help individuals identify their life stressors. In discussing results with clients who have completed the test, she carefully describes how to interpret results and other factors that might suggest the need for further counseling for stress management.

− Meg, a career counselor, develops a computerized initial decision-making program that is designed for clients to take home and complete at their leisure. Although it is her intention that clients will bring the results of this initial exploration to the next counseling session for further discussion, she fails to include this information in the software. Several clients complete the program at home but fail to return for further counseling. Meg assumes that these clients must not be committed to the career exploration process, and she does not attempt to follow up or contact them.

E.4. Release of Information to Competent Professionals

a. *Misuse of Results.* **Counselors do not misuse assessment results, including test results, and interpretations, and take reasonable steps to prevent the misuse of such by others. (See C.5.c.)**

+ A counselor in an agency becomes aware that one of his colleagues uses a paper-and-pencil personality inventory for purposes for which it was not designed. The counselor talks to his colleague privately and expresses his concern. The colleague, who had been unaware of her misuse of the inventory, agrees to seek further training in the instrument before using it again.

− A counselor in private practice routinely gives a battery of psychological tests to all of her clients before she begins counseling with them. The cost to clients of this testing is considerable. When one of her colleagues questions her rationale for this practice, she replies that clients gain confidence in her and in the counseling process when they have something concrete such as test results.

b. *Release of Raw Data.* **Counselors ordinarily release data (e.g., protocols, counseling or interview notes, or questionnaires) in which the client is identified only with the consent of the client or the client's legal representative. Such data are usually released only to persons recognized by counselors as competent to interpret the data. (See B.1.a.)**

+ A counselor administers a projective test to a 7-year-old child who refuses to speak. The results indicate an unusual pattern, and the counselor is unsure how to best interpret this. With the written consent of the child's parents, she sends the test protocol to a professor in a neighboring state who is an expert in projective testing, with a request for assistance in understanding how to interpret the child's results.

— A school counselor conducts a self-esteem group for children. She typically asks children to draw their families in a simplified genogram format. She decides to share one child's drawing with his teacher, without discussing it first with either the child or his parents.

E.5. Proper Diagnosis of Mental Disorders

a. *Proper Diagnosis.* **Counselors take special care to provide proper diagnosis of mental disorders. Assessment techniques (including personal interview) used to determine client care (e.g., locus of treatment, type of treatment, or recommended follow-up) are carefully selected and appropriately used. (See A.3.a. and C.5.c.)**

+ Mel is an intake counselor in a psychiatric hospital. Each time a new patient is admitted, Mel is responsible for formulating an initial diagnosis and suggesting an appropriate course of treatment. If he believes that he does not have sufficient data to make this assessment at the conclusion of the intake interview, he schedules further sessions so that he can make an accurate diagnosis and formulate a treatment plan.

— Craig works with clients who have serious psychological disturbances, but he takes few steps to formulate a formal diagnosis. When he is required by a third-party payer to include a diagnosis, Craig routinely assigns a diagnosis of depression with mild to moderate severity. He claims that what these clients need is a caring counselor who will listen to them, not one who diagnoses and categorizes them.

b. *Cultural Sensitivity.* **Counselors recognize that culture affects the manner in which clients' problems are defined. Clients' socioeconomic and cultural experience is considered when diagnosing mental disorders.**

+ Sean is a counselor who works in a culturally and racially diverse school. As a certified special education counselor, he is responsible for diagnosing students who may need to placed in special education classes. He proceeds cautio realizing that the cultural context needs to be taken into consideration in making accurate diagnoses.

— Terrence is hired to work as a counselor in an agency with a diverse client population. He fails to take into account their socioeconomic and cultural backgrounds in making diagnoses and developing treatment plans. Many clients are economically impoverished. These clients are often late for appointments and seem to Terrence to be disoriented. He tends to assign severe diagnoses to these clients. He mentions to one of his colleagues that this agency's caseload seems to include an inordinate number of clients who are seriously maladjusted.

E.6. Test Selection

a. *Appropriateness of Instruments.* **Counselors carefully consider the validity, reliability, psychometric limitations, and appropriateness of instruments when selecting tests for use in a given situation or with a particular client.**

+ The manager of an employment agency asks her counseling staff for advice on the purchase of an attractive new test of manual dexterity. The counselors evaluate the test manual and advise against purchasing the test because there is limited evidence that the test is valid.

— A counselor has administered a personality inventory to a Mexican American client. The counselor is aware that this inventory contains several race-related or race-sensitive items, enough to make its use questionable with Mexican American clients. The counselor is also aware that the test manual contains instructions on how to adjust the scoring for minority clients so that the standard norms and profile can be used. The counselor considers doing this, but decides it would be a waste of his time because this particular client seems so well acculturated.

b. *Culturally Diverse Populations.* **Counselors are cautious when selecting tests for culturally diverse populations to avoid inappropriateness of testing that may be outside of socialized behavioral or cognitive patterns.**

+ The faculty of a graduate counseling program meet to discuss tests to be used in the selection of candidates for admission to the program. They realize that the Miller's Analogy Test may not be suitable for some candidates and decide to search for alternative assessment strategies.

− Kim Sung, a high school senior, has lived for only a few years in this country. He is fluent in oral communication and reads well, and has achieved a high score on a college entrance examination. He meets with his school counselor to discuss his plans for going to college and asks for assistance in exploring possible careers. The counselor administers a personality inventory and a career interest inventory. The results of the career interest inventory indicate a preference for legal work, and Kim Sung says that he thinks he might like to be a lawyer. The counselor points out that according to the personality inventory he is unassertive and noncompetitive, and that these traits would make it impossible for him to succeed as a lawyer.

E.7. Conditions of Test Administration

a. *Administration Conditions.* **Counselors administer tests under the same conditions that were established in their standardization. When tests are not administered under standard conditions or when unusual behavior or irregularities occur during the testing session, those conditions are noted in interpretation, and the results may be designated as invalid or of questionable validity.**

+ During the administration of a standardized test, a malfunction in the timer causes the time to be 7 minutes short for a subtest. The problem is discovered a week later when the timer is used again. The principal is reluctant to report the matter to the national testing center, but the counselor insists that it be reported, pointing out how this could adversely affect the total test results.

− The director of testing at a university is scheduled to administer the LSAT. En route to the test site, the director has a flat tire. She arrives late and the students, who were already anxious, are quite upset. To offset the students' distress, she decides to give them 30 minutes extra time beyond that allotted in the directions for the testing. She does not report these events to the testing service.

b. *Computer Administration.* **Counselors are responsible for ensuring that administration programs function properly to provide clients with accurate results when a computer or other electronic methods are used for test administration. (See A.12.b.)**

+ Before using a computer-administered-and-scored test with clients, a counselor goes through the entire test-taking and scoring process herself to ensure that the computer program works properly.

− Over the course of a school year, 50 students take a computerized assessment of vocational interest. The counselor, who had neglected to master the operation of the program or test the accuracy of the results, routinely makes a small error in operating the program. As a result, students are given inaccurate information.

c. *Unsupervised Test Taking.* **Counselors do not permit unsupervised or inadequately supervised use of tests or assessments unless the tests or assessments are designed, intended, and validated for self-administration and/or scoring.**

+ An elementary school counselor is administering a timed, individually administered test designed to detect learning disabilities. She takes precautions to prevent interruptions during the testing session so as not to disturb the child's concentration or invalidate the test results.

− A school counselor is administering a portion of an achievement test to a small group of students who were absent on the day the test was originally given. During the testing session, the counselor is called to answer a phone call and leaves the students alone in the room for 10 minutes while she takes the call.

d. *Disclosure of Favorable Conditions.* **Prior to test administration, conditions that produce most favorable test results are made known to the examinees.**

+ A student is scheduled to take a college entrance examination. The counselor learns that the student is upset over the recent death of his grandmother. She suggests that the student postpone taking the examination, explaining that the results could be influenced by his emotional state.

– A counselor is administering an achievement test to a group of ninth graders. Toward the end of the test, the counselor notices that one student has put her head down on the desk. When questioned, the student says that she has a terrible headache and feels nauseated, but that she has completed the test as best she was able. The counselor does not tell her that she could retake a different form of the test at a later date.

E.8. Diversity in Testing

Counselors are cautious in using assessment techniques, making evaluations, and interpreting the performance of populations not represented in the norm group on which an instrument was standardized. They recognize the effects of age, color, culture, disability, ethnic group, gender, race, religion, sexual orientation, and socioeconomic status on test administration and interpretation and place test results in proper perspective with other relevant factors. (See A.2.a.)

+ A Mexican American transfer student is recommended for a low-ability class placement based on his poor performance on a mental ability test. The school counselor learns that Mexican Americans are not represented in the norm group for the test and that the student has always performed well academically. The counselor puts together a variety of more appropriate measures to use as a basis for placement.

– Frank is a Vietnam war veteran who has been hospitalized many times for depression. He applies for vocational rehabilitation assistance to pursue job training. He has been unable to hold a job for longer than a few months since he was discharged from military service. The counselor administers an interest inventory. The results do not indicate a strong interest in any of the occupational areas. The counselor fails to consider Frank's history and mental status in interpreting the results, and tells Frank that he might want to consider just getting steady work instead of seeking job training.

E.9. Test Scoring and Interpretation

a. *Reporting Reservations.* **In reporting assessment results, counselors indicate any reservations that exist regarding validity or reliability because of the circumstances of the assessment or the inappropriateness of the norms for the person tested.**

+ A high school student with a learning disability is disappointed with his low score on the social sciences subtest of a scholastic aptitude test. The student places great faith in the test results and says that he will give up his plans to become a history teacher. The counselor explains that the test results may have been affected by the learning disability and helps the student explore a range of factors that could have a bearing on his career plans.

− A counselor is mailed a sample copy of a new vocational interest inventory that is in the process of being standardized. The counselor peruses the inventory, is favorably impressed, and decides to use it in vocational counseling with one of his clients. He fails to tell this client that the test results may be unreliable.

b. *Research Instruments.* **Counselors exercise caution when interpreting the results of research instruments possessing insufficient technical data to support respondent results. The specific purposes for the use of such instruments are stated explicitly to the examinee.**

+ The director of testing at a community college has been contacted by a testing company that wants to use college freshmen as part of the item analysis group. The director agrees to help and explains to student volunteers that they are participating in the development of this test and that they won't be able to get any meaningful information from the results.

− A counselor administers a newly developed ability test to a prospective college student. The test's predictive validity has not been established. In interpreting the scores, the counselor does not inform the student about the test's limitations and proceeds to draw inferences from the test results about the student's chances for success in college.

c. *Testing Services.* **Counselors who provide test scoring and test interpretation services to support the assessment process confirm the validity of such interpretations. They accurately describe the purpose, norms, validity, reliability, and applications of the procedures and any special qualifications applicable to their use. The public offering of an automated test interpretations service is considered a professional-to-professional consultation. The formal responsibility of the consultant is to the consultee, but the ultimate and overriding responsibility is to the client.**

+ A counselor is hired as a consultant to a large department score. She is asked to do something to determine which job applicants are prone to tardiness and absenteeism due to hypochondriacal tendencies (calling in sick). The counselor proposes a correlational study comparing results from instruments that measure hypochondriacal tendencies with actual employee promptness and attendance over a 10-month period. The counselor explains that until and unless sufficient correlation can be found between actual employee performance and test data, no individual employee's test result can be considered relevant to the problems of tardiness and absenteeism.

− A counselor contracts to provide test scoring and interpretation to an employment agency. He has met with a representative of the agency, and they have reached agreement regarding the particular tests that will be administered to agency clients. He scores a test for a client who has a physical disability. Although this test has limited validity for individuals who are physically disabled, he does not note this limitation in his interpretation of the results.

E.10. Test Security

Counselors maintain the integrity and security of tests and other assessment techniques consistent with legal and contractual obligations. Counselors do not appropriate, reproduce, or modify published tests or parts thereof without acknowledgment and permission from the publisher.

+ A provision for test security is that no test booklets are to be taken out of the testing room by anyone. One of the proctors starts to leave the room with a test booklet. The counselor reminds him of the rule and has him leave the test booklet in the room.

− A counselor determines by empirical study that a test of academic motivation can be constructed by drawing selected items from each of several published personality and interest inventories. She constructs and begins to utilize her test without obtaining permission from the publishers of these inventories to use their items.

E.11. Obsolete Tests and Outdated Test Results

Counselors do not use data or test results that are obsolete or outdated for the current purpose. Counselors make every effort to prevent the misuse of obsolete measures and test data by others.

+ Harriet is hired as a counselor in a university admissions office. She notices that Graduate Record Exam (GRE) results are routinely used as a criterion for admission to graduate programs without giving consideration to the date of the testing. She calls to the attention of her director that results more than 10 years old should not be used for this purpose, and the director agrees to make the needed change in procedures.

− A counselor discourages a 36-year-old reentry college student from pursuing a degree in electrical engineering because of a low algebra score on an achievement test taken when she first started college at the age of 20.

E.12. Test Construction

Counselors use established scientific procedures, relevant standards, and current professional knowledge for test design in the development, publication, and utilization of educational and psychological assessment techniques.

+ A counselor educator who is designing a test takes specific steps to reduce bias against certain cultural groups. In developing the test, she makes use of current professional knowledge and also has other experts evaluate the test.

– A counselor develops a computer program that generates a profile of suicide risk. She relies on a common-sense justification for the program's interpretation. For example, the program describes self-reported feelings of depression as elevating suicide potential. The counselor rents an exhibit booth and sells the program at a state professional conference.

SECTION F: TEACHING, TRAINING, AND SUPERVISION

Study and Discussion Guide

✦ *Counselor Educators and Trainers: How can appropriate relationship boundaries between counselor educators and students be determined? What ethical, professional, and social relationship boundaries between counselor educators and students do you see as important? What about boundaries between supervisors and supervisees?*

✦ *Counselor Education and Training Programs: As a student, what do you want to know about the program to which you are applying, prior to admission? What kinds of information do students need to be provided at the beginning of their training programs?*

✦ *Self-Growth Experiences: What role should therapeutic experiences play in a graduate counseling program? Should these experiences be a basic part of the program or merely recommended? What do you see as the problems, if any, in combining experiential training experiences with didactic course work? What guidelines might you like to see regarding students' levels of self-disclosure?*

✦ *Counseling for Students and Supervisees: What do you see as the rationale for prohibiting counselor educators or supervisors from serving as counselors to students or supervisees over whom they hold administrative, teaching, or evaluative roles? What is your opinion about the ethics of supervisors or counselor educators entering into counseling relationships with former supervisees or students?*

✦ **Clients of Students or Supervisees:** *What kinds of information do student interns in field placements need to provide to their clients?*

F.1. Counselor Educators and Trainers

a. *Educators as Teachers and Practitioners.* **Counselors who are responsible for developing, implementing, and supervising educational programs are skilled as teachers and practitioners. They are knowledgeable regarding the ethical, legal, and regulatory aspects of the profession, are skilled in applying that knowledge, and make students and supervisees aware of their responsibilities. Counselors conduct counselor education and training programs in an ethical manner and serve as role models for professional behavior. Counselor educators should make an effort to infuse material related to human diversity into all courses and/or workshops that are designed to promote the development of professional counselors.**

➕ Ellen teaches a variety of courses including practicum, family therapy, counseling techniques, and multicultural counseling. As a member of the counseling department, she is partly responsible for the admission of students to the program, and she participates in the process of evaluating students for retention at various points in the program. In all of her classes she combines experiential and didactic components. She strives to make theory come alive by focusing on practical applications. Because of her approach to teaching she gains a good deal of information about her students' values, attitudes, and life experiences. For example, in her family therapy class, her students explore how their family-of-origin experiences influence them today. In her multicultural class, she challenges students to examine their cultural biases and prejudices and how these might impact their work with culturally diverse populations. In order to role model professional behavior, Ellen explains to her students her bases for evaluation in teaching her courses and in serving on the admissions and retention committee. She is aware of the differential in power and clarifies how she functions in various roles.

➖ A master's degree program in counseling requires students to complete a course in multicultural counseling. The department members make little effort to infuse material related to human diversity in the core courses, assuming that students will learn about diversity issues in the required multicultural course.

b. *Relationship Boundaries With Students and Supervisees.* **Counselors clearly define and maintain ethical, professional, and social relationship boundaries with their students and supervisees. They are aware of the differential in power that exists and the student's or supervisee's possible incomprehension of that power differential. Counselors explain to students and supervisees the potential for the relationship to become exploitive.**

+ In a counselor education program that involves experiential as well as didactic course work, the faculty are committed to helping students become aware of the power differential that exists between teachers and students. They form a committee, composed of both faculty and student representatives, to develop a set of guidelines to minimize any potential abuse of this power.

− Ben, a supervisor, is particularly fond of one of his hard-working supervisees. The supervisee comes to Ben for a couple of counseling sessions to deal with his anxiety over losing his part-time job. He is worried that he may have to drop out of his graduate program because of financial hardship. Ben offers to give him an interest-free loan to help him through this difficult time. Ben tells the supervisee that he can repay the loan once he is out of school.

c. *Sexual Relationships.* **Counselors do not engage in sexual relationships with students or supervisees and do not subject them to sexual harassment. (See A.6. and C.5.b)**

+ Mark is a middle-aged professor in a counseling program. He has recently gone through a painful divorce. He feels emotionally vulnerable and finds himself attracted to one of his students. He seeks counseling to deal with his feelings and is very careful to maintain appropriate professional behavior with the student.

− Wanda often flirts with her male supervisees. She has a tendency to joke with them and send them verbal and nonverbal messages with sexual overtones. Although her behavior makes the supervisees uncomfortable, they believe that there is nothing they can do to correct the situation.

d. *Contributions to Research.* **Counselors give credit to students or supervisees for their contributions to research and scholarly projects. Credit is given through coauthorship, acknowledgment, footnote statement, or other appropriate means, in accordance with such contributions. (See G.4.b. and G.4.c.)**

+ A professor is writing an article that describes his research on student attitudes toward gender socialization. He invites two of his doctoral students to participate in the analysis of the data. He acknowledges both students in the article for their contributions.

− Bill, an untenured faculty member, scrambles to complete a journal article before he is reviewed for tenure consideration. Although one of his graduate assistants did considerable work on the article with Bill, he knows that faculty review committees tend to give less weight to coauthored than to single-authored journal articles. Bill decides to put only his name on the article and to explain the situation to his graduate student.

e. *Close Relatives.* **Counselors do not accept close relatives as students or supervisees.**

+ Herb is a faculty member in a counselor education program. His wife Thelma had earned her master's degree in counseling before they met. Now she wants to return to school to obtain her doctorate in counselor education. The university at which Herb teaches is located in a small town, and the nearest other counselor education doctoral program is in a city that is a 3-hour drive away. Herb and Thelma discuss the difficulties that could be involved if she were to apply and be accepted into the program where Herb teaches. They conclude that it would be difficult for her to avoid taking courses with him and realize that her enrollment would put his colleagues in an uncomfortable position. They decide that Thelma will apply to the city university, and if she is accepted they will have to make some sacrifices to accommodate her goals.

    ‐ Lee's daughter is enrolled in the same graduate program in which he is a professor. Lee allows her to enroll in a family counseling course that he is teaching. The course involves experiential activities dealing with the family history of students. Lee thinks that he and his daughter can be good role models by being open and honest with the students about their family dynamics.

f. *Supervision Preparation.* **Counselors who offer clinical supervision services are adequately prepared in supervision methods and techniques. Counselors who are doctoral students serving as practicum or internship supervisors to master's level students are adequately prepared and supervised by the training program.**

    + Diane, a counselor educator, supervises doctoral students who serve as practicum supervisors to master's level students. She has developed a supervision course that the doctoral students must take before they function as supervisors. In addition, she meets with these doctoral students each week in a small group. In these meetings, the students discuss what they are learning, and Diane helps them with any problems they encounter in providing supervision.

    ‐ Beverly accepts a part-time position as a clinical supervisor for a practicum group. Although she has never taken a course or workshop in supervision and has no on-the-job training as a supervisor, she believes she can draw on her wealth of experience as a counselor to help her do a good job as a supervisor.

g. *Responsibility for Services to Clients.* **Counselors who supervise the counseling services of others take reasonable measures to ensure that counseling services provided to clients are professional.**

    + Greta conducts weekly supervision meetings with a small group of students. She expects them to bring up any problems they are facing in their field placements. She encourages role-playing and helps students develop alternatives to dealing with difficult clients. Supervision sessions focus on client dynamics, and on supervisees' self-awareness, especially of ways that their own countertransference issues might interfere with effective counseling.

- Brian, who functions as a field supervisor, feels that he is greatly overworked in his agency. Although he agreed to accept two graduate students as interns, he finds it difficult to make the time to meet with them to discuss their cases. Both of his supervisees have told him that they need more supervision than they are getting from him. Brian says that there is merit in letting students learn by struggling on their own.

h. *Endorsement.* **Counselors do not endorse students or supervisees for certification, licensure, employment, or completion of an academic or training program if they believe students or supervisees are not qualified for the endorsement. Counselors take reasonable steps to assist students or supervisees who are not qualified for endorsement to become qualified.**

+ Although Steve earned high grades in his academic courses, certain personality patterns are interfering with his ability to form good relationships with the staff and his clients at the agency where he is doing his field work. The campus supervisor meets with Steve and the field supervisor to identify specific areas of concern. The three of them develop an action plan aimed at modifying some of Steve's behaviors. They plan to meet periodically to evaluate how well the plan is working.

- Sean is applying for a position as a counselor in a community counseling center. He asks his department chairperson for a letter of recommendation. The chairperson feels that in good conscience she is unable to endorse him as a viable candidate for this position. However, she fears that Sean, whom she sees as a litigious type, will cause trouble for the department. She decides to write him a brief letter of recommendation, hoping that the potential employer will be able to read between the lines of her lukewarm endorsement.

F.2. Counselor Education and Training Programs

a. *Orientation.* **Prior to admission, counselors orient prospective students to the counselor education or training program's expectations, including but not limited to the following: (1)**

the type and level of skill acquisition required for successful completion of the training, (2) subject matter to be covered, (3) basis for evaluation, (4) training components that encourage self-growth or self-disclosure as part of the training process, (5) the type of supervision settings and requirements of the sites for required clinical field experiences, (6) student and supervisee evaluation and dismissal policies and procedures, and (7) up-to-date employment prospects for graduates.

+ Prospective students who indicate an interest in applying to a counseling program are provided with an informational pamphlet. The pamphlet describes the philosophy of the program; admission, retention, and dismissal policies and procedures; skill and knowledge acquisition required for graduation; and the curriculum. A section details evaluation procedures and identifies training components that include self-growth and self-disclosure as being separate from graded components. Another section describes the required field experiences and explains the program's criteria for selecting sites and site supervisors. At the end of the pamphlet, results of a recent follow-up study of graduates are summarized to give readers information about their employment prospects after graduation. Students who apply for admission are asked to view a videotape, created by the program faculty and students, that provides similar information prior to their admission interviews.

− In the brochure sent to prospective students by a counseling department, two master's degree programs are outlined. Plan A is a traditional program. Plan B enables students to complete the program more quickly by enrolling in a special summer practicum. Some students select Plan B, and after they arrive on campus, advanced students advise them to switch plans because of the lack of clients during the summer practicum.

b. *Integration of Study and Practice.* **Counselors establish counselor education and training programs that integrate academic study and supervised practice.**

+ The faculty who teach in a master's degree program in counseling hold a retreat to assess their program's balance between didactic and experiential learnings. They identify the components in required courses that provide students with opportunities for supervised practice, and conclude that their students need more skill-building opportunities before they enter practicum and internship. They make a commitment that full-time faculty will teach the introductory core courses and will infuse role-play and other opportunities to translate theory into practice. They also decide to add to the curriculum a counseling techniques course, with emphasis on supervised practice, that students will take concurrently with the theories course.

— Students in a master's level counseling program are permitted to waive their second semester of practicum if they write a thesis. Program faculty realize that this option adversely affects the preparedness to practice of students who select it. However, they are reluctant to give up the opportunities for publishing that students' thesis work provides for them.

c. *Evaluation.* **Counselors clearly state to students and supervisees, in advance of training, the levels of competency expected, appraisal methods, and timing of evaluations for both didactic and experiential components. Counselors provide students and supervisees with periodic performance appraisal and evaluation feedback throughout the training program.**

+ Students are informed before they enter a counseling program that they will be expected to acquire competency in group work, and that although experiential learning in this skill area will be required, self-disclosure will not be graded. A full-time faculty member teaches the didactic component of the group counseling course, and her syllabus clearly indicates the grading requirements. An adjunct professor teaches the experiential component, which involves the students in co-leading a small group in which they explore some of their own personal concerns. The adjunct professor supervises these groups and offers feedback, but does not evaluate students on their performance as group members or leaders or on their level of self-disclosure in the groups.

— Shirley is a graduate student in counseling. Last semester, she enrolled in a course entitled "Introductory Counseling

Skills," which was taught by a part-time faculty member. Class time was devoted to lectures and discussions of a variety of counseling approaches. Grades were based on class participation and an objective examination, and no opportunities were provided for students to demonstrate or receive performance feedback on their development of counseling skills. This semester she is enrolled in an advanced counseling techniques class. On the first class day, the professor assured students that he would give them periodic performance evaluation. However, he has yet to do so, and there are only 4 weeks remaining in the semester.

d. *Teaching Ethics.* **Counselors make students and supervisees aware of the ethical responsibilities and standards of the profession and the students' and supervisees' ethical responsibilities to the profession. (See C.1. and F.3.e.)**

+ Faculty in a counselor education program believe that professional ethics should be infused throughout the curriculum. During the introductory course, class time is devoted to studying the ACA Code of Ethics and Standards of Practice. A formal ethics course is required and the courses in research methods, psychometric procedures, group process, and practicum deal with specialized applications of ethics. Finally, during their internships, students meet weekly with their supervisor in a small group format to discuss cases and explore any problems they might be encountering in their field placements. At the initial meeting, the supervisor asks his supervisees to carefully review the ACA Code of Ethics and Standards of Practice. He encourages them to bring to the weekly meetings any concerns they have, especially as they apply to ethical concerns they are confronting at their sites.

− The professor who teaches the specialty course in school counseling offers only superficial coverage of the ACA Code of Ethics and Standards of Practice. He believes that the code and standards are too generic to be of much use to school counselors, and that school counselors rarely encounter the difficult ethical dilemmas that are faced by mental health counselors in the community.

e. *Peer Relationships.* **When students or supervisees are assigned to lead counseling groups or provide clinical supervision for their peers, counselors take steps to ensure that students and supervisees placed in these roles do not have personal or adverse relationships with peers and that they understand they have the same ethical obligations as counselor educators, trainers, and supervisors. Counselors make every effort to ensure that the rights of peers are not compromised when students or supervisees are assigned to lead counseling groups or provide clinical supervision.**

+ As one component of a practicum in group counseling, the graduate students colead a self-exploration course in the undergraduate program. The groups they lead are supervised by an instructor with whom they meet weekly for group supervision. The supervisor emphasizes the importance of ethical and professional behavior on the part of these student leaders.

− Advanced master's students function as facilitators of small groups in a beginning skills-development course. Some of the facilitators know the beginning students, and in one particular class there is a great deal of conflict because the beginning students feel they are being pressured to reveal their personal problems. They approach the course instructor with their concern, but he decides not to intervene. He tells them that he might escalate the problem if he were to step in, and that there is much to learn from dealing with conflict.

f. *Varied Theoretical Positions.* **Counselors present varied theoretical positions so that students and supervisees may make comparisons and have opportunities to develop their own positions. Counselors provide information concerning the scientific bases of professional practice. (See C.6.a.)**

+ A professor regularly invites other professors and practitioners with differing theoretical approaches to lecture to her class in counseling methods in order to encourage students to adopt a broad perspective. The assigned text gives equal coverage to a wide variety of counseling theories. Students are required to write a term paper that compares and contrasts two of the major theories and sets forth the student's own theory of counseling.

- A professor views behavioral counseling as mechanistic and dehumanizing. She does assign students to read the textbook chapter on behavioral counseling and briefly discusses this approach. However, she devotes the major portion of the semester to the Adlerian approach, of which she is an adherent.

g. *Field Placements.* **Counselors develop clear policies within their training program regarding field placement and other clinical experiences. Counselors provide clearly stated roles and responsibilities for the student or supervisee, the site supervisor, and the program supervisor. They confirm that site supervisors are qualified to provide supervision and are informed of their professional and ethical responsibilities in this role.**

+ A professor in the counseling department is appointed field placement director. She meets with all field supervisors to determine their qualifications and willingness to supervise practicum students properly. She meets with the students when they begin their placements and clearly defines their roles and responsibilities. The students then meet with their field supervisors to develop a contract outlining goals, objectives, and strategies. The director periodically visits the sites to ensure that supervisors and students are adhering to the contract and are functioning in an ethical and professional manner.

- A graduate student starts an internship at a career counseling agency in the community. Nobody there seems to know what the student is supposed to be doing; he is encouraged to "work up some goals," but there are no suggestions or structure. The student complains of the excessive ambiguity to his university supervisor, but the supervisor does not feel comfortable about intervening. The student continues to attempt to define his own role and responsibilities.

h. *Dual Relationships as Supervisors.* **Counselors avoid dual relationships such as performing the role of site supervisor and training program supervisor in the student's or supervisee's training program. Counselors do not accept any form of professional services, fees, commissions, reimbursement, or remuneration from a site for student or supervisee placement.**

+ An agency counselor is hired part time by a graduate counseling department to function as a university supervisor for
interns. When he becomes aware that two students in one of
his supervision groups have been placed at his agency, he informs the department chairperson of this situation. Arrangements are made for these two students to be supervised by
another faculty member.

− A faculty member has worked closely with the Metropolitan
Counseling Center to develop the center as a field placement site
for graduate counseling interns. After 2 years, Metropolitan
regularly receives three interns per semester. The director of the
center is pleased with the quality of the interns' work. He tells
the faculty member that he is grateful for all her work, which
has enabled the center to serve more clients, and that he wants
to honor her with a monetary award. The faculty member feels
that she deserves this recognition and accepts the award.

i. *Diversity in Programs.* **Counselors are responsive to their
institution's and program's recruitment and retention needs for
training program administrators, faculty, and students with
diverse backgrounds and special needs. (See A.2.a.)**

+ A counseling department announces an opening for a faculty
position. The department actively recruits qualified candidates
representing a variety of cultural and ethnic backgrounds.

− A master's degree in counseling is offered at a university that
is located in a major metropolitan area with a culturally and
racially diverse population. The faculty members in the program include two white males and one white female. The student body is comprised almost exclusively of white females.
When asked why their students are not more representative
of the city's population, the faculty respond that they don't
know what they can do about the situation because minority
students are not attracted to a program taught by white
faculty members.

F.3. Students and Supervisees

a. *Limitations.* **Counselors, through ongoing evaluation and appraisal, are aware of the academic and personal limitations of**

students and supervisees that might impede performance. Counselors assist students and supervisees in securing remedial assistance when needed, and dismiss from the training program supervisees who are unable to provide competent service due to academic or personal limitations. Counselors seek professional consultation and document their decision to dismiss or refer students or supervisees for assistance. Counselors assure that students and supervisees have recourse to address decisions made to require them to seek assistance or to dismiss them.

✛ Rachel, a counselor educator, observes a graduate student, Ken, as he counsels clients in his first practicum. She becomes concerned about his lack of counseling skills. Despite feedback, Ken fails to improve. He maintains rigid control of the interview while anger breaks through in the form of sarcasm. In response to a suggestion from Rachel that he explore his anger in counseling, Ken becomes defensive. Rachel, after informing Ken of her intentions, asks two other faculty members to observe his counseling sessions. They agree that his counseling skills are deficient, and in consultation with Ken, they develop a plan for remediation.

— Marla, a 55-year-old graduate student in counseling, has received very high grades in her didactic course work. In her practicum, she demonstrates only limited capacity to relate to clients. Her practicum supervisor attempts to talk with her, but Marla is not receptive to feedback. In fact, Marla accuses the supervisor of being biased against older students. The supervisor, afraid that he might trigger an age discrimination lawsuit, gives Marla a passing grade in practicum.

b. *Self-Growth Experiences.* Counselors use professional judgment when designing training experiences conducted by the counselors themselves that require student and supervisee self-growth or self-disclosure. Safeguards are provided so that students and supervisees are aware of the ramifications their self-disclosure may have on counselors whose primary role as teacher, trainer, or supervisor requires acting upon ethical obligations to the profession. Evaluative components of experiential training experiences explicitly delineate predetermined academic standards that are separate and

not dependent upon the student's level of self-disclosure. (See A.6.)

+ Jane is a counselor educator who teaches the introductory counseling skills course. A significant portion of the course is devoted to having students learn and practice basic counseling skills, working in dyads and videotaping their work. At the beginning of the semester, Jane thoroughly explains to students that she will be reviewing the videotapes with them, with a focus on the skill development of the student who is in the counselor role. She clarifies that she will not be evaluating the self-disclosures of the student in the client role, and that she will keep these disclosures confidential. She does alert students, however, that her ethical obligations to the profession require her to act in certain circumstances, such as hearing a student client reveal information that might lead her to believe that there was a danger to the student or to others. She also reiterates the grading criteria as outlined in her syllabus, including the fact that students are not graded on their performance in the client role.

− Students enrolled in a graduate course in group counseling are expected to learn by doing. They are expected to form a group and to discuss their personal problems in the group. The professor who teaches the course expects students to trust that he will respect their confidentiality. However, students know that he chairs the department's student review and retention committee. They wish he would be more explicit about his criteria for evaluating them in the course and for continuation in the program.

c. *Counseling for Students and Supervisees.* **If students or supervisees request counseling, supervisors or counselor educators provide them with acceptable referrals. Supervisors or counselor educators do not serve as counselor to students or supervisees over whom they hold administrative, teaching, or evaluative roles unless this is a brief role associated with a training experience. (See A.6.b.)**

+ Denise, a practicum student, demonstrates excellent counseling skills during the first half of the semester. After spring break, however, her supervisor notices that she is struggling to attend to clients and seems preoccupied during sessions. The supervisor shares his observations with Denise, who reveals that her husband asked her for a divorce a week ago. Denise asks the supervisor to counsel her through this difficult time. The supervisor explains that he cannot serve as her counselor and provides her with the names of several referrals.

— A counselor educator also has a part-time private practice. One of her graduate students approaches her after class and says that the course has brought up some personal issues for him. He asks to be a client in her private practice. She agrees to see him as a client in her practice.

d. *Clients of Students and Supervisees.* **Counselors make every effort to ensure that the clients at field placements are aware of the services rendered and the qualifications of the students and supervisees rendering those services. Clients receive professional disclosure information and are informed of the limits of confidentiality. Client permission is obtained in order for the students and supervisees to use any information concerning the counseling relationship in the training process. (See B.1.e.)**

+ A supervisor requires counselor interns in an agency to give each of their clients a written professional disclosure statement. The interns review the statement with clients at the beginning of the initial session to ensure that clients know of their qualifications and the fact that they are being supervised. They also inform their clients that they meet with both a field supervisor and a campus supervisor to discuss their cases.

— Rod, an intern, is assigned to counsel with a client who was referred to the university clinic by a therapist in the community. At this client's request, the therapist has forwarded her counseling records on the client. Rod reads the records and sees that the client is described as being slow to trust and concerned about her confidentiality. Rod fears that if he tells her that he will be discussing his cases with his supervisor, she will not be self-disclosing. He decides to withhold this information from her.

e. *Standards for Students and Supervisees.* **Students and supervisees preparing to become counselors adhere to the Code of Ethics**

and the Standards of Practice. Students and supervisees have the same obligations to clients as those required of counselors. (See H.1.)

+ Madelyn is about to begin her internship in counseling. She carefully reviews the ACA Code of Ethics and Standards of Practice before she reports to her internship site. She reviews with her site supervisor her ethical obligations as they pertain to her internship work. Over the course of the semester, Madelyn brings in to supervision sessions any ethical dilemmas she encounters.

− Robin, a counselor intern, has begun a dating relationship with one of the members of the group she is leading. When a fellow intern challenges her on the ethics of this behavior, Robin replies that because she is only a student, she is not bound by the ACA Code of Ethics and Standards of Practice.

SECTION G: RESEARCH AND PUBLICATION

Study and Discussion Guide

Research Responsibilities: If you were involved in setting up a research project to assess the effectiveness of counseling with clients, what ethical considerations might guide your project?

Informed Consent: What might you want to tell clients who were participating in a research program designed to test for outcomes? What steps might you take to obtain informed consent?

Reporting Results: What steps do you need to take in reporting results in order to ensure that you give accurate information and minimize misleading results?

Publication: If you were preparing and submitting a journal article for publication, what ethical considerations might you need to address? What issues might you need to take into account if you had a coauthor?

G.1. Research Responsibilities

a. *Use of Human Subjects.* **Counselors plan, design, conduct, and report research in a manner consistent with pertinent ethical principles, federal and state laws, host institutional regulations, and scientific standards governing research with human subjects. Counselors design and conduct research that reflects cultural sensitivity and appropriateness.**

+ A counselor educator's research protocol requires an extended period of time from each subject. For some subjects the experience may be very fatiguing and frustrating. The investigator arranges the procedure so that there is a brief rest period at the end of each hour if the subject desires one. At the recommendation of the university's human subjects committee, she adds an allowance for ample time to confer with all subjects as they finish to offer support, answer questions, and provide information about the study.

− A counselor educator conducts a study designed to assess counseling students' awareness of the ethical obligations of their professors. The counselor educator interviews a number of students, presenting them with a series of vignettes describing the behaviors of professors in situations that have ethical implications. Student subjects are asked to evaluate the professors' behaviors, which in some vignettes are clearly unethical. In reporting the results of the study, the counselor educator states that Asian American students were found to have a lower level of ethical awareness than Euro-American students. He failed to consider that in some Asian cultures it is deemed impolite to challenge the behavior of authority figures.

b. *Deviation From Standard Practices.* **Counselors seek consultation and observe stringent safeguards to protect the rights of research participants when a research problem suggests a deviation from standard acceptable practices. (See B.6.)**

+ A counselor is conducting research to assess the impact of certain techniques on establishing trust and developing cohesion in group counseling. She questions whether one of the techniques that she wants to use is consistent with stan-

dard practices. Before implementing the technique, she consults with the review board at her university and also seeks
peer consultation.

➖ A researcher's design has been approved by the university's
research with human subjects committee, and she begins to
implement her study. She discovers that one of the interventions she is employing is causing the research participants an
unexpectedly high level of anxiety. She fails to consult with
colleagues, and because she is under time pressures to complete and publish her study, she does not redesign her procedures to add safeguards to protect the rights of participants.

c. *Precautions to Avoid Injury.* **Counselors who conduct research
with human subjects are responsible for the subjects' welfare
throughout the experiment and take reasonable precautions
to avoid causing injurious psychological, physical, or social
effects to their subjects.**

➕ The director of a community mental health agency wants to
study the personality traits and presenting symptoms of clients seeking services. All clients are asked to complete an
extensive test battery as part of the intake procedure. Clients
who complete the battery are given a full explanation of the
purpose of the testing and are carefully monitored to ensure
that they experience no adverse effects.

➖ An investigator studies the effects of feedback on changes in
communication style in a small group. Participants are encouraged to be as honest as possible and not hold back when
reporting their feelings about others. No clear guidelines for
feedback are established. The investigator does not monitor
for any negative impact on the subjects.

d. *Principal Researcher Responsibility.* **The ultimate responsibility for ethical research practice lies with the principal
researcher. All others involved in the research activities
share ethical obligations and full responsibility for their
own actions.**

➕ The administrators of a school district grant permission to a
researcher to study the impact of parental divorce on achievement test scores of elementary school children. The study re-

quires the assistance of the school counselors on each campus. Before agreeing to help, the school counselors read the proposal carefully to be sure that the study falls within ethical guidelines and that their student clients' rights are protected.

— A counselor in the Air Force allows the videotaping of her interviews with basic trainees as part of a research study. The videotaped interviews will subsequently be analyzed. Because the study has been approved by her commanding officer, the counselor does not feel obligated to decide for herself if the research falls within ethical guidelines.

e. *Minimal Interference.* **Counselors take reasonable precautions to avoid causing disruptions in subjects' lives due to participation in research.**

+ A counselor working in a college residence hall wants to study social communication among roommates. The most rigorous design for the purpose of this investigation requires splitting certain roommates and temporarily reassigning them to other rooms. However, the counselor creates a design that will not disrupt students' social relationships because the ratio of expected benefit to risk does not justify the more rigorous design.

— It becomes clear to Aaron that his doctoral research is disrupting the lives of participants in his study in ways that he had not anticipated. Several subjects have reported that they are feeling agitated and are having difficulty getting to sleep at night. Aaron is under presssure to complete his dissertation research, and he does not want the validity of his study to be threatened. Therefore, he decides not to change his design.

f. *Diversity.* **Counselors are sensitive to diversity and research issues with special populations. They seek consultation when appropriate. (See A.2.a. and B.6.)**

+ A doctoral student's research study involves working with the elderly in an inpatient facility. Because the student is committed to respecting the rights of the elderly people in her study and because she wants to do quality research, she consults with a professor who is nationally recognized as an expert on counseling the elderly. The expert suggests several minor changes in the design that the student incorporates into her proposal.

— A counselor is conducting research to determine why ethnic minority clients drop out of treatment prematurely in his agency. He makes home visits to clients who were no shows and asks them to respond to a series of questions, some of which are highly personal. He perseveres with these home visits despite the resistance he encounters from the interviewees.

G.2. Informed Consent

a. *Topics Disclosed.* **In obtaining informed consent for research, counselors use language that is understandable to research participants and that (1) accurately explains the purpose and procedures to be followed; (2) identifies any procedures that are experimental or relatively untried; (3) describes the attendant discomforts and risks; (4) describes the benefits or changes in individuals or organizations that might be reasonably expected; (5) discloses/appropriate alternative procedures that would be advantageous for subjects; (6) offers to answer any inquiries concerning the procedures; (7) describes any limitations on confidentiality; and (8) instructs that subjects are free to withdraw their consent and to discontinue participation in the project at any time. (See B.1.f.)**

+ A researcher obtains two groups of student volunteers as subjects for an experiment in group process. He carefully explains the study's purpose and procedures, potential risks and benefits, and limitations that the group format places on confidentiality. After he begins the group process, several subjects express their anxiety about the strong feelings expressed in the group. The researcher listens to their concerns and reiterates that they are free to drop out of the experiment at any time.

— A graduate student in counseling is designing a research study to assess the impact of a tutoring program for students on academic probation. Although her informed consent document is written in language that research participants are able to understand, she fails to include any information about alternative procedures that might be advantageous for the subjects. She also states that once they agree to be a part of this tutoring and research program, they cannot terminate until the program has been completed.

b. *Deception.* **Counselors do not conduct research involving deception unless alternative procedures are not feasible and the prospective value of the research justifies the deception. When the methodological requirements of a study necessitate concealment or deception, the investigator is required to explain clearly the reasons for this action as soon as possible.**

+ Subjects participate in a simulated counseling interview. Although the purpose of the experiment is to study subjects' reactions to the interviewer, subjects believe that it is the content of the interview that is under investigation. After completing the dependent measures, all subjects are informed of the true purpose of the study and the reason for the deception.

− An investigator wants to study the impact of nonreinforcement on class participation. In a general psychology lecture section, the teaching assistant is instructed not to reinforce orally correct responses to questions by certain student subjects. The impact of the nonreinforcement is judged in terms of these students' willingness to volunteer responses to the teaching assistant's questions. When the study is completed, the researcher fails to hold a debriefing session to explain the teaching assistant's behavior.

c. *Voluntary Participation.* **Participation in research is typically voluntary and without any penalty for refusal to participate. Involuntary participation is appropriate only when it can be demonstrated that participation will have no harmful effects on subjects and is essential to the investigation.**

+ A counselor wants to study the depth of self-disclosure that occurs in a therapy group. Because the experience of participating in such a group can be emotionally intense, the counselor decides that only volunteer participants will be used. All subjects will be informed of the nature of the experiment and potential risks. As an additional precaution, the counselor will screen each volunteer for sufficient ego strength and emotional stability.

— A professor is teaching a course in which the students will be suitable subjects for an experiment. The study requires subjects to complete a personality inventory. The inventory results will be compared with subjects' behavior in small task-oriented groups. The professor makes it mandatory that students complete the inventory and participate in the task groups, even though these requirements are not specifically related to the content of the course.

d. *Confidentiality of Information.* **Information obtained about research participants during the course of an investigation is confidential. When the possibility exists that others may obtain access to such information, ethical research practice requires that the possibility, together with the plans for protecting confidentiality, be explained to participants as a part of the procedure for obtaining informed consent. (See B.1.e.)**

+ Client files are to be reviewed as part of a research project investigating the content of session notes. Counselors who have agreed to participate in the project are instructed to use pseudonyms or false initials for clients when writing the records. They are also instructed to explain to clients the nature and purpose of the research, the procedures for protecting their confidentiality, and the possibility that they might inadvertently include the client's name in the records. Clients are assured that only the researcher, who shares the counselor's ethic of confidentiality, will see the records. Records of only those clients who have given their informed consent are used in the research study.

— A counselor publishes an article that consists primarily of case study analyses in a professional journal. Although the names of clients have been changed, in one case study certain details make it possible for some readers to ascertain the identity of a client who is a public figure. The counselor had obtained consent from this client and the others whose cases were described, but had assured them that their confidentiality would be absolutely maintained.

e. *Persons Incapable of Giving Informed Consent.* **When a person is incapable of giving informed consent, counselors provide an appropriate explanation, obtain agreement for participation, and obtain appropriate consent from a legally authorized person.**

+ Phil, a doctoral student, is conducting research with first graders. He provides an explanation about the project in language the children can comprehend and obtains their consent. He also explains the research procedures to the children's parents and obtains their written consent.

− A counselor is doing research on factors related to self-esteem with fourth-grade children. Although he explains to the children the general nature and purpose of the study, he assumes he does not need to obtain parental consent because he is merely observing behavior and is not conducting any interventions.

f. *Commitments to Participants.* **Counselors take reasonable measures to honor all commitments to research participants.**

+ Students in a counselor educator's class volunteer to participate in a study that involves their completing a paper-and-pencil inventory of attitudes toward ethical behaviors. The educator tells the participants that when the study is completed, she will provide them with a summary of the results. After she analyzes the data, she mails each student a description of her findings and conclusions.

− A researcher promised a group of subjects that he would provide them with a summary of his results. However, when he analyzes his data and fails to find significance, he abandons the project and neglects to send any information to the subjects.

g. *Explanations After Data Collection.* **After data are collected, counselors provide participants with full clarification of the nature of the study to remove any misconceptions. Where scientific or human values justify delaying or withholding information, counselors take reasonable measures to avoid causing harm.**

+ Abe, a counselor educator, conducted a research study using undergraduate students in a human services program as volunteer subjects. He provided participants with general information about the nature and purpose of the study. After the study was completed, he conducted a debriefing session aimed at correcting any possible misperceptions that participants may have held.

– Karen felt that it was essential to the integrity of her research design to withhold certain information from the participants. She promised to provide them with an explanation of procedures and a summary of results after the study was competed. After she finished the study, she failed to communicate with them. Several participants were left with the impression that they had performed poorly and perhaps had caused the study to be unpublishable.

h. *Agreements to Cooperate.* **Counselors who agree to cooperate with another individual in research or publication incur an obligation to cooperate as promised in terms of punctuality of performance and with regard to the completeness and accuracy of the information required.**

+ Two colleagues sign a contract with a publisher to coauthor a book on the men's groups they have been leading together for several years. They meet on a regular basis and submit drafts of chapters to each other for editing. They are diligent in fulfilling their commitments to each other and to the publisher.

– Ray promised his colleague, Sally, that he would write up for publication the results section of a research study they had conducted together. Despite Sally's repeated requests, Ray did not complete his section until 6 months after their agreed-upon deadline. He did not carefully check the accuracy of his computations, and Sally found several errors that needed to be corrected.

i. *Informed Consent for Sponsors.* **In the pursuit of research, counselors give sponsors, institutions, and publication channels the same respect and opportunity for giving informed consent that they accord to individual research participants. Counselors** are aware of their obligation to future research workers and ensure that host institutions are given feedback information and proper acknowledgment.

+ The director of a community mental health agency gives permission to Hal, a graduate student, to conduct a research study on how agency counselors spend their time. As they have agreed, when Hal completes his study he provides the director with a description of his findings and conclusions.

− The dean awards funding to a counselor educator to conduct a research project. The dean's stipulation is that the counselor educator will write a brief report that can be distributed to department members because the project is of general interest and relevance. The counselor educator completes the project but fails to submit the report he had agreed to write.

G.3. Reporting Results

a. *Information Affecting Outcome.* **When reporting research results, counselors explicitly mention all variables and conditions known to the investigator that may have affected the outcome of a study or the interpretation of data.**

+ The guidance director and a counselor in a school system collaborate on a research study investigating school dropout rates. The guidance director summarizes the data on the past year's dropouts. The counselor knows that some schools have included summer dropouts in their reports whereas others have not. The counselor tells the guidance director about this discrepancy, and the data analysis is revised.

− A researcher studying hospitalized psychiatric patients finds that about one third of the subjects refuse to participate in the experiment. In reporting the findings, the researcher states that the data were obtained on a given number of subjects but fails to state that this number reflects only two thirds of the total defined group.

b. *Accurate Results.* **Counselors plan, conduct, and report research accurately and in a manner that minimizes the possibility that results will be misleading. They provide thorough discussions of the limitations of their data and alternative hypotheses.**

Counselors do not engage in fraudulent research, distort data, misrepresent data, or deliberately bias their results.

+ A researcher, well known for espousing a particular theoretical position, conducts an experiment that only partially
supports her point of view. In the discussion section of the
report, the researcher interprets the data first in light of their
support of her favored theory, then in light of support for an
opposing theory. She concludes the paper with the statement
that the choice of interpretation may depend on the reader's
own theoretical orientation.

− A researcher discovers that her data do not meet the assumptions for the statistical test of significance that is being used.
She reports the results without mention of this discovery.

c. *Obligation to Report Unfavorable Results.* **Counselors communicate to other counselors the results of any research judged
to be of professional value. Results that reflect unfavorably
on institutions, programs, services, prevailing opinions, or
vested interests are not withheld.**

+ A high school counselor conducts a study to determine whether
seniors have engaged in unprotected sex. The administration
in this district takes particular pride in the sex education program that has been offered to junior high students for the past
7 years. The results of the counselor's study show that an unexpectedly high number of students appear to be oblivious to
the threat of sexually transmitted diseases. The results are made
available in a pamphlet to other counselors, to students, and
to parents. The administration decides to revise the sex education curriculum to reemphasize the prevention of sexually
transmitted diseases.

− A school counselor surveys substance abuse by students at an
affluent high school. The results suggest that substance abuse
is widespread. This information could be upsetting to parents. The counselor takes the principal's hint that the results
should go unreported.

d. *Identity of Subjects.* **Counselors who supply data, aid in the
research of another person, report research results, or make
original data available take due care to disguise the identity**

of respective subjects in the absence of specific authorization from the subjects to do otherwise. (See B.1.g. and B.5.a.)

+ A counselor who has submitted an article for publication used real names and photographs of persons and events to dramatize their rehabilitation. The counselor obtained the written permission of each of the individuals and shared with them a copy of the proposed article before submitting it to the journal.

− A researcher is studying correlates of depression as evidenced by certain types of profiles on the Minnesota Multiphasic Personality Inventory (MMPI)-II. Counselors from a community mental health agency are asked to submit MMPI profiles. One counselor, pressed for time, photocopies the profiles without editing out identifying data and without obtaining client permission to send the material.

e. *Replication Studies.* **Counselors are obligated to make available sufficient original research data to qualified professionals who may wish to replicate the study.**

+ A counseling department has a policy that all theses and dissertations completed by students in that department must include the raw data in an appendix so that another investigator might be able to perform a different analysis. The data must be presented in such a way as to protect the anonymity of individual subjects.

− A well-known researcher publishes an article that demonstrates positive results from an application of a counseling technique he has developed. He fails to report the very narrow subject selection criteria that may have stacked the deck in favor of positive results. He misplaces the raw data that might enable others to check the methodology of the study.

G.4. Publication

a. *Recognition of Others.* **When conducting and reporting research, counselors are familiar with and give recognition to previous work on the topic, observe copyright laws, and give full credit to those to whom credit is due. (See F.1.d. and G.4.c.)**

+ A counselor replicates a study that was terminated by the death of the original researcher. In reporting this investigation, the counselor acknowledges the original researcher as author of the hypothesis and design of the study.

– In presenting at a state conference, a counselor reports on her successful work with chemically dependent individuals in the workplace. The counselor presents this work as if it were original, without crediting earlier projects that have been reported in the professional literature.

b. *Contributors.* **Counselors give credit through joint authorship, acknowledgment, footnote statements, or other appropriate means to those who have contributed significantly to research or concept development in accordance with such contributions. The principal contributor is listed first and minor technical or professional contributions are acknowledged in notes or introductory statements.**

+ Three counselor educators write a descriptive study about brief solution-focused therapy. In the manuscript they submit for publication, all three counselor educators are listed as coauthors. The order of presentation of their names is determined in relation to the contribution of each to the project.

– In a graduate course in counseling theories, students are assigned to write a paper critiquing the philosophy and theory of an outstanding authority. Later, the professor writes a textbook and uses a student's paper with only minor editing. No mention is made of the student's original work.

c. *Student Research.* **For an article that is substantially based on a student's dissertation or thesis, the student is listed as the principal author. (See F.1.d. and G.4.a.)**

+ Charles, a doctoral student, works together with his major professor to write an article that is based on Charles' dissertation. When Charles writes the first draft of the manuscript and sends it to the professor, she sees that her name appears as the principal author. She corrects the copy by listing Charles as principal author.

— Kim has completed her master's degree project. Her professor suggests to her that an article could be derived from the project and offers to assist her in writing it. Once the article is completed, primarily by Kim but with significant assistance from the professor, the professor suggests that he be listed as the principal author. He tells her that readers will take the article more seriously if a professor is the principal author.

d. *Duplicate Submission.* **Counselors submit manuscripts for consideration to only one journal at a time. Manuscripts that are published in whole or in substantial part in another journal or published work are not submitted for publication without acknowledgment and permission from the previous publication.**

+ A counselor draws heavily on a published journal article on adolescent development in a chapter of a book she is writing. She contacts the journal's publisher and obtains permission to reproduce tables from the journal article in the book chapter. She acknowledges the author of the journal article in appropriate citations throughout the chapter.

— An assistant professor is employed in a publish-or-perish institution. Knowing that the process of acceptance, revision, and publication of an article can easily take more than a year, he submits the same article to three journals simultaneously.

e. *Professional Review.* **Counselors who review material submitted for publication, research, or other scholarly purposes respect the confidentiality and proprietary rights of those who submitted it.**

+ A counselor educator serves on the editorial board of a professional journal. All manuscripts are subjected to blind review; that is, the editorial board members do not know the identity of authors of manuscripts. The counselor educator receives a manuscript that is of great interest to him because he is scheduled to present a workshop in 2 weeks on the very topic addressed in the manuscript. Although he believes his workshop presentation could be strengthened by including material from the manuscript, he realizes that it is unethical for him to appropriate the material.

➥ A counselor educator is the editor of a professional journal. One month she receives an unusually large number of submissions, and in her haste to get the manuscripts out to editorial board members she fails to delete data that could identify the author of one article.

SECTION H:
RESOLVING ETHICAL ISSUES

Study and Discussion Guide

✦ *Informal Resolution: If you had reasonable cause to believe that another professional was violating an ethical standard, what informal means might you initially take to resolve the situation?*

✦ *Consultation: When might you seek consultation regarding a matter of suspected violations by another professional?*

✦ *Steps in Resolving Ethical Dilemmas: What are some ways you can use the ACA Code of Ethics to assist you in resolving ethical dilemmas? If you were confronted with a difficult ethical issue, what steps might you take in resolving the problem? What ethical responsibilities do you have when you become aware of unethical behavior of a colleague?*

H.1. Knowledge of Standards

Counselors are familiar with the Code of Ethics and the Standards of Practice and other applicable ethics codes from other professional organizations of which they are members, or from certification and licensure bodies. Lack of knowledge or misunderstanding of an ethical responsibility is not a defense against a charge of unethical conduct. (See F.3.e.)

✦ Karen is a professional member of ACA and is a licensed professional counselor in the state where she practices. She specializes in sex education and therapy, and is a member of the American Association of Sex Educators, Counselors, and Therapists (AASECT). When the revised 1995 ACA Code of Ethics and Standards of Practice are published, she reads the documents carefully to ensure that she understands them. She reviews the codes of ethics of AASECT and her state licensure body, and compares their standards to those of ACA. She discovers that according to the ACA Code of Ethics, counselors are expected to contribute a portion of their activity to pro bono service. Although the other two codes do not mention pro bono work, Karen decides to offer a series of free educational seminars for parents on how to talk to your teenager about sex.

— Jason Jones, an ACA member, advertises himself as Dr. Jones although his EdD degree is in educational administration. When a complaint is filed against him with the ACA Ethics Committee for violating standard C.3.a. (Accurate Advertising), he attempts to defend his actions by stating that he was not aware that this new standard had appeared in the 1995 revised Code of Ethics.

H.2. Suspected Violations

a. *Ethical Behavior Expected.* **Counselors expect professional associates to adhere to the Code of Ethics. When counselors possess reasonable cause that raises doubts as to whether a counselor is acting in an ethical manner, they take appropriate action. (See H.2.d. and H.2.e.)**

+ An employment service supervisor is concerned that a new counselor, who has said that he likes a challenge, is spending more and more time with a few difficult-to-place clients to the exclusion of others seeking counseling. The supervisor confers with the counselor, who redistributes his time more equitably for a few weeks. Then, once again he begins to focus on just a few challenging clients. The supervisor, uncertain what to do at this point, consults with another supervisor at a different agency.

— A career counselor is aware that one of her colleagues, who failed to attend in-service training on a new career interest inventory, has been interpreting the results of that inventory to clients. The counselor is a friend of the colleague and knows that the colleague is under considerable stress at home. Therefore, the counselor does nothing to correct the situation.

b. *Consultation.* **When uncertain as to whether a particular situation or course of action may be in violation of the Code of Ethics, counselors consult with other counselors who are knowledgeable about ethics, with colleagues, or with appropriate authorities.**

+ Nguyen is a counselor for a private rehabilitation counseling service. The director of the service has instituted a new set of record-keeping procedures, and Nguyen questions whether the procedures are ethical. He calls and consults with his former professor with whom he completed his ethics course. He also calls a colleague who served for many years on the ethics committee of the state rehabilitation counseling association.

− Lorraine is a counselor in a mental health agency. One of her colleagues rountinely assigns almost every one of his clients a diagnosis of adjustment disorder for insurance purposes. Lorraine questions the ethical propriety of this practice. However, she is relatively new to the agency, and the colleague has been there for several years. Therefore, Lorraine assumes that she must be incorrect in her concern and does nothing.

c. *Organization Conflicts.* **If the demands of an organization with which counselors are affiliated pose a conflict with the Code of Ethics, counselors specify the nature of such conflicts and express to their supervisors or other responsible officials their commitment to the Code of Ethics. When possible, counselors work toward change within the organization to allow full adherence to the Code of Ethics.**

+ Nguyen, the counselor in the preceding scenario, determines after consultation that the new record-keeping procedures of his employer, the rehabilitation counseling service, do violate ethical standards. He takes his concerns to the director of the service, pointing out the ethical standards in question and describing the results of his consultations. The director agrees to appoint a committee to review the procedures and modify them if necessary, and asks Nguyen to serve on the committee.

− Roger works as an outplacement counselor for a large corporation. Although some of the outplacement procedures used by the corporation are in conflict with Roger's understanding of ACA's Code of Ethics, he says nothing. He assumes that because he is just a small cog in a giant corporation, no one will listen to his concerns.

d. *Informal Resolution.* **When counselors have reasonable cause to believe that another counselor is violating an ethical standard, they attempt to first resolve the issue informally with the other counselor if feasible, providing that such action does not violate confidentiality rights that may be involved.**

+ Pat, a counselor in private practice, meets Eugene at a meeting of a local professional association. As they converse, they discover a shared professional interest in learning more about hypnotherapy. Pat offers to send Eugene a copy of some materials. Eugene hands her one of his new business cards. Later, Pat reads the card and realizes that it contains misleading information about the services that Eugene, with his master's degree and state licensure, is qualified to offer. She calls Eugene and expresses her concerns. Eugene agrees to destroy his business cards immediately and obtain a new set that advertises accurately.

− Pat, the private practitioner in the preceding scenario, reads Eugene's business card and immediately files a written, formal complaint against Eugene with the ACA Ethics Committee. She does not contact Eugene first to attempt to resolve her concerns informally.

e. *Reporting Suspected Violations.* **When an informal resolution is not appropriate or feasible, counselors, upon reasonable cause, take action such as reporting the suspected ethical violation to state or national ethics committees, unless this action conflicts with confidentiality rights that cannot be resolved.**

+ Toni learns that an ACA member who teaches psychology part time at a local community college has been recruiting his students as clients for his private practice. She calls the member and attempts to express her concern, but he refuses to discuss it with her. She informs him that she is ethically obligated to take action and then reports the suspected violation to the ACA Ethics Committee.

− Susan, a high school counselor, has reasonable cause to suspect that the junior high counselor who works in her district has sexually harassed several female student clients. She consults with a fellow professional who urges her to take action to rectify the problem, but Susan refuses to act because she must continue to work with the junior high counselor as a colleague.

f. *Unwarranted Complaints*. **Counselors do not initiate, participate in, or encourage the filing of ethics complaints that are unwarranted or intend to harm a counselor rather than to protect clients or the public.**

+ Alan is a counselor educator at a state university. He consults with Vicky, who works at a private university in the same city, about his anger at his department chair who is an ACA member. Alan says he believes that the department chair is unethical and he is considering filing a complaint with the ACA Ethics Committee. It is apparent to Vicky that Alan's anger may be justified but has nothing to do with the department chair's ethical conduct. She shares her perception of the situation with Alan and encourages him to take appropriate action rather than file an unwarranted complaint.

− Bob is a counselor in private practice who has been very successful at supplementing his income by giving stress management workshops. Arlette opens a private practice in a neighboring community and begins giving seminars on a similar topic. Attendance at Bob's workshops decreases markedly. In retaliation, he files an ethics complaint against Arlette with the state licensing board, even though his charges are unwarranted.

H.3. Cooperation With Ethics Committees

Counselors assist in the process of enforcing the Code of Ethics. Counselors cooperate with investigations, proceedings, and requirements of the ACA Ethics Committee or ethics committees of other duly constituted associations or boards having jurisdiction over those charged with a violation. Counselors are familiar with the ACA Policies and Procedures and use it as a reference in assisting the enforcement of the Code of Ethics.

+ Candace is shocked to learn that a former client has filed a complaint against her with the ACA Ethics Committee. Although Candace firmly believes the complaint is unjustified, she takes the matter seriously. She reads the ACA Policies and Procedures for Processing Complaints of Ethical Violations, consults with an attorney, and writes a response that gives the fullest possible description of events in question. She submits documentation to support her response.

— Curtis is very surprised to learn that a former client has filed a complaint against him with the ACA Ethics Committee. Looking back on his work with the client, he begins to question whether he made the best possible judgments. He refuses to respond to the Ethics Committee because he doesn't want to give them any ammunition that might be used against him.

PART III

ISSUES AND CASE STUDIES

The brief vignettes in Part II of the casebook are intended to clarify the meaning of the individual ethical standards. Part III takes a broader perspective and presents 10 chapters highlighting key ethical issues that counselors encounter in their work. Some of these chapters were written by us; others were contributed by experts on particular topics. The issues include

+ client rights and informed consent;
+ ethical issues in multicultural counseling;
+ confidentiality;
+ competence;
+ working with multiple clients;
+ counseling minor clients;
+ dual relationships;
+ working with suicidal clients;
+ counselor training and supervision; and
+ the relationship between law and ethics.

Each chapter is followed by one or more case studies in which counselors confront ethical dilemmas related to the issue discussed and make decisions—sometimes wisely, sometimes unwisely. The case studies are more detailed than the vignettes in Part II and more illustrative of the complex realities of actual practice. Each case includes an analysis of how the Code of Ethics might be used to help the counselor solve the dilemma and ways in which the counselor's actions complied with and/or violated the code.

The case studies are not actual cases from the Ethics Committee files, which are confidential. However, they have been written by current and former members of the Ethics Committee and other professionals who are particularly knowledgeable about ethics. To the extent possible, they are representative of the types of actual cases that are encountered by the Ethics Committee and by practitioners in the field.

As we noted in the Introduction, formal complaints to the ACA Ethics Committee very rarely allege a single violation of the Code of Ethics. Rather, cases typically involve claims of violations of multiple standards. In this respect, the case studies presented here are also quite realistic. Each one raises a number of considerations that need to be studied in light of more than one standard to conduct an ethical analysis. We invite readers to grapple with the complexities of the cases and to discuss and debate the issues they raise.

Chapter One

CLIENT RIGHTS AND INFORMED CONSENT

Gerald Corey and Barbara Herlihy

The counseling relationship is founded on trust. Trust is a deeply personal experience that defines the counseling relationship and provides a context for the therapeutic process (Pope & Vasquez, 1991). One of the best ways to build trusting relationships with clients is to respect their many rights and to inform them of their choices. Clients have the right to receive the information they need in order to become active participants in the therapeutic relationship (Corey, Corey, & Callanan, 1993).

The right to informed consent is perhaps the most basic right of clients in counseling. The process of informed consent begins when the counseling relationship is initiated and continues throughout the relationship. Standard A.3.a. of the Code of Ethics specifies that counselors need to disclose to clients (1) the purposes, goals, techniques, rules of procedure, limitations, and potential risks; (2) implications of diagnosis, the intended use of tests and reports, fees, and billing arrangements; and (3) an explanation of confidentiality and its limits. According to this standard, clients also have the right to obtain clear information about their case record, to participate in their ongoing counseling plan, and to refuse any recommended services and be advised of the consequences of doing so. Other factors that may affect the client's decision to enter the therapeutic relationship are the potential benefits of counseling, the responsibilities of the counselor and of the client, legal and ethical parameters that could define the relationship, the qualifications and experience of the counselor, and the approximate duration of the counseling relationship.

Obviously, informed consent is not a simple procedure. The challenge for counselors is to strike a balance between giving clients too much and too little information (Corey et al., 1993). Too much information can be overwhelming, but it is too late to disclose information after a problem or concern has already arisen. It seems to us that counselors may err in either direction, depending on the setting in which they work. For example, counselors who work in inpatient facilities are aware that clients are often required to sign an array of consent documents before being admitted to the hospital, at a time when they are likely to be under great stress and may have diminished capacity to make well-considered decisions. Some school counselors, however, may give only the briefest explanation of such elements of informed consent as the limits of confidentiality or the purposes and potential uses of tests.

Of course, the types and amounts of information, as well as the style of presentation, are governed by many factors. Some of these include legal requirements (such as due process), system policies and procedures (many agencies and institutions have standard forms), the capacity of clients to understand the information, and whether the client is an adult or a minor. What is important is to provide clients with opportunities to ask questions, and to provide information in language that is understandable to them.

In addition to following the letter of the Code of Ethics, counselors will do well to consider the spirit that underlies informed consent in deciding what to tell their clients. Clients should be provided with enough information to enable them to make wise choices. This includes choosing whether to enter into counseling, selecting their counselor, and making choices about their treatment plans. It is important that clients be active participants in the therapeutic relationship. Clients are often unaware of their rights (Corey et al., 1993; Rinas & Clyne-Jackson, 1988), and they may not have given any thought to their own responsibilities in solving their problems. In seeking the expertise of a professional, they may unquestioningly accept whatever their counselor suggests, without realizing that the success of this relationship depends largely on their own investment in the process.

It is important to address the client's expectations of the counseling process. Clients often ask how long counseling will last. Although counselors cannot give a specific amount of time, we can address the client's concerns and provide appropriate information. Clients are sometimes unaware that they are likely to experience uncomfortable emotions associated with counseling, and they may harbor expectations of quick relief and happiness. Generally, putting informed consent information in writing is a good method to help ensure client understanding. Counselors in all settings are advised to develop disclosure statements or informed consent documents that they can give to their clients. An excellent model has been offered by Wittmer and Remley (1994). Clients can take this information home and bring to the following session any questions or concerns they may have.

With these guidelines in mind, we can now turn to two case studies that illustrate their application in actual practice. The counselors in the cases work in very different settings — one in a rehabilitation agency and the other in a university counseling and research center — yet they each discover how difficult it can be to keep the client's welfare foremost when dealing with complex systems whose various constituencies have competing needs.

Case Study 1

PRESSURES FROM ALL SIDES: A REHABILITATION COUNSELOR'S DILEMMA
Mary Ellen Young

Kate was delighted to be hired as a vocational rehabilitation counselor by the Metropolitan Rehabilitation Company immediately after she graduated from her master's degree program in rehabilitation counseling. A client named Brad was one of her first referrals.

Brad had been a construction worker all his life. He started working at the age of 16, helping on a construction site near his home. He was raised by a single mother, and the money he earned helped her pay the bills and support his younger siblings. By the time he was 17, he had dropped out of high school and was working full time. He did not regret leaving school because his grades had never been very good and the money really helped. He also liked the other men he worked with and appreciated the fact that they were willing to teach him the trade. He particularly like doing structural work on tall buildings as they were going up. By the time he was 20, he was a skilled worker with a formal apprenticeship behind him. He met and married Pam, and they had two children.

Brad was on the job when a rope broke, causing him to fall from a scaffolding 20 feet above the ground. He hit his head and sustained an injury to his spinal cord that resulted in incomplete paraplegia or partial paralysis of his lower extremities. After being treated in a trauma center, Brad was sent to a rehabilitation hospital where he learned to use a wheelchair. His major concern was whether he would walk again. After several months of physical therapy, he was able to walk a short distance using two canes. However, he was sent home with his wheelchair for primary mobility. His doctor documented that he had a mild brain injury, with some short-term memory loss. He was trained to use a memory notebook as a compensation strategy.

While Brad was still in the hospital, he received a letter from an attorney who stated that he should be informed of his rights to recover damages because of his employer's negligence. Brad hired this attorney to represent him should the need arise.

Because his injury was job related, Brad qualified for worker's compensation to cover his medical expenses and wage loss. At the suggestion of the hospital social worker, he also applied for Social Security Disability Insurance. This could eventually provide additional income and qualify him for Medicare. Following his discharge from the rehabilitation hospital, Kate visited Brad at home, informing him that the insurance company had hired her company to help him return to work.

After her initial interview with Brad, Kate received a series of phone calls. The first was from the attorney whom Brad had hired. The attorney told Kate that Brad was too disabled to pursue employment at this time and that Kate should not contact him again.

The second call was from the claims adjuster who told her that she should get Brad back into sedentary work with the construction firm as soon as possible to minimize the long-term costs to the insurance company.

The third call was from Brad's wife, Pam, who expressed concern that Brad not be forced into going back to work too soon. His income from his construction job had been good when he was working, but periods of employment had been interspersed with periods of unemployment and limited income. Pam thought that because of the severity of Brad's injury, he should continue to draw benefits that could provide a steady income to the family. She also expressed her concerns about medical expenses unrelated to the injury as well as other family medical expenses, should Brad not be covered by medical insurance in the future.

Finally, Brad called and tearfully told her that he did not want to spend the rest of his life as a cripple and that he wanted to get back to work as soon as possible.

Unsure what to do next, Kate spoke with her supervisor. The supervisor reminded her that Brad's insurance carrier did a lot of work with their company and suggested that she work with the employer to get him back to work as soon as possible, at least on a part-time basis.

Questions for Thought and Discussion

If you were in Kate's place, how would you deal with the apparently conflicting desires and needs of all the parties involved in Brad's case? How can Kate keep the welfare of her client foremost, when so many competing demands are being made on her? Who should decide what is in Brad's best interest? What are the elements of informed consent that Kate needs to be concerned with, in working with Brad? If you were to apply the ethical decision-making model to this dilemma, how might you rank the moral principles? What might this ranking suggest, in terms of the decision you might reach or actions you might take?

Analysis

The practice of vocational counseling in a situation such as a worker's compensation injury is fraught with ethical challenges. In this case, the client's employer, the insurance company, the attorney, and even the counselor's employer may all have a financial stake in Brad's outcome, that is, whether or not he will return to work. The decisions that Brad makes will also have far-reaching impact on the family's financial resources and plans for the future. A counselor, particularly a newly trained counselor, may have difficulty keeping the client's best interest at the forefront of the counseling process. The Code of Ethics stresses that the "primary responsibility of counselors is to respect the dignity and to promote the welfare of clients" (A.1.a.). Kate will need to keep this in mind as she negotiates the minefield of a potentially litigious situation.

Whether or not Brad returns to work, or when he will return, depends on many factors including the course of his medical recovery, his transferable skills, his ability and willingness to explore new vocational areas and obtain additional training, and his overall ability to cope with this traumatic life event. On one side, pressure to return to work as soon as possible will come from many directions.

Brad, himself, is eager to get back to work. Both Kate's employer and the insurance company that is paying Kate's employer support this goal, although their motivations are different.

On the other side, a system of compensation and benefits exists so that Brad and his family will not be financially devastated by this work-related injury. His wife's concern about his returning to work too soon is valid. His attorney is acting on his behalf to obtain the highest possible financial compensation for his injury. The Code of Ethics, under Career and Employment Needs, states that counselors do not place clients "in positions that will result in damaging the interest and welfare of clients, employers, or the public" (A.1.e.). Involving Brad's wife in the counseling process as a "positive resource" may also be recommended and is supported by the Code of Ethics (A.1.d.). Because rehabilitation is usually funded by a service delivery system, numerous parties may be involved in both the process and outcome of rehabilitation counseling services. Payers for services (whether the state rehabilitation agency, an insurance carrier, or an employer) usually require extensive reporting to establish accountability for money expended in terms of the client's return to work or positive vocational outcomes. Such information is needed to document the favorable cost/benefit ratio of the program and to justify continuation of services. However, this system creates a potential ethical dilemma for the counselor because there are additional limits to confidentiality beyond those in a traditional counseling relationship. Brad has a right to full disclosure from Kate about what the counseling process will entail and an explanation of the limits of confidentiality, as well as his right to refuse any recommended service and to be advised of the consequences of that refusal (A.3.a., B.1.g., D.4.). Kate must inform him that it is her responsibility to report his progress to the insurance company and to do so honestly, accurately, and without bias (C.5.c.).

Finally, Kate must be particularly concerned about her supervisor's response to her questions about the dilemma. Her continued employment with Metropolitan Rehabilitation Company implies that she is in agreement with her employer's policies. According to the Code of Ethics, counselors should "reach agreement with employers as to acceptable standards of conduct" (D.1.l.). Kate will need to establish a dialogue with her supervisor to resolve these issues. If the supervisor continues to pressure her to act in an unethical manner, she may need to seek employment elsewhere.

Questions for Further Reflection

1. When counselors work in complex systems with multiple and competing demands (such as rehabilitation companies, hospitals, schools, business and industry, or agencies), how can they ensure that they are keeping their clients' welfare foremost?

2. When working in complex systems, do counselors need to serve as advocates for their clients? How is the advocate's role different from the traditional counselor's role, and what problems or ethical dilemmas might arise when serving as a client advocate?

Case Study 2

A QUESTION OF INFORMED CONSENT
J. Melvin Witmer and Thomas E. Davis

Megan, a 16-year-old high school junior, sought counseling at her school because she became extremely anxious when she was expected to perform in social situations. Her anxieties were causing physical problems, including weight loss and sleeplessness, and were interfering with her academic work. The school counselor met with her several times, but since no progress was being made, the counselor referred Megan to the Center for Counseling and Research at the local university. The center was directed by the counselor education program and provided clinical and research experiences for students and faculty.

During the intake session, Bill (a counselor intern supervised by a faculty member) provided Megan with a brief orientation to the counseling services. Because she was still a minor, Bill informed her that her parents' permission was required. Megan was reluctant to agree to this because she was unsure how her parents would react to her seeking counseling outside the school setting. However, when assured that her parents would not be told details of personal information she disclosed, she agreed to have one of her parents accompany her to the first session.

At this initial meeting, the counselor explained to Megan and her mother the policies and procedures of the counseling center regarding client rights and responsibilities and confidentiality. He explained that sessions might be observed by his supervisor and that their sessions might be part of ongoing research being conducted by the center. It was agreed that the purpose of the sessions should be to help Megan become more competent and comfortable in social situations and manage the stress that she felt when she anticipated such situations.

Bill gave Megan a working diagnosis of social phobia. In the fourth session he chose to use the eye movement desensitization and reprocessing (EMDR) procedure, and he continued its use over the next three sessions. The procedure had become quite popular, although still considered by some as experimental and by others as controversial, for easing the emotional trauma surrounding several social situations from childhood. Bill anticipated that EMDR would eradicate the traumatic thoughts, feelings, and pictures that he believed were contributing to Megan's social phobia.

During the 3 weeks of treatment, Megan experienced additional symptoms of fear and nightmares. She avoided social situations in which she would have to perform, such as band, and English class, where she was assigned to give a speech. She began skipping these classes by going to the library. When her mother learned about this through a telephone call from the school counselor, she contacted Bill at the center and asked for an appointment.

At the appointment, with Megan and Bill's supervisor present, the mother reported that she was very concerned about the lack of therapeutic progress and frustrated by the inadequate amount of information that she had been given regarding Megan's treatment. She was angry that even though she had been told that the counseling might be part of ongoing research, little else had been shared with her or her daughter about the method of counseling that was being used. She stated that she was considering filing a complaint and asked about procedures for doing so.

Questions for Thought and Discussion

What primary issues does this case raise for you? What elements must the informed consent process include in order for consent to be obtained in a fully ethical manner? If you were the counselor or the supervisor in this case, what might you want to tell Megan and her mother during their appointment to discuss their concerns? What obligations do the

counselor and supervisor have to inform Megan's mother about her op-
tions, if she decides she wants to make a complaint against them?

Analysis

This case raises issues related to competence, informed consent, and client participation in research that may have deviated from standard practice.

A primary concern is whether the client was adequately informed of the services that were to be delivered. Informed consent requires that the client consents voluntarily, is mentally competent to make the decision to participate, and understands the information provided by the counselor, including the particular modality or modalities to be used in treatment. In this case, because Megan was only 16 years old, her mother was required to give consent. It appears that the first two elements of informed consent were met: the mother was competent and consent was voluntary. It is questionable, however, whether Megan and her mother were adequately informed of the risks as well as the benefits of treatment (A.3.a., G.2.a.).

The Code of Ethics states that counselors and their clients work jointly to devise "integrated, individual counseling plans that offer reasonable promise of success and are consistent with abilities and circumstances of clients" (A.1.c.). In this case, Megan's mother seems to have been unclear about the general method of intervention used in the treatment of her daughter.

The counselor should have informed the client of rights relative to the purpose, goals, techniques, and other pertinent information. Counselors must "take steps to ensure that clients understand the implications of diagnosis, the intended use of tests and reports, fees, and billing arrangements" (A.3.a.). In addition, clients have the freedom to choose whether to enter into a counseling relationship and to determine which professionals will provide counseling. These choices should be based on adequate information given to the client by the counselor. The lack of specific information given to the mother and daughter in this case might suggest that the information provided was not sufficient to allow for freedom of choice.

Another concern is that the method was, by some standards, experimental in nature. With little information about the course of treatment and what the client might expect, the mother had cause for concern. Typically, counselors deem the standard treatment of a social phobia to be some form of behavioral or cognitive/behavioral modality. The use of eye movement desensitization and reprocessing would be considered a deviation from standard practices. In such a case, the counselor should "seek consultation and observe stringent safeguards" (G.1.b.).

It seemed that little if anything about the nature of the intervention was shared with Megan or her mother. This lack of communication seems to have set into play a potential violation of Standard G.1.c. This standard requires counselors to "take reasonable precautions to avoid causing injurious psychological, physical, or social effects" to research participants. Megan experienced increased fear, nightmares, and avoidance of social situations, and she began skipping classes in school. Did the counselor explain to her that occasionally in the counseling process clients get worse before they get better?

Two additional issues to be addressed in this case are the role of the supervisor and the competency of the student counselor to use EMDR. Were both the supervisor and the counselor competent to use the EMDR procedure? Was the supervisor aware of Bill's decision to use it, and did the supervisor carefully monitor the work? Appropriate education, training, and supervised experience are required for counselors to practice in a new specialty area (C.2.b.).

Was Megan's right to confidentiality appropriately balanced against the mother's right to know? Whenever parental permission is required, the counselor has an obligation to provide some level of general disclosure to the parent but at the same time an obligation to protect the client's confidentiality (B.3.).

If Megan's mother had filed a formal complaint with the ACA Ethics Committee, the committee most likely would have found that the counselor did not meet the minimum standards for informed consent. It does not appear that adequate information was offered about the method of treatment. Although Megan and her mother understood that Megan might be a participant in an ongoing research study, little was offered to them about the specifics of the intervention. The committee might issue a formal reprimand to the counselor and supervisor, and require the supervisor to submit a proposed protocol for informed consent to be used with future clients of the center.

Questions for Further Reflection

1. What needs to be included in an initial informed consent statement? What should be added or reiterated as the counseling relationship progresses?

2. How does informed consent with minor clients differ from informed consent with competent adults? What steps can be taken to safeguard a minor client's confidentiality and, at the same time, respect a parent's right to know?

CHAPTER TWO

ETHICAL ISSUES IN MULTICULTURAL COUNSELING

Derald Wing Sue

The demographic landscape of the United States is changing at a rapid pace. U.S. Census figures have indicated that racial/ethnic minorities will become a numerical majority some time between the years 2030 and 2050. The implications for counselors cannot be avoided. Increasingly, we will come into contact with culturally different clients who may not share our world view of what constitutes normality and abnormality. The strategies and approaches we have been taught to use in counseling may be ineffective and even antagonistic to the life-styles of our culturally different clients (Paniagua, 1994). Counselors who are not trained in working with culturally different clients, and who attempt to provide services, may be guilty of unethical practice (Ponterotto & Casas, 1991).

Because the counseling profession continues to emphasize a monocultural approach in training, research, and practice (Sue, Arredondo, & McDavis, 1992; Sue & Sue, 1990), many counselors appear to be ill prepared to deal effectively with cultural diversity. Some multicultural specialists have accused the profession of engaging in cultural oppression by using unethical and harmful practices in working with culturally different clients. In the past, our professional organizations have been negligent in their failure to adopt ethical guidelines that are multicultural in scope. Advocates of multiculturalism believe that omission of such standards and failure to translate multicultural awareness into actual practice are inexcusable and represent a powerful statement of a low priority and lack of commitment given to cultural diversity (Ibrahim & Arredondo, 1990).

The revised (1995) ACA Code of Ethics and Standards of Practice represent a much-needed step in rectifying the serious inadequacies of previous codes. It remains to be seen, however, whether these statements represent hollow words or an actual commitment to the concepts of multiculturalism and diversity. If translated into meaningful action, the code and standards may have some very important implications.

The Preamble to the Code of Ethics immediately and forcefully includes the following statement: "The American Counseling Association is an educational, scientific, and professional organization whose members are dedicated to the enhancement of human development throughout the life-span. Association members *recognize diversity in our society and embrace a cross-cultural approach* [italics added] in support of the worth, dignity, potential, and uniqueness of each individual."

This statement makes clear several important points. First, its prominence in the Preamble suggests the importance of ACA's commitment to multiculturalism and its central place in the Code of Ethics. No longer are multiculturalism and diversity an afterthought or tangential to ethical practice. Professional organizations that purport to value cultural diversity must include a forceful and meaningful statement of their positive stand toward multiculturalism.

Second, it suggests that counselors need to realize that diversity and cultural pluralism are a social reality. To operate monoculturally and monolingually, as if our society and clients were all the same, is delusionary. Unfortunately, many of our educational institutions, mental health organizations, and worksites continue to take an ethnocentric view of the world. The United States is the most culturally diverse country in the world but continues to be one of the most parochial.

Third, the Preamble will, hopefully, help us recognize that diversity and multiculturalism are two different concepts. It is possible to have a diverse organization, society, school system, or clientele and still be monocultural in practice. Thus diversity is not enough to assure a truly multicultural system of helping. Stating that ACA members "embrace a cross-cultural approach" suggests that multiculturalism should be valued positively, not just tolerated, by counselors. It also suggests that culturally appropriate strategies of helping must be developed.

Nondiscrimination and Ethical Practice

Statements regarding nondiscriminaton are included throughout the Code of Ethics and Standards of Practice. For example, Standard A.2. states that counselors "do not condone or engage in discrimination based on age, color, culture, disability, ethnic group, gender, race, religion, sexual orientation, marital status, or socioeconomic status."

It is becoming increasingly clear that the values, assumptions, beliefs, and practices of a monocultural society are structured to serve only one narrow segment of the population (Sue, Ivey, & Pedersen, 1996). Psychology in the United States has been severely criticized as being ethnocentric and inherently biased against racial/ethnic minorities and women. Many critics have decried the great harm done to our minority citizens by our systems of education and counseling/psychotherapy. Rather than educate or heal, rather than offer enlightenment and freedom, and rather than allow for equal access and opportunities, historical and current practices have restricted, stereotyped, damaged, and oppressed the culturally different in our society.

These discriminatory practices seem to have a twofold origin. First, they may reside in conscious and unconscious biases, stereotypes, and value systems that are imposed on the culturally different client. Studies show that minorities are generally given less preferred forms of treatment, shunted into dead-end educational and vocational programs, and given more negative psychological evaluations than their majority counterparts (Sue & Sue, 1990).

Second, and more insidiously, some policies and practices may have the unintended consequence of unfair discrimination. How counseling services are advertised, the location of the services, and how services are delivered may be similar for everyone, but biased. In this respect, the nondiscrimination standards may cause confusion among helping professionals. In many institutions a belief prevails that if policies are applied equally to all groups, they cannot be discriminatory. Likewise, many counselors proudly proclaim that they treat everyone the same in counseling. Yet equal treatment can be discriminatory. For example, institutions of higher education often rely on SAT scores for admission. The requirement to attain a certain score is applied to all students regardless of race, culture, or ethnicity. This is equal treatment, but many studies now show that a disproportionate number of minority students are victimized and that such tests do not have predictive value for many groups.

Likewise, counselors need to realize that working with minority clients may require differential approaches. Treating people differently is not necessarily preferential, especially when it provides for equal access and opportunity. The counseling profession must develop new theories, practices, policies, and organizational structures that are more responsive to *all* groups.

Ethical Multicultural Practice

As professional counselors, we must recognize that culture is central to everything that we do. It is not isolated or ancillary. Both clients and counselors are the carriers of their own cultures. On a personal level, it is undeniable that race, culture, and ethnicity are functions of every person's development. Each of us is a racial/cultural being. No one group has exclusive ownership of these group identity factors.

Further, we need to recognize that multicultural relationships are not limited to those between Black and White, Asian and White, or Hispanic and White. Multiculturalism speaks to the need to discuss interethnic relations as well, including Asian-Black, Black-Hispanic, Hispanic-American Indian, and others. With changing demographics, it is clear that various racial minority groups need greater understanding among themselves as well (Sue, 1993).

In addition, if we believe that many problems reside outside the person (prejudice and discrimination) and not within (person-blame), ethical practice dictates that professionals develop alternative helping roles that are aimed at *system intervention*. The traditional counseling role has been primarily confined to a one-to-one, remediation-oriented, in-the-office form of help, but recognition that problems may reside in the social system dictates use of nontraditional roles. These roles may include adviser, advocate, consultant, change agent, facilitator of indigenous support systems, and facilitator of indigenous healing systems (Atkinson, Thompson, & Grant, 1993). Most counselor education programs do not train us in these roles, yet they are some of the most effective in multicultural helping.

Our ability to move toward ethical multicultural practices appears to lie in three primary goals. First, we need to become more culturally aware of our own biases, values, and assumptions about human behavior. Second, we need to become increasingly aware of the cultural values, biases, and assumptions of various diverse groups in our society. Third, we need to begin to develop culturally appropriate individual and system intervention strategies.

Attaining these goals is fundamental in meeting the challenge of ethical multicultural practice. On a professional level, how we meet the challenge will determine the viability and health of the counseling field. On a personal level, how we meet the challenge also foretells the legacy we will leave our children. Race, culture, ethnicity, and gender are fundamental aspects of each of us. They are not solely minority or women's issues. Continuing to deny the impact and importance of these variables is to deny social reality itself. Let us meet the challenge honestly not only because it is good for our profession but also because *it is the ethical thing to do.*

It requires more than good intentions to meet this challenge, as the following two case studies illustrate. In both cases, the counselors wanted to do the right thing when they were confronted with minority client issues. Nonetheless, in the final analysis, both of them were ethically remiss.

Case Study 3

A CASE OF JUSTIFIED DIFFERENTIAL TREATMENT
Derald Wing Sue

Janice, a 27-year-old White counselor, recently accepted her first counseling position at a community mental health clinic in a large urban metropolis. She had been born and raised in a small, predominantly White community where she had minimal experience with multiracial populations. Realizing that she lacked experience in dealing with Asian Americans, African Americans, and Latino/Hispanic Americans, Janice made attempts to rectify this deficiency while she was in graduate school by taking courses in multicultural counseling and minority mental health issues. She did quite well in these courses and felt positive about her receptivity to exploring her own biases and values. She saw herself as an open and honest individual who opposed discrimination and prejudice.

Her self-image was challenged, however, when she discovered that she harbored a strong aversion to interracial and especially Black-White relationships. She was placed in a very uncomfortable situation when a fellow graduate student, who was Black, asked her for a date. Janice accepted the invitation but found that she was ashamed of being seen in public with him, and when alone with him could not dispel fears of being sexually assaulted. She continued seeing him for several dates because she didn't want him to think she was discriminating or was a racist. She secretly acknowledged that she had prejudices but promised herself that she would not allow them to interfere with her work as a counselor.

As in her personal life, this resolve was severely tested during one of her couple counseling sessions. Malachi, a recently divorced African American man, and Teresa, his White woman friend, had come to the clinic at her urging. Teresa had come under increasing pressure from Malachi to make their relationship more permanent through marriage, but she felt conflicted and unable to make a decision.

During their initial sessions, Janice found that she was having difficulty being objective without taking sides. She identified strongly with Teresa, and wondered whether Malachi had considered the best interests of any children they might have together in the future. After all, the children would suffer discrimination, not just the couple.

At some level, Janice realized that her unresolved issues about interracial relationships might potentially compromise her therapeutic integrity. Yet she did not want to discriminate and treat this couple differently by refusing to give them the counseling help they had requested. As a result, she continued working with them for an extended period of time, until Malachi refused to attend further sessions.

Questions for Thought and Discussion

If Janice were your colleague and she came to you for consultation in this case, what might you be inclined to say to her? If you believed that Janice was not competent at this time to work with a particular population, what suggestions might you give her? Imagine that you are in a situation similar to that of Janice. With what kinds of clients might you have difficulty because of your biases, prejudices, assumptions, or values? If you were to recognize that a client was tapping into your strong feelings in ways that could impede the counseling process, how might you proceed? What steps can you take to enhance your knowledge and skills so that you can work more competently with clients whose world views are different from your own?

Analysis

Several multicultural as well as therapeutic issues are raised by this case. First, counselors who are not trained in working with a multicultural population and who work with members of that group may be guilty of unethical practice. Janice's completion of two courses in multicultural counseling may not have been sufficient for her to gain competence. Multicultural competence requires more than cognitive introduction to the topic. It dictates long-term and continuing education and life experiences with the specific population. Standard A.2.b. states that counselors "will actively attempt to understand the diverse cultural backgrounds of the clients with whom they work" and that these attempts should include, but not be limited to, "learning how the counselor's own cultural/ethnic/racial identity impacts his/her values and beliefs about the counseling process." In this case, Janice does appear unprepared to work with African Americans.

It is clear that Janice continues to harbor strong feelings against interracial relationships. She recognizes that her biases may be (and probably are) interfering with her therapeutic effectiveness, and she apparently finds biracial children disturbing. Her strong feelings of alliance with Teresa may not really be identification so much as projection of her racist or biased attitudes and feelings. Counselors have an ethical responsibility to avoid imposing such biases on their clients.

Janice is confused about what nondiscrimination is about. If she reads Standard A.2.a., which states that counselors "do not condone or engage in discrimination based on age, color, culture, disability, ethnic group, gender, race, religion, sexual orientation, marital status, or socioeconomic status," she may unwittingly believe that treating minority clients differently might be an indication of discrimination. Janice seems to be reenacting her biases in the counseling session. She did not want to go out with the Black student, but acquiesced so as not to treat him differently or appear racist. She continued to see the interracial couple for the same reasons. Yet her good intentions not to let her racial biases interfere with helping them were unsuccessful.

Ethical multicultural practice dictates that we are able and willing to understand that we all harbor biases, prejudices, and irrational thoughts/beliefs/feelings that might hinder our ability to work with certain client populations. Janice's case is not unlike many others.

For example, what about a straight male counselor who works with a gay client but harbors strong moral convictions that the gay "lifestyle" is immoral? What about a feminist counselor who works with a chauvinistic male client? These situations, like interracial relationships, may tap into strong feelings, values, and biases that only serve to impede the counseling process and, perhaps, work against the benefit of clients.

Janice needs to realize that the nondiscrimination standards do not necessarily imply equal or similar treatment for all clients. The spirit of this standard implies fair treatment. Fair treatment may dictate differential approaches that recognize the counselor's limitations and the unique needs of clients. In order to allow for equal access and opportunities, counselors often have to modify their approaches and strategies when working with culturally different clients.

Janice should recognize that we all have biases and prejudices. Acknowledging them and discovering how they affect her counseling is crucial to the development of multicultural effectiveness. Ethical practice on her part suggests several possible scenarios: (1) she can seek consultation with another helping professional about the situation, (2) she can seek continuing education about interracial matters, or (3) she can refer the couple to another counselor with multicultural expertise. In Janice's case, the last option seems indicated until her own biases and fears can be adequately resolved.

Questions for Further Reflection

1. Janice is not an ill-intentioned person; she is a victim of her cultural conditioning. What biases or fears do you have, and how might they interfere with your ability to counsel effectively with clients whose backgrounds are different from your own?

2. What kinds of life experiences do you think counselors need to have in order to achieve interpersonal intercultural competence?

Case Study 4

A CROSS-CULTURAL IMPROPRIETY
Beth A. Durodoye

Stephanie is a white counselor in a high school whose student body is predominantly African American and Hispanic. She has been assigned to supervise Carl, a master's level practicum student, for the semester. Carl is also White. One of his duties has been to contact and inform potential students of the purposes and goals of the gifted-and-talented program.

Two months into Carl's internship, Stephanie noticed that he had few contacts with African American students, and that some of the contacts he did have were negative. She felt concerned and scheduled a supervision session with Carl. During the course of their conversation, he made several disturbing remarks, such as that he was of the opinion that most of the African American students with whom he had spoken had learning disabilities. He stated that he found the African American boys, in particular, to be "unprepared, lazy, and inarticulate." He offered no explanation or proof for the statements he made. Carl added that he had little patience for working with African Americans, although the internship had made him aware of his preference for working with Hispanic students. Carl went on to say that he wanted a fulfilling internship experience and hoped that Stephanie would help him accomplish this goal.

Stephanie listened attentively to Carl and nodded her head in agreement. She added that she understood African Americans "work at a different pace than other students and also need more guidance." She did not elaborate further on this statement. She advised Carl to refer the African American students to a doctoral intern who was also working in the guidance office. She then reassigned Carl to administrative duties and class observations of troubled African American students.

At the completion of Carl's internship, Stephanie's written report to his internship professor stated that she had "some concern about Carl's work with some of the minority students, but he is open to alternative ways of handling troublesome situations." She indicated that this situation had "no bearing on his ability to be a successful school counselor."

A week before the semester break, an irate mother of one of the African American students contacted the school district office to question her child's "racist treatment and referral" in matters concerning the gifted-and-talented program. She was referred to Stephanie, and after a conference that the mother found unproductive, she spoke with the district's supervisor of guidance and counseling. The mother remained dissatisfied, and after being informed of her avenues of recourse, she filed a complaint with the ACA Ethics Committee charging Stephanie with violating standards A.2.a., A.2.b., F.1.f., F.1.g., and F.1.h.

Questions for Thought and Discussion

If you were Stephanie's colleague and she were to consult with you regarding Carl's assumptions about and perceptions of African American boys, what might you suggest that she do? If you were a member of the ACA Ethics Committee, might you find Stephanie guilty of violating the Code of Ethics? What determination might you make regarding sanctions? If you believe that Stephanie needs to acquire increased cross-cultural competence, what steps might you recommend that she take?

Analysis

Standard A.2.a. states that counselors "do not condone or engage in discrimination based on age, color, culture, disability, ethnic group, gender, race, religion, sexual orientation, marital status, or socioeconomic status." In this case, it seems clear that Stephanie condoned her supervisee's discrimination through passive acceptance. If the complaint were considered by the Ethics Committee, the committee would find her in violation of this standard.

Standard A.2.b. states that counselors "will actively attempt to understand the diverse cultural backgrounds of the clients with whom they work" and that these attempts should include "learning how the counselor's own cultural/ethnic/racial identity impacts his or her values and beliefs about the counseling process." Stephanie's patronizing statements concerning students who were ultimately in her care demonstrated a lack of understanding and self-awareness. The Ethics Committee would also note that since the supervisee's biases were not addressed, his reassignment to observation of troubled students may have served to further perpetuate his stereotypes. The committee would also find Stephanie guilty of violating this standard.

Standard F.1.f. states that counselors "who offer clinical supervision services are adequately prepared in supervision methods and techniques." The Ethics Committee would consider that Stephanie was willing to schedule extra time with Carl to discuss her concerns, although she did not address the race issue, and that she also implemented a referral process. On the basis of the information given, the committee would not be able to determine whether she was inadequately prepared in supervision methods and techniques.

Standard F.1.g. states that counselors "who supervise the counseling services of others take reasonable measures to ensure that counseling services provided to clients are professional." Stephanie correctly implemented the referral process when it was apparent that her supervisee was not prepared to work with clients of a different background, although her motivations were not clear. Was the referral action taken to quickly smooth over an uncomfortable situation, or because the supervisee was truly deemed incompetent to assist the students? The Ethics Committee would decide that the counselor did not violate this standard.

Standard F.1.h. states that counselors "do not endorse students or supervisees for certification, licensure, employment, or completion of an academic or training program if they believe students or supervisees are not qualified for the endorsement. Counselors take reasonable steps to assist students or supervisees who are not qualified for endorsement to become qualified."Stephanie was sufficiently concerned about her supervisee's competencies to reference them in her letter to his university supervisor, yet no steps were taken to assist the supervisee to explore this situation and its ramifications for his work in the field. The Ethics Committee would conclude that Stephanie was in violation of this standard.

It is likely that the Ethics Committee would issue a reprimand to Stephanie and recommend that she successfully complete a cross-cultural counseling course. A further recommendation would be that she discontinue the supervision of practicum students until after she completes the course and arranges for cross-cultural supervision. After a period of 1 year, the committee would review the outcomes of their recommendations.

Questions for Further Reflection

1. What level of competency is appropriate for counselors preparing to work with cross-cultural populations?

2. How does institutional racism in the counseling profession affect counselors in the United States? What responsibilities do counselors have to act as change agents?

CHAPTER THREE

CONFIDENTIALITY

Barbara Herlihy and Gerald Corey

Confidentiality is essential to the counseling relationship. In order for genuine therapeutic work to occur, clients need to feel free to explore their fears, hopes, fantasies, hurts, and other intimate and private aspects of their lives. They need to know that their counselor is trustworthy and will treat their revelations with respect. The counselor's confidentiality pledge is the cornerstone on which this trust can be built.

Confidentiality is both one of the most basic of our ethical obligations and, at the same time, one of the most problematic. Professional counselors increasingly confront confidentiality issues created by complex legal requirements, developing technologies, new service delivery systems (such as health maintenance organizations and preferred provider networks), and a culture that places greater and greater emphasis on the rights of service recipients.

An entire section (Section B) of the Code of Ethics is devoted to confidentiality. The first standard in this section states that counselors "respect their clients' right to privacy and avoid illegal and unwarranted disclosures of confidential information" (B.1.a.). Some counselors have taken this obligation so literally that they believe they should maintain a client's confidentiality even when the client asks them to share information with others. It is important to remember that confidentiality belongs to the *client*, not to the counselor. It may be waived only by the client (or the client's authorized representative) (B.1.b.).

Confidentiality needs to be discussed with clients when counseling is initiated and throughout the relationship as needed (B.1.g.). We have an obligation to tell our clients that what they reveal in the counseling relationship will be kept confidential, *except in certain circumstances*. Confidentially is not absolute, and other obligations may override our pledge. Ethically conscientious counselors must constantly navigate through a complicated array of exceptions, some legal and others ethical in their bases. These exceptional circumstances include sharing information in order to provide best possible services or to protect someone in danger. They also include group or family counseling, counseling minors, and obeying court orders. It is little wonder that counselors encounter dilemmas of confidentiality so frequently and that we find them to be the most difficult type of dilemma to resolve (Hayman & Covert, 1986).

Exceptional Circumstances

Sometimes is it permissible to share information with others in the interest of providing the best possible services to clients. These circumstances include

- ✦ when clerical or other assistants handle confidential information;
- ✦ when the counselor consults with experts or peers;
- ✦ when the counselor is working under supervision; and
- ✦ when other mental health professionals request information, and the client has given consent to share.

Clerical assistants and other employees or subordinates of the counselor may handle confidential client information, and there is no ethical problem in their doing so. However, counselors need to be aware that they are *responsible* for any breach of confidentiality by someone who assists them (B.1.h.). This speaks to the importance of training subordinates about confidentiality and carefully monitoring office procedures.

Counselors are certainly encouraged to consult with colleagues or experts when they have questions or concerns about their work with a client. If possible, consultation should be managed without revealing the identity of the client, and clients should be informed beforehand of the counselor's intention to seek consultation. Supervision raises a different circumstance, one in which the client's identity cannot be concealed. The supervisor needs to have access to client records, may observe an actual counseling session through a one-way mirror, or may review audio- or videotapes of sessions.

Again, though, the purpose is to ensure quality service, and the ethical obligation is to inform clients fully that supervision is taking place.

Confidential information may also be shared with other helping professionals, when the client requests it or gives permission. This often occurs when clients (or counselors) move to a different location and records are sent to a new therapist. It also routinely occurs in inpatient settings where treatment teams share client information during staffings. The benefits of coordinating the efforts of various professionals are obvious, but clients need to be informed as to what information about them is being shared, with whom, and for what purposes (B.1.i.).

Sometimes it is permissible to breach confidentiality in order to protect someone who is in danger. These circumstances include

+ when the counselor suspects abuse or neglect of a child, an elderly person, a resident of an institution, or others who have limited ability to care for themselves; and
+ when the client's condition poses a clear and imminent danger to self or others.

Both federal and state laws mandate the reporting of suspected child abuse or neglect, and statutes often include a requirement to protect others who may have diminished capacity to care for themselves. This reporting obligation is clear and leaves little room for judgment calls by counselors.

Our confidentiality requirement "does not apply when disclosure is required to prevent clear and imminent danger to the client or others" (B.1.c.). A legal duty to warn and protect an identifiable or foreseeable victim may exist when a client threatens violence toward another person or persons. This duty, which arose out of the *Tarasoff* (1974) case in California, has created considerable consternation among helping professionals. The *Tarasoff* precedent has been applied in some states, but there is variation on several dimensions, such as whether a counselor *may* warn or *must* warn, to whom a warning should be given, and under what circumstances. According to the Code of Ethics, we must disclose when legal requirements demand it and consult with other professionals when we are uncertain (B.1.c.). This suggests that counselors must be familiar with their state laws regarding a duty to warn and should not hesitate to consult with an attorney as well as with experts when they are in doubt.

A duty to warn also may exist when a client is suicidal and poses a danger to self. Counselors struggle with the demands of deciding when to take a client's threats or hints seriously enough to report the condition. This issue is addressed in further detail in chapter eight, Working With Suicidal Clients.

In recent years, mental health professionals have asked for clarification from their professional associations as to whether an ethical duty to warn may exist when a client is HIV positive or has AIDS and may be putting others at risk (Harding, Gray, & Neal, 1993; Hughes & Friedman, 1994). The ACA Code of Ethics contains a new standard that addresses this question. When a counselor has confirmed information "that a client has a disease commonly known to be both communicable and fatal," the counselor is justified in disclosing information to an identifiable third party who is at a high risk of contracting the disease. We should not take this action, though, until we have ascertained that the client has not already informed the third party and does not intend to do so in the immediate future (B.1.d.). The first case study in this chapter illustrates some of the dilemmas that counselors encounter around this issue.

In some situations, counselors must clarify that confidentiality cannot be guaranteed. These circumstances include

- ✦ when counseling groups or families, or whenever there are more than two people (counselor and individual client) in the room; and
- ✦ when the client is a minor.

The confidentiality pledge is different in working with groups than it is when working with individual clients. Although group counselors can make their own promise not to disclose certain information, they cannot guarantee the behavior of group members. Thus group counselors must not only "clearly define confidentiality and the parameters for the specific group being entered" but also "explain its importance, and discuss the difficulties related to confidentiality involved in group work. The fact that confidentiality cannot be guaranteed is clearly communicated to group members" (B.2.a.). Counselors who work with families also encounter some unique confidentiality dilemmas. Issues that arise when counselors work with multiple clients are further addressed in chapter five.

When clients are minor children, their parents or guardians may have rights to certain information. Although, ethically speaking, children should be able to expect confidentiality, their legal rights are more limited. In addition, the counseling process can sometimes be enhanced by including parents or guardians. This reality is acknowledged in Standard B.3, which also notes that the overarching concern is for the minor client's best interests. Chapter six focuses specifically on ethical issues in working with minor clients.

Counselors, like all citizens, must obey orders given to them by a judge or official of the court — which creates an exception to our confidentiality pledge. However, when counselors are called to testify in court and their clients ask them not to reveal information gained in counseling sessions, counselors should ask the court not to require the disclosure and explain the potential harm that could be done to the counseling relationship (B.1.e.). When disclosure is required, only essential information should be revealed (B.1.f.). Whether or not a counselor will be able successfully to request in court to withhold information may depend on the privileged communications provisions in the state where the counselor practices. Confidentiality is an *ethical* obligation, whereas privileged communication is a *legal* concept that protects clients from having their confidential communications revealed in court without their permission. State laws vary considerably with respect to which mental health professionals' communications are privileged, and under what circumstances. Counselors must know the laws in their own states.

Records

We need to remember that not only are clients' communications confidential, but also counseling *records*. Section B.4. sets forth several guidelines for maintaining, storing, transferring, sharing, and disposing of records. Despite counselors' best efforts, it is possible for the confidentiality of records to be inadvertently breached, particularly when counselors are not aware of the confidentiality implications of new technologies. The second case study in this chapter provides an illustration of just such an occurrence.

Case Study 5

CONFIDENTIALITY AND CLIENTS WITH HIV/AIDS
Jorge Garcia

Mary is a 30-year-old single woman of African American descent. Due to a rare neuromuscular disability that she has suffered for the past 4 years, she experiences weakness and some minor speech problems. During the last year she has made significant progress. She has regained strength in her legs and is able to endure standing and walking for longer periods of time. Her speech has improved to a point where verbal communication with others is virtually not a problem. Finally, after years of depression, Mary is starting to feel more optimistic. She has begun to plan a new career and has enrolled in graduate school.

Three years ago she began a relationship with John, whom she met through common friends. She felt that he was a positive influence in her life and that he motivated her to study. During the past year there were times when he would be ill and once he had to be hospitalized, but the rest of the time he was healthy and strong, and she did not see any signs of serious illness. When he was hospitalized, she visited him at the hospital and talked to the doctors and nurses who gave her reassurance but never told her what his condition was. Mary had a close relationship with John's mother, and although they provided support for each other they never talked about the nature of John's medical condition.

About a month ago, John suddenly became very ill and was taken to the hospital for intensive care. Mary was informed, and she went to visit him, again without knowing his exact condition. The next day she received a phone call from John's sister who told her that he had died the night before. Mary was shocked, stating that she had never expected something like this to happen because she had not seen any serious symptoms of illness in John. His family invited her to talk and showed surprise that she did not know that he had contracted HIV about 8 years ago and had developed AIDS symptoms within the last 2 years. They had assumed she knew, and that was the reason they had never talked to her about it. Mary also learned that John had been receiving treatment, which included counseling services from a professional counselor. She now feels betrayed and angry at John who never told her of his condition. She has gone for laboratory tests, which were positive because she and John did not practice safe sex methods.

Feeling completely overwhelmed and in despair, Mary has sought counseling services. She wonders why John never informed her of his diagnosis, and also why the professionals treating him never approached her, particularly John's counselor who probably knew that she was John's girl friend.

Questions for Thought and Discussion

If you had been John's counselor in this case, would you have asked him about his sexual partners and his sex practices? If he were to tell you that he had a sexual relationship with Mary, what might you say to him? If John remained steadfast in his decision not to tell Mary about his condition, how might you work with him? Would you have informed Mary of his HIV status if he refused to do so? What might you want to include in your professional disclosure statement about your policies pertaining to maintaining or breaching confidentiality in cases involving HIV/AIDS?

Analysis

This case illustrates one of the most controversial ethical dilemmas involving counseling HIV-positive clients, which is the need to weigh the confidentiality rights of the client against the right of the public to know in order to prevent the spread of the disease. The main issue is whether mental health professionals have a duty to warn third parties about HIV infection. So far there is not a legal duty to warn, but if such legislation is passed, professional organizations have suggested that the duty should not be imposed or should include immunity from civil and criminal liability for providers who make decisions in good faith about whether or not to disclose confidential information (APA, 1991).

The ACA Code of Ethics includes confidentiality rights under Section B. Standard B.1.d. addresses disclosure when clients have contagious, fatal diseases. Although this standard does provide guidelines, in the case of AIDS it is very difficult to identify who in particular is at risk, and to assess the degree to which individuals who have intimate relationships with persons with HIV are in imminent danger. Assessment and identification require careful and responsible decisions. The standard states that disclosure may be considered only when the counselor knows the identity of a person who is at a high risk of infection. Disclosure should be made only when the client has not informed the third party and is not intending to do so in the immediate future. This guideline gives counselors *permission* to breach confidentiality, but does not constitute a *duty* to warn because such a provision would put counselors in a very vulnerable position.

Based on this discussion, was John's counselor in violation of the ACA Code of Ethics by not informing Mary of her partner's condition? Under Standard B.1.d., the counselor would have been justified in disclosing John's condition to her. However, in order for the Ethics Committee to find the member in violation of this standard, Mary would have to prove that she was in clear and imminent danger because of John's conditon. It is not the client's illness but his behavior that may pose danger to others. This includes the practice of unsafe sex and not disclosing one's condition to sexual partners.

Mary would have to prove that the counselor (a) knew her identity, (b) had compelling reason to believe she was in imminent risk of contracting the disease, and (c) had made no effort to have John inform her of his condition or had failed to ascertain John's willingness to inform her.

The counselor would need to provide evidence that he did not know that Mary was John's sexual partner, that John never admitted engaging in behaviors that could put partners at risk of contracting HIV, or that John had provided convincing information that he had revealed his condition to his sexual partner (even though it turned out that he hadn't done so).

In this case, there is a possibility that John's counselor committed a violation of the Code of Ethics. Regardless of whether Mary decides to pursue a complaint against him, and regardless of how an ethics committee might rule on that complaint, many questions remain unanswered. If John's counselor had warned Mary when he learned her identity, would the warning have come soon enough to have been effective? Mary's successes in regaining her physical and mental health and her optimism for life are now jeopardized by her HIV-positive status. How can Mary's counselor best be helpful to her? Mary may remain symptom free for years. If she enters into a sexual relationship with a new partner at some future time, and if she is careless about safe sex practices, her counselor may be faced with the same question that arose earlier—whether to issue a warning or to maintain the client's confidentiality.

Questions for Further Reflection

1. Suppose you were counseling an individual with AIDS who had not notified his or her sexual partner. How much time do you think you could or should ethically devote to persuading the client to inform the partner before you breached confidentiality?

2. Do you think that counselors have an ethical responsibility to check to see whether their HIV-positive client has been truthful when the client claims that he or she is practicing safe sex or has notified partners? What considerations do you need to take into account in pondering this question?

Case Study 6

A COMPUTER-AIDED VIOLATION OF CONFIDENTIALITY
James P. Sampson, Jr.

Jim, a college sophomore, was proud of his skill with computers. He frequently was asked to help fellow students in solving difficult computer problems. For Jim, one of the ultimate challenges was to gain access to restricted files on one of the networked campus computers via a computer located in the library. His goal was to gain access, read the contents of a file, and then exit without being detected. By successfully pitting his skill against that of university personnel, he believed he could prove that he was as smart as his peers expected him to be. He justified his actions by rationalizing that he never copied files or deprived the owner of access by erasing or corrupting the file.

To avoid detection, Jim used a series of computer accounts and passwords of other students who could be easily observed signing on at the computer lab. He was careful never to copy files into his own personal account or to use the computer in his room at the residence hall. He was also careful not to brag openly about his success, and told only a couple of close friends. In the previous semester he had gained access to a faculty member's research data by determining the account number from a log of publicly available electronic mail addresses and then systematically entering likely passwords over a period of 3 weeks. He also accessed records from the financial aid department by observing two sequences of letters and numbers, which he correctly guessed to be an account number and password, taped to the side of a computer monitor in the financial aid office.

One aspect of Jim's part-time job involved delivering mail to and from various campus offices. While waiting to pick up mail from the counseling center secretary, he noticed a monthly statement for computer charges for an account named *CASENOTE* on the desk of the center's receptionist. Later that evening, Jim began systematically entering likely passwords. After only a few tries, he gained access to the CASENOTE account by using the last name of the counseling center director as the password.

Jim began browsing through case notes on several counseling center clients. The notes for one client were particularly interesting to Jim. A student named Mary had a long history of bulimia that had become increasingly severe over the past 2 months. Because Jim's older sister had experienced problems with bulimia, he was familiar with some of the related issues. Jim shared this story with his roommate, Guillermo, who recognized Mary as someone who was in one of his classes.

A week later, as Guillermo and Mary were leaving class, Guillermo began a conversation with Mary. After experiencing little success in keeping the conversation going, Guillermo tried to show some concern by asking if her eating disorder was improving. Because Mary had told no one on campus about her problem except her counselor, she became very upset at this breach of confidentiality, and turned and walked away. The next day she went to see her counselor to describe the incident and to ask how this could have occurred. Unable to get a satisfactory explanation from her counselor, Mary complained in writing to the counseling center director.

Questions for Thought and Discussion

If you were Mary's counselor and she came to you asking how this breach of confidentiality had occurred, what might you say to her? If you were the director of the counseling center and Mary presented you with a written complaint, how might you respond to her? How might you deal with Mary's counselor? What issues does this case raise for you with respect to keeping client records on a computer? What safeguards can you implement to ensure that your confidential records are protected from unauthorized access?

Analysis

The Code of Ethics states that counselors are responsible for maintaining the confidentiality of counseling records, including computerized records (B.4.b.). Even though Mary's counselor was not directly involved in disseminating confidential information, she did use a computer system that was inherently vulnerable to unauthorized access, ultimately leading to an ethical violation. The director of the counseling center, who had responsibility for supervising the design and use of information systems in the center, also contributed to this ethical violation.

A number of steps could be taken to prevent problems like the one that occurred here. First, confidential information should not be maintained on a computer system that can be generally accessed through a computer network. Second, identification information for computer accounts containing client data needs to be considered confidential and treated as such. Third, account names and corresponding passwords for confidential data should be kept obscure to decrease the likelihood of unauthorized access. Fourth, passwords for accounts containing client data should be changed regularly to limit exposure if security is compromised.

This ethical violation might have been avoided if staff had a greater awareness of the positive and negative aspects of using computer technology in the delivery of counseling services. Greater awareness of potential problems can help counselors assume a proactive role in preventing ethical dilemmas.

Questions for Further Reflection

1. Technology has evolved and will continue to evolve at a rapid pace. What steps can counselors take to ensure that ethical practice keeps pace with advancing technology?

2. What safeguards do you have in place to ensure that your confidential records—computerized or not—are protected from unauthorized access?

CHAPTER FOUR

COMPETENCE

Gerald Corey and Barbara Herlihy

Trust as a key element in creating and maintaining the counseling relationship has been emphasized in earlier chapters on client rights and confidentiality. The concept of trust is equally foundational to any discussion of competence because it defines the context in which clients enter into a therapeutic relationship. "When clients put their trust in us as professionals, one of their most fundamental expectations is that we will be competent" (Pope & Vasquez, 1991, p. 51). Clients, as help seekers, place themselves in a vulnerable position, allowing their counselors to hear their most personal secrets and learn about their most private struggles. This trust that clients bestow upon counselors is a source of power that must not be abused; clients need to be able to rely on their counselor's competence as a helper.

Counselors have an ethical obligation to practice "within the boundaries of their competence, based on their education, training, supervised experience, state and national professional credentials, and appropriate professional experience" (C.2.a.). Competence in counseling is difficult to define. Counseling is not a unitary profession. Counselors work with a wide spectrum of clients and client concerns in very diverse settings that require different skills and competencies. No professional counselor can be competent in every aspect of potential practice. Appropriate education, training, and experience in working with children do not qualify us to work with older adults, competence in individual counseling does not qualify us to conduct groups or work with families; and expertise in working with clients who suffer from depression does not qualify us to work with borderline patients. Competence in providing counseling services does not necessarily imply competence in areas such as consulting, as the first case study in this chapter demonstrates.

How can boundaries of competence be determined and assessed? Mental health professionals have long struggled with this question, and their efforts have taken varied forms, including the development of standards for training, credentialing, continuing education, and new specialty areas of practice as well as self-monitoring.

Obviously, training is a basic component in developing competence to counsel. Key issues include determining who should be selected for training and by what selection methods, what should be taught and by which methods, and what procedures should be used to ensure that only competent counselors are graduated from training programs. Although ethical issues in training and supervision are more fully addressed in chapter nine, one reality that is particularly germane to the development of competence is that training institutions may vary considerably in the quality of training provided. Two bodies that have offered national standards for training counselors are the Council for Accreditation of Counseling and Related Programs (CACREP) and the National Board for Certified Counselors (NBCC). Regional accreditation of universities is another method of quality control.

CACREP, established in 1981 by the American Association for Counseling and Development as an independent accrediting body, accredits programs that have undergone a rigorous review. Thus graduates of CACREP-accredited programs can be reasonably assumed to possess certain competencies. However, the majority of counselor training programs are not CACREP accredited. The NBCC has identified content areas in which prospective counselors should receive instruction, has set requirements for supervised experience, and requires the successful completion of an examination. Again, however, certification by NBCC is voluntary, and the majority of practicing counselors do not hold this credential. Regional accreditation provides another mechanism to establish adequacy of training, and counselors may advertise only their highest degree earned in counseling or a related field from a "college or university that was accredited when the degree was awarded by one of the regional accrediting bodies recognized by the Council on Postsecondary Education" (C.3.a.).

Each of these approaches to ensuring quality in counselor training has its limitations, so that successful graduation from a training program does not guarantee competency. It should be noted, however, that the variability across training programs is not necessarily negative as long as graduates are aware of their limitations and their boundaries of competence (Keith-Spiegel & Koocher, 1985).

Credentials are presumed to exist as a tangible indicator of accomplishment with implications for assessing the competence of the credential holder. The state licensure movement has been significant in this respect. Licensure assures clients that their counselors have completed minimal educational requirements, have had supervised experience, and have successfully completed an examination or other form of screening. Licensure requirements vary from state to state, however, and the possession of a license does not ensure that practitioners will competently *do* what their credential permits them to do (Corey et al., 1993). The second case study in this chapter describes the pitfalls into which a counselor falls when he attempts to open a private practice, even though he is fully licensed and possesses the appropriate credentials.

Licensure laws typically require that professionals complete continuing education requirements in order to renew their licenses. Continuing education is also an ethical obligation. Standard C.2.f. states that counselors recognize the need for continuing education to keep abreast of current information and developments, and that they "take steps to maintain competence in the skills they use, are open to new procedures, and keep current with the diverse and/or special populations with whom they work." As with other means of attempting to assess competence, there are limitations to what continuing education requirements can accomplish. It is difficult to monitor the quality of continuing education offerings or their relevance to a particular counselor's needs. The number of clock hours obtained may have little relationship to how much the counselor has actually learned and integrated into practice.

Without an agreed-upon definition of competence, it is difficult for ethically conscientious counselors to determine exactly where their boundaries of competence lie and to recognize when they are in danger of exceeding them. In the absence of formal criteria for evaluating competence in specific practices or specializations, counselors must carefully assess whether they should accept or continue to work with certain clients or refer them. Consultation with other professionals is also a prudent and ethically appropriate measure (C.2.e.). While learning skills in new specialty areas, counselors "take steps to ensure the competence of their work and to protect others from possible harm" (C.2.b.). These steps might include further formal education or training, and/or working under supervision.

Because competence is so difficult to define and assess, careful self-monitoring may be the most effective method for counselors to ensure that they are providing the highest quality of services. Counselors are ethically obligated to "monitor their effectiveness as professionals and take steps to improve when necessary" (C.2.d.).

It is incumbent on each of us to strive to maintain self-awareness and to be alert to any signs of burnout or impairment. Our obligations to clients necessitate that we seek assistance for our own problems that are interfering with our professional effectiveness, and that if necessary, we limit, suspend, or terminate our professional responsibilities until we are restored to full functioning (C.2.g.). We believe that the importance of maintaining a connectedness with peers cannot be overemphasized in this regard. Peer consultation groups can provide a source of support to counter the loneliness that is often associated with the work of the counselor, especially the private practitioner. Keith-Spiegel and Koocher (1985) have observed that the impaired mental health professional is most typically a professionally isolated individual. Peers can help us see our blind spots, offer new perspectives on ethical and practice issues, and provide us with opportunities to share information about resources and effective therapeutic procedures.

The ultimate answer to maintaining competence most likely lies in our ability to explore our own motives and relationships insightfully. As Keith-Spiegel and Koocher (1985) have noted, this ability is not easily taught and never perfected, yet it is among the most critical to the effective ethical functioning of the professional counselor. The development of competence is an ongoing process that is never really completed.

Case Study 7

Competent to Consult?
Janice L. Smith and Michael L. Baltimore

Marsha was a university professor and part-time private practitioner. She had an excellent reputation in her community for offering diagnosis and treatment planning workshops for practitioners seeking third-party reimbursement from insurance companies. Two counselors in a community mental health agency attended one of Marsha's seminars and asked her if she was interested in consulting with their agency about treatment planning and completing insurance reimbursement forms for their clients. She responded enthusiastically. A week later, the director of the agency contacted her and asked her to provide a series of in-service sessions with 10 master's level counselors to assist them in their diagnosis and treatment planning with agency clients.

Although Marsha had expertise in diagnosis and insurance reimbursement, she had no formal training or supervision in agency consultation. Because of her extensive knowledge base and experience in providing workshops she believed that with some self-instruction she could provide ethical and professional services to the agency. She considered asking colleagues for information about the consultation process but was concerned that she might lose respect in her professional community if she sought advice. She called the director and accepted his offer. They did not discuss how Marsha might report back to the director or how her work might be evaluated.

In fulfillment of her 6-month contract, Marsha met biweekly with staff members to discuss cases and to help ensure that the agency was providing diagnosis and treatments plans that increased the likelihood of third-party reimbursement. She paid scrupulous attention to ethical and professional guidelines in the area of consultation. She first established a written contract with the agency stipulating that staff member participation was strictly voluntary and confidential. It was agreed that she was acting strictly in a consultant capacity; that is, she was performing her consultation functions as a peer and was not responsible for the actions of her consultees. They, in turn, were not bound to follow her advice.

Marsha and the consultees agreed to maintain confidentiality regarding client information. To ensure agency clients' freedom of choice and informed consent, Marsha required that all clients be given written material describing her involvement in discussing confidential case material during treatment team meetings and in reviewing client files and insurance documents. She explained how she planned to tailor her consultations to ensure that at the end of her contract consultees would feel comfortable in carrying out their responsibilities independently, without her assistance. Staff members were quite impressed by Marsha's expertise in third-party reimbursement issues and treatment planning, and with her ethical consultation practices. They felt very comfortable sharing clinical concerns about their cases and conveyed their enthusiasm about her consultations to the agency director.

At the conclusion of the consultation contract, Marsha was contacted by the agency director. He arranged to meet with her to discuss the group's general performance in diagnosis and treatment planning and the effectiveness of her consultation. At their meeting, Marsha was surprised when the director requested information about the quality of each participant's treatment plans. He explained that the agency was about to decrease the size of its staff and that her opinion would be useful in making staffing decisions. The director told her that he considered her to be highly competent in the evaluation of professional counseling skills.

Marsha, having had ample opportunity to review the staff members' clinical performance, decided to comply with the director's request. She felt obligated to him because he had hired her and had negotiated her consultation contract. She reasoned that because the reduction in staff was going to occur with or without her input, she ought to do what she could to save the jobs of the staff clinicians she believed were the most skilled practitioners and should also be the most successful in obtaining third-party reimbursement for agency clients.

Several months later, two former employees who had participated in the consultation group filed a complaint with the ACA Ethics Committee, charging Marsha with ethical misconduct. They based their complaint on her disclosures to the director about individual staff members' performance.

Questions for Thought and Discussion

In what ways do you think that Marsha may have exceeded the boundaries of her competence in accepting the consultation contract? What criteria might she have used to assess her competence to consult? What steps would you recommend to her, if she were to ask your advice regarding how to acquire competency in agency consulting? How do you think the Ethics Committee might rule on the complaint? What ethical standards might committee members consider to be relevant in reaching their decision?

Analysis

Marsha appropriately fulfilled her ethical responsibility to ensure that agency clients were informed of her consultation relationship with staff members and her access to confidential client information (A.3.a.). Consultees, however, have similar rights. Agreements about the goals and processes of the consultation, voluntary participation, freedom of choice, and clear understandings as to what types of information will be disclosed by the consultant are critical at the beginning of the relationship for all persons concerned. This is particularly true when a third party such as a superior is involved in the process.

Marsha established at the outset that information shared in the consultation meetings was confidential for both clients and consultees. No evaluative component was established. The consultees, despite their voluntary participation in the consultation activities, were not give the freedom to choose whether to participate in consultation meetings with knowledge that their individual clinical performances might be evaluated and disclosed to the agency director. Therefore, Marsha violated the privacy rights of all participants by sharing information with the director that was not germane to the purposes of the consultation (B.6.a.).

Despite the wealth of experience that counselors may have, they are ethically bound to seek education, supervision, and consultation when developing new specialty areas of practice (C.2.b.). Although Marsha was an experienced practitioner and presenter in the area of treatment planning and insurance reimbursement, she had no previous agency consultation experience. The issue here is not that she decided to study consultation issues on her own. She failed to consult with appropriate professionals regarding a new area of practice and acted incompetently because she was not knowledgeable about confidentiality and informed consent issues for the consultees. If she had sought consultation, she might have been better prepared to discuss evaluating staff with the director at the time she negotiated her contract.

Based on the information given, the ACA Ethics Committee would find that Marsha behaved unethically by violating consultee confidentiality in performing her consultation duties (B.6.a.) and by failing to request consultation/supervision when using a new skill (C.2.b.) Her competence to evaluate practitioners is not in question because she possessed the professional skills to perform this function. However, she did not understand that she was violating her consultees' rights and neglecting her primary responsibility to promote the welfare of her consultees when she divulged information that ultimately affected their employment status (A.1.a.).

Questions for Further Reflection

1. What are counselors' ethical and professional obligations regarding confidentiality and informed consent in consultation situations? What information should be shared with the consultees at the outset of the consultation relationship?

2. What steps should counselors take to ensure their competence when they practice in new specialty areas?

Case Study 8

ETHICAL PITFALLS IN MANAGED CARE
Larry Golden

After completing his master's degree in counseling, Martin worked at the Family Service Center, an agency where he received the 3,000 hours of supervised practice required for licensure in his state. He passed the state board examination and became a licensed professional counselor. Only then, in accordance with state licensing regulations, did Martin hang out his shingle and open his independent private practice.

Martin wanted to provide the best possible counseling services to his clients. He also wanted —and needed—to earn a good living. During the first few months he struggled, unaware of the extent to which managed care had impacted the private practice of counseling. He placed ads in the yellow pages of local telephone directories, gave free talks at PTA meetings and to various civic clubs, invited referral sources out to lunch, and attempted several other strategies to build a client base. Very few referrals came.

Martin pursued an opportunity to become a network provider with HealthCo, a managed care company. He accepted the company's $45.00 per hour payment, although it was considerably less than his usual fee, and agreed to comply with HealthCo's approach to managed care. He was delighted when HealthCo referrals began to come on a regular basis.

In some respects, Martin was pleased with the services provided by the managed care company. When he ascertained that a client who presented with depression was also suffering from anorexia, he realized that he needed to refer the client because he lacked training and supervised experience with this disorder. He called his HealthCo case manager, who arranged a referral to a psychiatrist in the network who specialized in eating disorders.

However, there were some aspects of the relationship with HealthCo that worried Martin. He was required to get telephone authorizations for client sessions, but it seemed that whenever he called, he was connected to a different case manager who identified himself or herself only by first name. The case managers began the telephone conferences by keying in Martin's client's social security number to gain access to the client's computerized file. Before he began to work with HealthCo, Martin had been required to give a diagnosis when completing paperwork for third-party payers, and he was comfortable with giving that information. But these case managers insisted that if they were to *manage*, they needed much more information. They inquired about clients' childhood traumas, marital problems, addictions, and other matters. Martin realized that this questioning was legal because the clients had signed HealthCo's disclosure form, but he wondered, Was it ethical? He became concerned about just what happened to the information he disclosed over the telephone.

Soon after these concerns began to emerge, one of Martin's clients ran out of insurance benefits. The case manager suggested that Martin space out the last 3 of the 20 allocated visits over a period of several months and/or arrange a referral to a community mental health center. Martin did not feel that these options were acceptable. The client needed weekly sessions, and considerably more than the three that remained. He also believed that she needed continuity of care, and that a transfer to a new counselor was not in her best interest. Martin attempted to explain his concerns to the case manager but was unsuccessful in convincing her to alter her decision. Because he could not consider abandoning a client and could not agree to make a referral, he decided, with some resentment toward HealthCo, to continue to see the client pro bono. This interaction caused Martin to wonder what professional credentials

HealthCo's case managers possessed. Were they qualified to make decisions about psychotherapy?

Soon thereafter, an 11-year-old boy named Joshua was referred to Martin under the boy's father's company insurance plan administered by HealthCo. Joshua was getting in fights at school. It quickly became clear to Martin that Joshua's parents were in conflict, so Martin recommended marital counseling. However, this particular HealthCo plan didn't cover marital counseling. Martin, beginning to feel frustrated with managed care, saw the parents in counseling and billed the sessions under Joshua's name. He justified his decision to himself by reasoning that, after all, gains in the marital relationship should surely yield benefits for Joshua.

Questions for Thought and Discussion

In what respects has Martin's behavior been in compliance with the Code of Ethics? Do you see any ways in which he has acted unethically? If Martin had been meeting regularly with a peer consultation group, how might such a group have helped him deal with the ethical issues and practice issues he encountered? If he had consulted with you regarding his concerns about HealthCo, what advice might you have given him? How can counselors in private practice best deal with managed care companies? Do you believe Martin was competent to open an independent private practice?

Analysis

An ethical issue first arose in this case when Martin ascertained that one of his clients was anorexic. He realized that he would be exceeding the boundaries of his competence if he continued to work with her, and he appropriately arranged a referral to a qualified provider. He acted in accordance with Standard A.11.b., which states that if counselors determine an inability to be of professional assistance to a client, they terminate the counseling relationship and refer the client; and with Standard C.2.a. which states that "counselors practice only within the boundaries of their competence."

Martin grew concerned about a possible breach of confidentiality via HealthCo's anonymous case managers and potential lapses in the company's computer system. Standard D.4 of the ACA Code of Ethics is pertinent here. It states that "When counselors work as subcontractors for counseling services for a third party, they have a duty to inform clients of the limitations of confidentiality that the organization may place on counselors in providing counseling services to clients. The limits of such confidentiality ordinarily are discussed as part of the intake session." Martin had a responsibility to ensure that he knew what information about clients he was required to provide *before* he agreed to become a HealthCo provider. It appears that he allowed his decision to affiliate with the company to be driven by his frustrations and financial needs, and he may have acted hastily. At this point, he needs to resolve his concerns directly with HealthCo, and determine whether he can ethically continue to be a network provider. If he decides to continue, he also has a responsibilty to ensure that his HealthCo clients are fully informed about the information he will be providing to the company. Ethically, he cannot rely solely on the fact that the clients have signed the company's disclosure form.

Martin began to grow disenchanted with the managed care company's policies and procedures and to have some concerns about the quality of care that he could provide under their aegis. He will be well advised to consider whether he can remain a network provider and continue to adhere to Standard D.1.l.: "The acceptance of employment in an agency or institution implies that counselors are in agreement with its general policies and principles."

It was only with resentment that Martin continued to see a client whose benefits had been exhausted. He acted in accordance with the Code of Ethics in refusing to abandon the client (A.11.a) and in agreeing to provide pro bono services (A.10.d.). However, he needs to seriously consider whether he will be able to work effectively in this counseling relationship or whether his feelings will interfere with his ability to provide the best services possible.

Regarding Martin's decision to see Joshua's parents and bill the sessions under Joshua's name, Martin has committed a serious error. His failure to provide a proper diagnosis is a violation of Standard E.5.a., and his misleading report to the insurance company is a violation of Standard C.5.c. Insurance fraud is a legal as well as an ethical issue. Martin's rationalizations in this case might well be the beginning of an ethical slippery slope for him. He might find it easier and easier to condone dishonest practices in the future. He might have been pleasantly surprised had he discussed his thinking with

HealthCo's case manager for Joshua and his family. Managed care companies want to be time efficient and may well have supported Martin's view that helping the parents was the quickest and most effective way to help the son.

The managed care industry confronts the practitioner with some difficult ethical issues. The industry is not inherently unethical, but there are no industry-wide ethical standards. Counselors are advised to consult the ACA Code of Ethics as well as their state licensure laws when questions arise in working with managed care systems. We will also be wise, if we wish to continue to work with managed care companies, to work to persuade them to hire only licensed practitioners as case managers and to develop industry-wide standards of ethical practice.

In Martin's case, an overarching question is whether he possessed sufficient competence to establish an independent private practice. Although he was fully qualified according to the requirements in his state, which allowed only licensed counselors to establish independent private practices, he was naive and uninformed about many issues related to managed care.

Questions for Further Reflection

1. In order to be successful as independent private practitioners, counselors need to have skills and knowledge not only as clinicians but also as business persons. How can counselors acquire the skills and knowledge needed?

2. Are independent private practitioners particularly vulnerable to burnout and/or impairment? What steps can they take to ensure their competence on an ongoing basis?

CHAPTER FIVE

WORKING WITH MULTIPLE CLIENTS

Barbara Herlihy and Gerald Corey

Within the counseling profession there is growing interest in working with couples, families, and groups. When counselors work with more than one client at a time, some new ethical considerations arise and existing ones become more complicated. Although the ACA Code of Ethics addresses working with multiple clients in several new standards, the ACA code is generic. Family counseling and group work are specialized areas, and the ACA standards cannot be truly comprehensive with respect to specific issues that need to be addressed when practitioners work with multiple clients. Counselors who work with families and groups are advised to familiarize themselves with the *AAMFT Code of Ethics* (American Association for Marriage and Family Therapy, 1991) and the *Ethical Guidelines for Group Counselors* (Association for Specialists in Group Work [ASGW], 1989), in addition to the ACA code.

Most of our general ethical obligations apply not only to individual counseling but also to family counseling and group work. We will discuss here only a few issues that seem to us to have particular relevance to working with multiple clients. These issues include client welfare and protection from harm, informed consent, confidentiality, counselor values, and competence.

Client Welfare and Protection From Harm

The primary responsibility of counselors is to promote the welfare of the client. When counselors offer individual counseling services, the question of who the client is does not arise as a precursor to determining what is in the client's best interest. However, this seemingly basic question can be difficult to answer when working with families or groups. As Corey et al. (1993) have noted, when the focus of counseling shifts from the individual to the family system, a new set of ethical questions arises. Whose interests should the counselor serve? To whom does the counselor have primary responsibility—an individual family member who may have originally sought counseling or the family as a whole? Standard A.8 provides some guidance on this issue, stating that when counselors "provide counseling services to two or more persons who have a relationship (such as husband and wife, or parents and children)," they need to clarify at the outset "which person or persons are clients and the nature of the relationships they will have with each involved person." Even when good-faith efforts at clarification are made, role conflicts can develop. When this happens, counselors "clarify, adjust, or withdraw from roles appropriately" (A.8.).

Client welfare considerations when working with individuals may at times suggest to a counselor that it might be helpful to involve the client's family in the counseling process. A family systems perspective is reflected in Standard A.1.d., which acknowledges that families are usually important forces in clients' lives and encourages counselors to "enlist family understanding and involvement as a positive resource, when appropriate."

In group work, ensuring client welfare can be particularly difficult because the group counselor has less situational control. Groups can be powerful catalysts for change. This potency, along with the difficulty of monitoring the moment-to-moment experiencing of members, means that groups can be risky. Screening and selection are important ethical considerations because the degree of compatibility of the group members will have a strong impact on the success of the group experience. Standard A.9.a. requires counselors to do their best to "select members whose needs and goals are compatible with [the] goals of the group, who will not impede the group process, and whose well-being will not be jeopardized" by participating.

Counselors in a group setting need to take "precautions to protect clients from physical or psychological trauma" (A.9.b.) A difficulty arises in practice when events that occur during a group's process are therapeutic to one member or to some members but are aversive to others. For example, emotions (including anger, sadness, and pain) are regularly elicited in groups, and facilitating emotionality is one of the most powerful change mechanisms in groups. However, an event that provides an emotional catharsis to one group member may provoke extreme discomfort in another (Lakin, 1994). Similarly in family therapy, ethical dilemmas can arise when an intervention that serves one person's best interests comes into conflict with the wishes or needs of another family member.

Informed Consent

Informed consent issues take on new complexity when applied to counseling with families or groups. When working with families, several questions arise: Who gives consent for the family? Which family members are actively seeking counseling and who in the family is a reluctant participant? Are there differences among family members in their capacity to understand what the counseling process may involve? How can family counselors adequately address, at the outset, the reality that there will inevitably be abrasive interactions during sessions, and how can counselors describe the ways they will deal with these events? It is not a simple task for counselors to give clear information to individual clients regarding the life changes they might anticipate through therapy; it is a real challenge for family counselors to describe potential changes in family relationships as well as changes that individual family members might make in conjunction with shifts in the system.

Lakin (1994) has suggested that many group counselors are relatively unskilled at describing for prospective participants what is likely to occur in group interactions, beyond generalities about hoped-for benefits. Indeed, there are limits to the extent that a group counselor can articulate — before the fact — the kinds of peer interactions that might unfold in a group context. Group counselors cannot anticipate the responses of group members in general, nor can they know in advance what the effects will be of dynamics that may be created by the interplay of personalities.

Confidentiality

Marriage and family counselors have unique confidentiality concerns. A particular issue that often emerges in practice is how to deal with family secrets, or information that one family member may have shared with the counselor during an individual session but has withheld from a spouse or parents or children. According to the Code of Ethics, the privacy rights of each family member must be protected. "In family counseling, information about one family member cannot be disclosed to another member without permission" (B.2.b.).

Questions about the confidentiality of counseling records can also arise. For example, a couple may come for marriage counseling and then later seek a divorce. In a child custody dispute, one marital partner may want the counselor to testify about what was discussed in counseling while the other partner may want the sessions kept confidential. Although the ruling of the court will have to guide the counselor in this example, the Code of Ethics guideline is that "access to records is limited to those parts of records that do not include confidential information related to another client" (B.4.d.).

Group counseling, like marriage and family therapy, raises some unique confidentiality issues. Confidentiality is different in group situations than it is in individual counseling, and it is difficult to enforce. Standard B.2.a. provides some guidelines for handling the issue of confidentiality in groups: "In group work, counselors clearly define confidentiality and the parameters for the specific group being entered, explain its importance, and discuss the difficulties related to confidentiality involved in group work." Prospective group participants have a right to know that confidentiality cannot be guaranteed in a group setting, and counselors have an ethical responsibility to communicate this fact clearly to group members (B.2.a.).

Counselor Values

According to the Code of Ethics, counselors must be "aware of their own values, attitudes, beliefs, and behaviors and how these apply in a diverse society," and we must take care to avoid imposing our values on clients (A.5.b.). This ethical imperative has some special applications to family and group counseling.

Corey et al. (1993) have noted that the counselor's values will have a crucial influence on how the counselor works with a couple or family. Of particular relevance are the counselor's personal values pertaining to such issues as marriage and divorce, traditional and nontraditional life-styles, conception, abortion, gender roles, extramarital affairs, homosexuality, and child rearing and the discipline of children.

Group counselors, like family therapists, are not value free. Certain values are inherent in the group process, such as self-disclosure, risk-taking behavior, learning to be direct and open, choosing for oneself, and increasing awareness and autonomy. It is essential for group counselors to examine their assumptions about human nature and the therapeutic process if they are to avoid imposing their beliefs and values on group members, even in subtle and unintended ways (Corey, Corey, & Callanan, 1990). It is important that counselors remain cognizant that their role is not to impose their own values on a family or a group but to help individual members find their own way and arrive at solutions that work for them.

On a related note, respecting diversity is relevant to both family counseling and group work. It is essential that counselors who work with clients who are culturally different from themselves take steps to learn about specific cultural values and practices that will impact the course of counseling, whether in family work or in a group context. For example, striving for autonomy may be an alien concept for certain families or group members, yet an uninformed counselor might influence family members or group participants to "get on with their independence" and assert their autonomy.

Competence

Counselors who want to work with couples and families should be aware that competence in marriage and family therapy involves more than the completion of one or two specialized courses. The American Association for Marriage and Family Therapy has developed academic standards for marriage and family therapists and has also recommended that trainees have supervised experience in working with families, experience in their own family-of-origin work, and personal therapy. Counselors who work with groups can assess their level of training by studying the "Professional Standards for the Training of Group Workers" that have been developed by ASGW (1991). These standards describe core skills and knowledge and make recommendations for supervised practice. Although these training standards for family counselors and group workers are helpful, it should be remembered that, as we noted in chapter four, the tasks of developing and maintaining competence are lifelong and are never really finished.

The issue of boundaries of competence and several other issues discussed here emerge in some interesting ways in the following case studies. In the first, a marriage and family counselor grapples with knowing a secret, and in the second, a group counselor implements a questionable intervention technique.

Case Study 9

A MARRIAGE AND FAMILY COUNSELOR
LEARNS A SECRET
Mary E. Moline

Diana, a private practitioner, began working with Mrs. Cole, who was referred for counseling by her family doctor. Her doctor had not been able to find any physiological basis for her complaint that on several occasions she had felt as though she were choking and could not breathe.

After several sessions, it became apparent both to Diana and to the client that these choking symptoms occurred when Mrs. Cole's husband came home from work. Through further exploration, Mrs. Cole came to realize that she felt a great deal of anger that she had not been able to express, and that her relationship with her husband was directly related to her choking. With Mrs. Cole's permission, Mr. Cole was invited for conjoint therapy.

During the first conjoint session, Diana noted that Mr. Cole was not being congruent when he discussed his relationship with his wife. He said that he loved her, but his nonverbal communications and tone of voice indicated otherwise. When Diana asked him if he had any feelings other than love for his wife, he became defensive and said "no." At this point, Diana told Mr. and Mrs. Cole that she wanted to see each of them separately. Concerned that Mr. Cole might become hostile and uncooperative, she neglected to discuss issues pertaining to secrets and how they are handled.

Mr. Cole did come for an individual session, during which he admitted that he had been having an affair for 8 months. He was adamant in stating that he would never reveal the affair to his wife. He added that, moreover, if the counselor had asked him about this during the conjoint session he would have denied it. He urged Diana not to bring up the affair during sessions with Mrs. Cole. He felt certain that his wife would leave him if she knew. He became very emotional when he spoke of their four young children, saying that he was a good father and did not want their lives disrupted. When Diana asked him if he was committed to the marriage, he said that he was, but he wanted very much to have this other relationship. He stated that his goal in counseling was to adjust to balancing two relationships and to reduce his stress, and he requested additional sessions to help him with these goals.

Questions for Thought and Discussion

If you were the counselor in this case, how might you deal with Mr. Cole's refusal to disclose his affair in a conjoint session? If you kept his secret, do you think that counseling with this couple stands much chance of being productive? If Diana were to approach you and ask for help in resolving her dilemma, what might you say to her? What recommendations could you offer regarding how she might proceed? If you were working with a couple, might you be willing to see each of them for individual sessions also? Why or why not?

Analysis

There are many ethical issues to be considered in this case. Perhaps the primary issues are confidentiality, neutrality, and competence.

The Code of Ethics clearly indicates that the counselor cannot reveal information given by one family member (Mr. Cole) to another member (Mrs. Cole) without his permission (B.2.b.). If the counselor does not reveal this information, however, she might be rendered ineffective as their family therapist. She might transfer her reactions to this secret into their conjoint sessions.

In order for Diana to be able to reveal the information to Mrs. Cole in an ethical manner, she would have had to have made it clear *before* treatment began that she did not keep secrets. This should have been part of her informed consent procedure. Sound, ethical practice would have been to make clear to both parties at the outset how she would handle issues of confidentiality (A.3.a.). Because she was ethically remiss and failed to do so, she now finds herself caught on the horns of a dilemma.

Assuming that Diana believes the information about Mr. Cole's secret affair is harmful to the counseling process, she might attempt to encourage Mr. Cole to reveal it himself. Another factor that has not been explored is the possibility that Mr. Cole's lover could be infected with a fatal, communicable disease such as AIDS. If that were the case and safe sex were not being practiced, Diana might be justified in sharing the information with Mrs. Cole (B.1.d.). If this is not the case, however, Diana is now stuck with the secret.

Diana might feel torn by conflicting obligations. Mrs. Cole was her original client, and much progress remains to be made with respect to the choking problem. Because she was referred to the counselor first, any interventions need to be aimed at helping her reduce her incidents of choking. At the same time, it is clear that Mr. Cole feels a great deal of stress and he wants help. The situation is complicated by the fact that Mr. Cole has a part in the inception of his wife's problem, yet he does not want to be honest about it. Moreover, he now wants the counselor to help him solve his problem of balancing both relationships. Will Diana be able to remain neutral or objective in working with them? According to some experts in the field of family therapy, a neutral position is necessary for a practitioner to work on behalf of both individuals. If the counselor sides with one person over another, this will affect her ability to gain trust and will decrease her chances of being helpful. It will be important for Diana to assess her degree of effectiveness in this case. If she believes she cannot serve them effectively as a couple, she will need to withdraw from her position as their counselor and refer them to another therapist (A.11.b.). It might be a good course of action to refer Mr. Cole to one therapist and Mrs. Cole to another.

Given the nature of the ethical dilemma that this counselor has created for herself, it seems appropriate to question her preparedness to work with couples and families. If she is not fully prepared to work from a systemic perspective, she should suspend her work with couples and families until she can receive further, specialized training (C.2.a., C.2.b.).

Questions for Further Reflection

1. What ethical considerations are involved in deciding the most appropriate form of treatment: individual, conjoint, or family therapy?

2. How can counselors assess their own neutrality when working with couples?

Case Study 10

A GROUP LEADER'S RISKY INTERVENTION
George T. Williams

Greg has been leading a group that is heterogeneous in composition, including five women and three men. Their ages range from 23 to 57 years. The group has contracted to meet for 12 weekly sessions, with each session lasting 1½ hours. The major theme for the group is enhancing intimacy in interpersonal relationships.

During the initial group screening process, each member met individually with Greg to develop a personal written contract regarding participation in the group. Contracts included each member's assessment of his or her own interpersonal relationships, goals, strategies for improving interpersonal communications and relationships, and the evaluation criteria to be used for determining whether members achieve their personal goals.

Through the first five sessions, much time was spent exploring each member's values, expectations of the group, fears about being in the group, and significant interpersonal relationships outside the group. Greg had also discussed the risks of potential life changes that may occur because of the group experience and had begun to help members assess their readiness to face these possibilities.

It is now the sixth session, and 28-year-old Joshua, who has remained rather quiet and guarded up to this point, becomes tearful. He states that he has begged Ellen, his live-in partner, to marry him but she has refused. She has told him that she has already been through one painful divorce and will never make that mistake again. He discloses to the group that he suspects Ellen is cheating on him. He says he has some strong religious convictions that "people should not get angry, but rather forgive." He further explains that through individual therapy he has become aware of his own codependency issues and how he has difficulty standing up to Ellen and expressing his feelings. Hesitantly, he reveals that he feels guilty for having thoughts of cheating back on her because such behavior would not be acceptable to his views on commitment or to his religion.

While listening to Joshua talk, Greg recalls how 34-year-old Desiree has talked for several weeks in group about her loneliness and not having had a date since she and her fiance ended their relationship almost 3 years ago. He decides to use an innovative technique to help both Desiree and Joshua with their personal struggles. He creates a role-play with Joshua speaking directly to Desiree. Joshua is coached to tell Desiree how beautiful she is and is encouraged to ask her out for a date. Greg believed the role-play could help Joshua learn assertiveness skills for expressing his feelings and help him overcome his codependency issues with Ellen. Greg was also considering Desiree's low self-esteem and how she might benefit by receiving positive strokes from a man complimenting her physical appearance.

Immediately following the role-play, Greg asked Joshua how it was to do the role-play. Joshua responded, "I really surprised myself. I was actually able to say what I felt inside, without holding back." Greg then asked Joshua if he was willing to complete a homework assignment that could help him continue practicing his interpersonal skills outside the group. After Joshua said that he was willing to do the assignment, Greg instructed: "Your assignment, which is to be completed by next week's group session and reported back to the group, is to call Desiree, invite her to dinner, and then actually take her to dinner. This may also help you to get the courage to be more independent from Ellen because it appears that she's been taking advantage of you."

Questions for Thought and Discussion

What distinctions do you see between therapeutic pressure and undue pressure in groups? What do you think of the group leader's decision to ask the two group members to explore their feelings via the role-play? If you had been Greg's coleader in this group, might you have intervened? If so, at what point?

Analysis

The group leader's careful attention to ethical considerations in forming the group was commendable. His extensive screening procedures were well in compliance with the Code of Ethics (A.9.a.). He also appears to have provided prospective group members with information they needed in order to give informed consent to join, and he was conscientious in alerting them to risks of potential life changes (A.3.a.).

Greg's intervention during the sixth session, however, was ethically questionable in several respects. Given Joshua's expressed values and religious convictions, was it appropriate for Greg to set up a role-play scenario encouraging Joshua to express romantic feelings to a woman other than his live-in partner? Was it appropriate to get Joshua's commitment to engage in behavior outside the group that conflicts with his values as part of the treatment plan? Counselors should not ask clients, individually or in a group setting, to change in directions they do not choose. Standards A.2.b. and A.5.b. speak to the need for counselors to respect differences in values and beliefs and to avoid imposing their own values on clients. This case raises another issue related to counselor values: that of gender bias. Greg's intervention seems to have been based on assumptions concerning the source of a female's self-esteem, and there is no evidence that he considered the effect that this intervention might have on Desiree.

The role-play was an experiment that the group leader created spontaneously as he considered the revelations that members had made or were making. It was an experimental procedure, and Greg should have considered Standard A.3. of the Code of Ethics, which deals with informed consent. Experimental treatment methods should be clearly indicated to prospective recipients *prior to* their involvement. The group leader also violated the spirit of informed consent when he asked Joshua to say whether or not he was willing to complete an outside homework assignment before knowing what the assignment might be. Joshua might well have felt severely conflicted over his homework assignment, wanting to please the counselor and group members by being assertive, yet not wanting to risk his relationship with Ellen or to act against his values and religious beliefs. When Greg placed Joshua in this position, he violated his ethical obligation to protect clients in a group setting from psychological trauma (A.9.b).

Several other questions are raised by this case. How does a group leader differentiate between therapeutic pressure in groups and undue pressure or coercion? Are there potential detrimental effects when group leaders encourage group members to engage in intimate intermember relationships outside of group?

When working with groups, counselors are often confronted with multifaceted dilemmas in helping members work on their own personal issues. The competent group leader needs to assess each member's values and goals and intervene with techniques that do not impose the leader's values.

> ## Questions for Further Reflection
>
> *1. How can counselors guard against the possibility of imposing their own values on clients, either individually or in a group setting? Are there subtle ways this can happen, outside the counselor's awareness?*
>
> *2. What safeguards need to be put in place when counselors use intervention techniques that are potentially powerful?*

CHAPTER SIX

COUNSELING MINOR CLIENTS

Wayne C. Huey

It is a basic tenet in counseling that all clients have a right to privacy and to expect confidentiality when they enter a counseling relationship. An atmosphere of trust and confidence between counselor and client is necessary if essential information is to be shared. Counselors also promote the principle of autonomy and strongly support the client's right of choice and self-direction.

However, freedom of choice and confidentiality are both predicated on the ability of the client to give voluntary, informed consent. If a client cannot comprehend what is being requested in a consent for disclosure or is unable to make a rational decision, valid informed consent cannot be given. For clients under the age of 18, the law in all states stipulates that they are not adults and, therefore, are not competent to make fully informed voluntary decisions (Davis & Mickelson, 1994). Consequently, whether or not unemancipated minor clients are developmentally capable of making informed decisions, their privacy rights legally belong to the parents or guardians. Herein lies the most pressing issue in counseling minors and one that constantly causes counselors to weigh conflicts between the minor's ethical right to privacy and the parent's or other authorized adult's legal right to know. Confidentiality issues create ethical dilemmas more frequently than any other issue in working with minors.

Every child, regardless of age, has a moral or ethical right to privacy in the counseling relationship. Therefore, the counselor should respect the minor client's right to control access to personal information, to the extent possible. However, confidentiality is never absolute for clients of any age. It involves degrees or conditions of confidentiality. The ethical consideration in working with minors is not whether to offer clients confidentiality, but rather if, and under what conditions or circumstances, information should be released to parents or other adults without the client's consent.

It is not uncommon for others to seek information about a minor that was disclosed in a counseling relationship. Demands come from a variety of sources other than the parents. In the school setting, for example, third parties such as teachers and administrators frequently want to know what's going on with a child whom the counselor is seeing. This quest for information is usually well intentioned, as are requests from parents. However, breaking the protective seal of confidentiality without just cause could be a death knell for school counseling programs. Students are likely to refuse to disclose any personal information if they fear it will be related to school officials or parents; that is, if they believe counselors will tell on them.

Because the legal rights for minors essentially reside with the parent or guardian, many counselors who work with minors feel torn between their ethical responsibility of confidentiality to the client and their legal responsibilities to the parents (Huey & Remley, 1989). Moreover, in the school setting, the concept of *in loco parentis* can create confusing ethical dilemmas for the counselor.

In the previous ACA *Ethical Standards* (1988), the issue of counseling minors was addressed in this statement: "When working with minors or persons who are unable to give consent, the member protects these clients' best interests." This reinforced the idea for some counselors that the best interest of the client was to protect from disclosure any information received because no mention was made of any ethical responsibilities to the parent or guardian. For other counselors, perhaps more in tune with liability issues, disclosing information to parents upon request was always considered to be in the minor client's best interest. It certainly was viewed by these counselors as being in their own best interest.

In the revised Code of Ethics, this standard has been expanded to include the statements that "parents or guardians may be included in the counseling process as appropriate," and "counselors act in the best interests of clients and take measures to safeguard confidentiality" (B.3.). It would be unusual and foolish for a counselor not to respect parents' rights and responsibilities for their children, but counselors now have more of an incentive to use their professional judgment in deciding whether and how to include parents.

Further endorsement for parent involvement is found in Standard A.1.d.: "Counselors recognize that families are usually important in clients' lives and strive to enlist family understanding and involvement as a positive resource, when appropriate." Although counselors working with minors have generally followed this guideline, the new standard emphasizes the appropriateness of eliciting family (parent) involvement. It further stresses the importance of establishing cooperative relationships with parents and/or other family members to facilitate the maximum development of the minor client. Initial reluctance on the part of clients, especially adolescents, to include other family members is not uncommon. The counselor may see advantages to be gained by including parents, but the minor client may not; and the counselor needs to respect the client's wishes unless a situation exists that mandates notifying the parents.

School counselors are often in the dual role of counseling minors and at the same time working with parents or teachers. The Code of Ethics cautions that when counselors are working with two or more persons who have a relationship, such as parents and children (or teachers and students), "counselors clarify at the outset which person or persons are clients and the nature of the relationships they will have with each involved person" (A.8). It is important not to underestimate the impact that a nurturing relationship between a student and a caring teacher can have on the client's positive development. Working with multiple clients, particularly where there is a power differential such as with parent and child or teacher and student, poses unique problems for the counselor. To deal with potentially conflicting roles, counselors "clarify, adjust, or withdraw from roles" as required (A.8).

Dual relationships frequently create ethical dilemmas for school counselors because of their job description and work environment. Some of these dilemmas pertain to confidentiality issues. Others concern having to perform duties with the potential for disciplinary actions; serving as counselor and teacher, counselor and coach or club sponsor; and having counseling relationships with other adults.

When the counselor's job description includes disciplinary functions related to a variety of duty assignments, such as bus or bathroom monitor, the ability to serve effectively as a personal counselor is potentially compromised. Students cannot be expected to confide in a counselor who assigned them to detention or reported their misbehavior to the parents.

The counselor as teacher, coach, or club sponsor also has the potential for creating dilemmas. Evaluative, supervisory and administrative duties pose possible situations that can conflict with the role of counselor.

Dual relationships with other adults or groups that may create dilemmas for school counselors include relationships with teachers, parents, administrators, and outside agencies. If counselors must adhere to policies that mandate reporting a variety of behaviors from sexual involvement to drug use, students will be reluctant to seek out the counselor for personal counseling. Such role conflicts are even more pronounced in small towns and rural areas where referrals are difficult. Standard A.6.a. provides specific precautions counselors can take to reduce the chance of harming clients when dual relationships are unavoidable, as is often the case in school settings. These safeguards include "informed consent, consultation, supervision, self-monitoring, and documentation." Counselors must clearly communicate their role to all populations served.

Some situations mandate that confidentiality be breached. Procedures for reporting suspected child abuse, suicidal threats, and client dangerousness to others are usually mandated by state laws or institutional guidelines. Counselors may still experience some dilemmas around particular cases of this type, but for the most part these exceptions to confidentiality are addressed adequately in the Code of Ethics, and counselors are somewhat comfortable in resolving these situations.

Guidelines for practice in resolving confidentiality issues relating to minors are fully explored in *Counseling Minor Clients* (Salo & Shumate, 1993). In general, a key to avoiding conflicts between a minor's privacy rights and a parent's demands for information lies in helping both parents and clients understand the scope of confidentiality prior to entering the counseling relationship. Although the legal rights may belong to the parent, it is ethically responsible to gain the minor's approval before making any disclosures of information. If a decision is made to reveal information to parents without consent of the client, the minor client should be involved in the decision-making process, informed before the information is released, and kept informed as further decisions are made. Further suggestions for ways to handle requests for confidential information from parents or guardians were made by Remley (1990). No matter how young the clients, they should have some control over the release of information that results from their choosing to engage in the counseling process. However, it should be kept in mind that children, especially younger ones, are often not nearly as concerned about confidentiality as the counselor is.

Standards A.1.d., A.8., and B.3. reinforce the notion that the parent-counselor relationship need not be adversarial, and in fact, parents can be valuable allies in counseling minors. The counselor, however, still retains the prerogative to decide when it is appropriate to include parents. The overriding concern is always for the client's best interests in resolving ethical dilemmas involving minor clients.

Case Study 11

A SCHOOL COUNSELOR IS CAUGHT IN THE MIDDLE
Mark Salo

Susan worked as a counselor in a large elementary school with students from kindergarten through sixth grade. Susan's primary duties included counseling individuals and small groups, teaching classroom guidance lessons, and consulting with parents, teachers, and administrators.

Shortly after the beginning of the school year, a parent called Susan and explained that her son, Nicholas, a fourth-grade student at Susan's school, was experiencing difficulties in school where none had existed before. Susan invited the mother, Juanita, to her office to discuss specific concerns. During this initial consultation Juanita divulged that her husband, Russell, had recently moved out of the house. Nicholas, being the oldest of three siblings, was especially upset with the situation and had shown recent outbursts of anger both at home and at school. Teachers had also notified Juanita that Nicholas' school work was slipping badly. Juanita tearfully revealed that her husband had physically assaulted her, and that although he had never abused the children, they were certainly affected. Susan and Juanita decided that Nicholas should begin to see Susan for counseling on a twice-weekly basis to help Nicholas deal with his anger and failing grades.

Susan saw Nicholas regularly for 5 to 6 weeks. During this time Nicholas revealed a great deal to Susan about himself and his family. He also came to realize that his angry outbursts and declining grades were related to the stress surrounding his family circumstances. At a follow-up meeting with Juanita, Susan was pleased to report that both Nicholas' grades and his school behavior had begun to improve.

An unexpected phone call from Nicholas' father alerted Susan to potential difficulties. Although Susan was cordial and professional, she became increasingly uncomfortable with Russell's press for information about both Nicholas and his mother. According to Russell, divorce papers had been filed by Juanita, and she was seeking full custody of the children. Russell became increasingly insistent in his demand to learn the content of all of Susan's sessions with both Nicholas and Juanita. During the conversation Russell alluded several times to his attorney's involvement and threatened to file a complaint with the ACA Ethics Committee for her noncompliance with his request. Although Susan closed the discussion by generally recounting Nicholas' improved behavior and academic performance, she was concerned that Russell might continue to push her for information she felt was confidential. A follow-up phone call to Juanita confirmed that legal papers had been filed. Juanita also told the counselor that both she and Nicholas wanted to keep the counseling records confidential and out of Russell's possession.

Questions for Thought and Discussion

Put yourself in the place of Susan, the counselor in this case. How do you believe you might react when pressed by Russell to reveal information about his son? What do you think of the way that Susan handled the situation? What, if anything, might you have done differently, and why?

Analysis

Susan's dilemma involved the confidentiality of information gained in counseling sessions and was compounded by the fact that Nicholas was a minor. She feared that revealing information to Russell could be damaging to both Nicholas and Juanita, and although Susan had no desire to get embroiled in a custody battle, she wanted to remain ethically responsible and legally sound. Susan reviewed the ACA Code of Ethics for guidance and found Section B: Confidentiality especially relevant to the case.

Standard B.1.a. states that counselors "respect their clients' right to privacy and avoid illegal and unwarranted disclosures of confidential information." Susan knew that revealing the records would go against Juanita's wishes and could be potentially damaging to the situation.

Standard B.3. provides further justification for withholding the records: "When counseling clients who are minors or individuals who are unable to give voluntary informed consent, parents or guardians may be included in the counseling process as appropriate." The standard further advises that counselors "act in the best interest of clients and take reasonable measures to safeguard confidentiality."

In addition, Standard B.4.a. states that counselors "maintain records necessary for rendering professional services to their clients and as required by laws, regulations, or agency or institution procedures." Susan knew that noncustodial parents do have access to school records as outlined by the Family Education Rights and Privacy Act (FERPA). However, the records in question were private counseling notes, seen only by Susan, and were stored away from school records in a locked filing cabinet.

An especially relevant point appears in Standard B.4.d., which states that counselors "recognize that counseling records are kept for the benefit of clients, and therefore provide access to records and copies of records when requested by competent clients, unless the records contain information that may be misleading and detrimental to the client. In situations involving multiple clients, access to records is limited to those parts of records that do not include confidential information related to another client." Susan felt that Juanita and Nicholas were multiple clients, and Russell should not have access to their records. Standard B.2.b. further confirmed Susan's conviction by stating that information about one family member cannot be disclosed to another member without permission, and that counselors protect the privacy rights of each family member.

Standard B.1.b. reminded Susan that the right to privacy may be waived only by the client or their legally recognized representative. Susan had confirmed with Juanita her desire to keep the notes confidential. However, Russell could still be a legally recognized representative, leaving a question that might take a judge's ruling to decide. Susan, upon consultation with her administrator and the school district's attorney, decided that if the custody case went to court, they would let the court decide the issue as supported by Standard B.1.e.: "When court ordered to release confidential information without a client's permission, counselors request to the court that disclosure not be required due to potential harm to the client or counseling relationship." In the event that a judge ordered the record to be revealed, Standard B.1.f. would guide Susan's response. She would reveal only essential information and would inform Juanita and Nicholas before disclosing.

This case illustrates how Susan used the Code of Ethics to guide her decision-making process in an ethical dilemma. It is important to remember that the Code of Ethics is not a legal document and that federal, state, and local laws supersede these guidelines. If Susan were court ordered to release her records, she should do so after stating her objections. The ACA Ethics Committee would not find a counselor in violation of the standards for complying with a court order.

Questions for Further Reflection

1. What if Nicholas had a caring and concerned teacher who approached this counselor, asking for information about his home situation to help her better understand Nicholas' academic and behavior problems? What might you tell the teacher?

2. In your own work as a counselor, how do you deal with situations that involve an apparent conflict between your legal and ethical obligations? How might you use the Code of Ethics to help guide you in your decision making?

Case Study 12

ENSURING A STUDENT'S WELFARE
Lynda L. Fielstein

Elena was a high school counselor in a rural area in the Southwest. One morning her principal, Ms. Brown, called her to report that a sophomore student, Randy, had come to school apparently intoxicated. His breath smelled of alcohol, and he seemed confused. The principal asked Elena to come down to her office to discuss the situation. They could not ascertain the severity of Randy's condition because the school nurse was not available on this particular day. Furthermore, Randy adamantly refused to reveal what he had consumed or how much.

In accordance with school policy, Ms. Brown called Randy's home to inform the parents. The grandfather answered the phone and explained that the parents were out of town for the day. He seemed indifferent to his grandson's situation and was reluctant to become involved. After some persuading, however, Ms. Brown convinced the grandfather to come and take Randy home.

After the grandfather and Randy left the school, the principal and counselor discussed the action they had taken. Ms. Brown, taking an administrator's point of view, believed they had acted appropriately. The school had discharged its duties properly by turning the student over to the parent or, in this case, guardian. However, the counselor had doubts that she had done enough to protect the welfare of the student.

Elena went back to her office and contemplated the situation. Had she behaved in a professional and responsible manner? Had she acted in the best interest of the student? As she reflected, she wondered whether more should have been done on the student's behalf. For one thing, she did not feel comfortable about leaving Randy with a grandparent who minimized the problem. How much alcohol had Randy consumed? What if he had ingested a combination of drugs and alcohol? What guarantee did she have that this guardian would be sensitive to warning signs that Randy might need medical attention? Had she assessed his mental condition? What if he were to drink more alcohol while at home? Randy is 16 years old and may have a driver's license. What if he decided to get behind the wheel of a car while intoxicated?

Questions for Thought and Discussion

If Elena were to consult with you at this point, what might you recommend that she do? It could be argued that this is a disciplinary matter and therefore the responsibility rests with the administrator, who is satisfied with the decision. Or does Elena, as a counselor, have a different or further responsibility to the student? How might you help her reason this through? What moral principles are involved here?

Analysis

Elena, believing that she had a further responsibility for Randy's safety, went back to the principal's office to discuss her concerns. At this juncture, Ms. Brown agreed that Elena should contact the grandparent and do what she felt was necessary. The counselor called the grandfather, and after a lengthy discussion, she persuaded him to take Randy to the hospital where qualified health personnel could assess his condition. It was determined that Randy did need medical attention.

Elena's actions were based on her knowledge of the ACA Code of Ethics. Initially, she did not have access to a school nurse so that she was unable to assess the severity of the student's condition. Later, she was unsure of the grandfather's ability to make sound, objective decisions concerning his grandson's welfare.

Standard B.3. states that when counseling minors, "parents or guardians may be included," but that counselors "act in the best interest of clients and take measures to safeguard confidentiality." Elena realized that confidentiality interests are superseded when "disclosure is required to prevent clear and imminent danger to the client" (B.1.c.). Because she could not determine whether potential harm to Randy was imminent, she acted responsibly in arranging to refer him to qualified medical professionals.

As this case illustrates, counselors must often do more than what is convenient or is considered appropriate by others. They must consider clients' best interests and act accordingly.

Questions for Further Reflection

1. What if the grandfather had refused to take Randy to the hospital? What should the counselor have done then?

2. What if the medical professionals had found that Randy was not at risk, and that he merely needed to sleep it off? If the parents had later become irate, accusing Elena of causing unnecessary medical expenses and bringing public embarrassment to their family, what might Elena say in her defense?

CHAPTER SEVEN

DUAL RELATIONSHIPS

Harriet L. Glosoff, Gerald Corey, and Barbara Herlihy

People naturally engage in several different roles, and they play these roles in a variety of settings (Super, 1990). Individuals who choose to go into the counseling profession are not expected to sacrifice their multiple roles or to restrain themselves from acting as neighbors, friends, employees, consultants, or relatives. However, whether it is ethical for counselors to assume any of these roles simultaneously with a *client*, or participate in a dual relationship, has generated a great deal of controversy among helping professionals. Many professionals assert that not all dual relationships can be avoided (Herlihy & Corey, 1992). This is particularly true in small, isolated communities: the smaller and/or more rural the community, the greater the likelihood that a counselor will be involved in some type of dual relationship (Sleek, 1994).

It has also been argued that not all dual relationships are harmful to clients. For example, some might question whether there is an ethical problem in accepting as a client a neighbor with whom one has little contact other than to wave hello or see occasionally at a local store (Haas & Malouf, 1995). However, most professionals will agree that the mixing of more significant roles such as counselor and employee or counselor and lover is clearly not appropriate. The important point is that whenever counselors play dual roles there is potential for a conflict of interest, loss of objectivity, and exploiting those persons who have sought help. Our discussion here provides an overview of various issues pertaining to sexual and nonsexual dual relationships and explores how these issues are addressed by the Code of Ethics.

Sexual Dual Relationships

Clearly, sexual relationships with clients are among the most serious of all ethical violations. Sonne and Pope (1991) reported that clients who had been sexually involved with their therapists often exhibit reactions similar to those of survivors of incest, such as role confusion, strong feelings of betrayed trust, and guilt. Virtually all codes of ethics categorically state that sexual relationships with clients are unethical, and licensure regulations and various state legislatures have added the force of law to ethical sanctions. For example, at least a dozen states have enacted laws that designate therapist-client sexual activity as a felony crime, as does the ACA Model Legislation for the Licensure of Professional Counselors (ACA, 1994). Nonetheless, these types of violations continue to be common (Neukrug, Healy, & Herlihy, 1992). In the past it has been evident to the members of the ACA Ethics Committee, as they deliberated on complaints received, that some unethical sexual behaviors were not directly addressed in the ethical standards. As a result, the current Code of Ethics contains several standards that speak to sexual dual relationships with current and former clients. The first of these standards states that "counselors do not have any type of sexual intimacies with clients," nor do they "counsel persons with whom they have had a sexual relationship" in the past (A.7.a.).

Former Clients. The question of whether sexual intimacies with former clients are ever acceptable has been extensively debated within the helping professions. Professional counselors agree that the fact that a counseling relationship has been terminated does not, in and of itself, present an adequate justification for changing a therapeutic relationship to a sexual one. Some professionals believe that the counselor-client relationship continues in perpetuity and that sexual relationships between counselors and former clients are *never* ethical. One rationale behind this line of thinking is that the seeds of the sexual attraction were planted during a therapeutic relationship in which information tends to flow one way, with clients being vulnerable and counselors disclosing little about themselves. Thus there will continue to be an asymmetry of power that will not be healthy for most former clients. In addition, research indicates that even those clients who have successfully terminated counseling tend to continue to work through unresolved transference issues for some time following treatment (Haas & Malouf, 1995).

Other professionals argue that although we need to remain aware of the potential for harm that exists due to residual transference and the continuing power differential, we also need to consider the wide range of circumstances that exist in the counseling field. They point to the real differences between long-term, intense personal counseling relationships and brief academic, career-oriented or other types of counseling. Haas and Malouf (1995) noted that prohibiting all future sexual contact with former clients, simply because they have been clients, speaks poorly of professionals' attitudes toward our clients' abilities to make their own informed decisions and could be viewed as a restriction of the client's autonomy. Many might also contend that it does not indicate great faith in the effectiveness of counseling.

Some individuals also assert that, even with those clients who were involved in less intense types of counseling situations, the issue is the length of time that needs to elapse before a counselor might justifiably enter into a sexual relationship with a former client. After receiving input from the ACA membership, Standard A.7.b. was proposed and adopted. This standard prohibits sexual intimacies with former clients for a minimum of 2 years after terminating the counseling relationship. Even after 2 years, counselors have a special obligation to examine carefully all factors involved, including their own motivations, and to demonstrate that there has been no exploitation. This new standard is in keeping with the ethical standards adopted by other related professional associations such as the American Psychological Association and the American Association for Marriage and Family Therapy.

Relationships With Others Who Are Not Clients. Most counselors engage in professional relationships, other than the counselor-client relationship, where there is a power differential and thus a potential for exploiting those who are in a vulnerable, subordinate position. Counselors may serve as employer, superior in the workplace, supervisor, or professor. Three standards address the potential for exploitation in these relationships. The first two speak directly to sexual dual relationships: sexual harassment is defined and is prohibited in the workplace (C.5.b.), and counselors "do not engage in sexual relationships with students or supervisees and do not subject them to sexual harassment" (F.1.c.). The third standard addresses both sexual and nonsexual dual relationships and states that counselors "do not engage in exploitive relationships with individuals over whom they have supervisory, evaluative, or instructional control or authority" (D.1.k.).

Nonsexual Dual Relationships

Although most of our professional literature has focused on the harm that can result from sexual relationships with clients, this does not mean that nonsexual dual relationships pose little threat to the well-being of clients and counselors. Nonsexual dual relationships may include "familial, social, financial, business, or close personal relationships with clients" (A.6.a.). Examples include combining the roles of teacher and counselor, or supervisor and counselor; bartering for goods or services; lending money to a client; providing therapy to a friend, an employee, or a relative; becoming friends with a client; and going into a business venture with a client.

As noted previously, not every combination of roles is detrimental. Many professionals consider mentoring counselor trainees or beginning counselors to be an integral part of their role. Mentors establish close working relationships, share research projects, co-author articles, and engage their proteges in social/business networks. Even in these situations, the complexity and multidimensional nature of dual relationships should be carefully explored, and potential risks must be weighed against benefits. There are few simple and absolute answers that neatly resolve dual relationship dilemmas. It is not always possible for counselors to play a singular role in their work, nor is it always desirable. It is likely that they will have to wrestle with balancing more than one role in their professional relationships. Thus it is critical that counselors give careful thought to the potential complications of dual relationships before they get entangled in ethically questionable relationships. The importance of consultation in working through these decisions cannot be overemphasized.

The ACA Code of Ethics cautions counselors to avoid dual relationships when possible. It notes that counselors "are aware of their influential positions with respect to clients" and avoid exploiting their clients' trust and dependency (A.6.a.). Interpersonal boundaries are not static but undergo redefinition over time, so that practitioners are presented with the challenge of managing boundary fluctuations and dealing effectively with overlap in roles. Given how closely counselors and clients work together, the idea of developing a friendship could be tempting. At one time or another, most of us have had a client we really liked and have thought it might be nice if we had met under different circumstances so that we could be friends. Similarly, most practitioners have been faced with close friends or relatives who have problems and who try to place the practitioner (intentionally or not) in the role of their therapist. The problem with this is that the underlying dynamics of friendships and therapeutic relationships are not the same. Friendships are built on mutual disclosure and support—on sharing joys and problems and being there for each other. Although therapeutic relationships are also based on trust, intimacy, and disclosure, they are not mutual (Haas & Malouf, 1995).

Risk Factors. Standard A.6.a. directs counselors to avoid relationships that "increase the risk of harm to clients." Thus counselors need to assess carefully whether a potential dual relationship could impair their judgment or objectivity and whether a potential for harm could be created if they were to enter into the relationship. Tomm (1993) has pointed out that it is not duality per se that constitutes an ethical problem; rather, it is the therapist's tendency to exploit clients that is central. Because of the imbalance of power, counselors are in a position to take advantage of clients.

Counselors must avoid any relationship, such as a friendship, that might impair their professional judgment. The duality of the relationship might make it difficult for counselors to confront clients when it is clinically appropriate to do so. It may be easy for counselors engaged in dual relationships to lose sight of the true motives behind their clinical actions with clients.

The risk of exploitation or diminished clinical judgment increases proportionately with the discrepancy in power, whether it is actual or perceived. Standard A.6.b. specifically addresses superior/subordinate relationships: "Counselors do not accept as clients superiors or subordinates with whom they have administrative, supervisory, or evaluative relationships." Students and supervisees are in a particularly vulnerable position with respect to their professors and supervisors. Several standards address relationship boundaries in teaching, training, and supervision and are discussed in chapter nine.

Bartering. Bartering is a dual relationship issue about which there has been little agreement among counseling professionals. Counselors who engage in bartering or trading goods or services in exchange for counseling services are often motivated to do so for benevolent reasons, typically to help clients who cannot afford to pay for services. Even with these altruistic intentions, bartering carries the potential for conflicts. On the one hand, bartering is an accepted practice in some communities and cultures. On the other hand, bartering may lead to resentment on the part of the client or the counselor. Services offered by clients are often not as monetarily valuable as counseling, and clients are at risk of becoming indentured servants as they fall further and further behind in the amount of time or money owed to the counselor (Kitchener & Harding, 1990). A client may also believe that counseling is not working and that, therefore, the counselor is not holding up his or her end of the bargain. Likewise, counselors may be dissatisfied with the timeliness or quality of goods or services delivered by clients and may feel that they are giving more to the exchange than they are receiving.

The standard that guides practitioners with respect to bartering states that counselors "ordinarily refrain from accepting goods or services from clients in return for counseling services because such arrangements create inherent potential for conflicts, exploitation, and distortion of the professional relationship" (A.10.c.). However, counselors may participate in bartering if the relationship is not exploitive, if the client requests it, if a clear written contract is established, and if bartering is an accepted practice among professionals in the community.

Conclusions

Much has been and continues to be written about dual relationships. It is a somewhat daunting but necessary task for conscientious counselors to be familiar with the Code of Ethics and to keep current with the professional literature. Some dual relationships can be avoided if potential problems are foreseen, but others can not. Regardless of the avoidability, the ethical counselor takes "appropriate professional precautions such as informed consent, consultation, supervision, and documentation" (A.6.a.) to help ensure that clients are not harmed.

The three case studies that follow may help to raise awareness of potential pitfalls. The first case study deals with a sexual dual relationship between a student and a professor; the second case study describes a situation that is unique to practicing in a rural setting; and the third case study illustrates how even well-intentioned counselors become enmeshed in problems when indirectly mixing friendship with counseling.

Case Study 13

CONSENTING ADULTS OR AN ABUSE OF POWER?
Holly Forester-Miller

Maria is a graduate student who is pursuing her master's degree in counseling. She hopes to enter a doctoral program after she graduates. Last semester, she was enrolled in a course taught by Professor Perry. Throughout the semester, Dr. Perry went out of his way to encourage her and praise her work. After she completed the course, he asked her to serve as a teaching assistant under his supervision for the next term. Maria felt honored that he thought so highly of her abilities, and she accepted the position.

As a teaching assistant Maria spent considerable time every week in the faculty office area and had frequent interactions with Dr. Perry regarding her work. Gradually, their conversations began to touch on personal issues. The personal interactions escalated to a point where Dr. Perry learned a great deal about Maria's private life and assisted her in making some important decisions, such as finding a new place to live.

Shortly after midterm, following a conversation in which Dr. Perry had emphasized to Maria that he thought her to be bright and competent, he made a sexual advance toward her. She was flattered that someone in his position could be interested in her. The next week, he asked her to come into the office on a Saturday to help him with some work, and she found herself alone with him. He told her that he found her beautiful and was very attracted to her. He began to kiss her. Maria felt complimented but a bit confused. She then willingly entered into a sexual relationship with him. They continued to work together regularly, with Dr. Perry supervising her work and constantly extolling her abilities. They began to have lunch together almost daily, and once a week went out to a local bar with a group of faculty members. Dr. Perry openly praised her work in front of his colleagues on these occasions.

257

About 6 weeks after the sexual relationship began, Maria started to question the relationship and her involvement with Dr. Perry. After considerable thought, she realized that she wasn't really attracted to him as a person, even though she admired his competencies as a professor and had enjoyed being so highly regarded by someone she admired professionally. She realized that her behavior was jeopardizing her relationship with her male friend who lived in another state, and concluded that she didn't want to lose that relationship.

The next day, she told Dr. Perry that she was no longer interested in having a personal relationship with him. He became upset and insisted that he was sure she would change her mind because he had been so good to her. No matter how hard she tried, the professor brushed aside her protestations. For the rest of the week, he continued to act as if nothing had changed. He was complimentary of her work, both in private and in front of others, and continued to behave flirtatiously when they were alone together.

Maria decided at this point to talk to a friend about the situation. She explained that, at this point, she wants out of the sexual relationship, but she is afraid that she will lose her assistantship on which she is now financially dependent. She needs to continue to meet regularly with Dr. Perry as her supervisor, and she will need to take a course from him next semester. She just can't afford to have a bad relationship with him. Although she willingly agreed to this relationship in the beginning, she now feels trapped and manipulated.

Maria asked her friend to keep their conversation in confidence, and she decided not to tell anyone else. Although her friend urged her to go to the department chair, Maria decided against doing this, fearing that such an action could affect her assistantship and her recommendations for doctoral studies.

At this point, Maria is continuing to deal with Dr. Perry on her own. When he suggests lunch or going out for a drink after work, she tells him she is very busy. She avoids him whenever possible, but when she is with him she feels uncomfortable and pressured. She sees no way out of her situation and believes this is her only option until she graduates.

Analysis

Standard F.1.b. of the Code of Ethics deals with relationship boundaries between students and their professors and the differential in power that exists in such relationships. It states that counselors "clearly define and maintain ethical, professional, and social relationship boundaries with their students and supervisees. They are aware of the differential in power that exists and the student's or supervisee's possible incomprehension of that power differential. Counselors explain to students and supervisees the potential for the relationship to become exploitive." The professor in this case clearly did not follow these guidelines in dealing with the student.

Some professionals, and graduate students, have questioned why relationships like this are considered unethical. They might respond to a situation such as the one presented in this case by saying, "This is graduate school, and she is a consenting adult. She chose to be with him." A professor, whether male or female, is in a position of power over the student. This allows the professor to have undue influence over that student even though the student may not realize it. And, as is clearly an issue in this case, does the student have equal power to decide to end the relationship? How can there be a mutually equal, consenting relationship when one of the individuals has the ability to decide the other's future through assigning grades, giving recommendations for future graduate study or employment, or other means of influence?

Standard F.1.c. states clearly that counselors "do not engage in sexual relationships with students or supervisees." It is obvious that this professor violated Standard F.1.c. as well as Standard F.1.b. He had a sexual relationship with her, and then after being told she wanted to discontinue the relationship, he continued to respond to her sexually, ignoring her requests. Because of the leverage he has, with the uneven power base, the question isn't whether she chose to be with him but whether she wants to be able to keep her assistant-ship and receive favorable grades and recommendations for further study. This is not a choice students should be put in a position to have to make.

Questions for Further Reflection

1. Students often look up to their professors and seek their guidance. In what ways is the influence a professor has over a student similar to the influence a counselor has over a client?

2. If a member of the faculty did not have a particular student in class, and was not currently and would never be the student's supervisor, might it then be acceptable for that professor to date the student? To have a sexual relationship with the student?

Case Study 14

AN UNFORESEEN IMPLICATION OF RURAL PRACTICE
Daniel L. Yazak

Mary Lynn, a divorced mother of three, has worked hard all her life. Her children are now grown, and she has recently left a large and often hectic urban counseling practice to move to a small town. She has established a practice that has a comfortable pace and has found a life-style more conducive to her personal life management and professional development. Her work load has decreased from an average of 30 clients a week to 15. Although her financial situation has changed substantially, so has the amount of time she spends dealing with third-party payers and managed care super-visors. All in all, she is very pleased with her decision to relocate to a rural area.

One of Mary Lynn's clients is Joyce, who has been coming for counseling for about 3 months to deal with the death of her hus-band who was killed in a hunting accident. The grieving process has been difficult for her, but she is making progress working through what Mary Lynn believes are appropriate and necessary stages of grief. Joyce had been commuting 50 miles to see a counselor before she was referred to Mary Lynn, and they are both pleased with the way the counseling relationship is progressing.

On her intake form, Joyce had given her occupation as *self-employed*. During the initial session, she had mentioned that she and her husband had owned a business in town until his death, and that she now operated it by herself. During that same interview, Mary Lynn had explained the appropriate boundaries for dual relationships, particularly in the areas of social, financial, business, or close personal relationships. Joyce had indicated that she understood the boundaries Mary Lynn wanted to establish, and each agreed to inform the other if a level of discomfort developed in any area of the relationship.

One evening, much to Mary Lynn's delight, her brother Bill calls her with exciting news: he is a finalist for a job that seems to be just what he is seeking. He tells her that the position is at a supervisory level, just what he needs to get started in his management career. What particularly appeals to him is that the job opening is in the town where Mary Lynn now resides. Both of them are excited about the possibility of seeing each other on a regular basis if he gets the job.

Later in the week, Joyce brings up a problem she is having that is related to her grieving process. It seems that one of the finalists for a supervisory position in her business reminds Joyce of her dead husband. The finalist has the same mannerisms and facial expressions, and even tells similar little jokes. Joyce is convinced that she can't have this person working for her, no matter what.

Questions for Thought and Discussion

Try to put yourself in Mary Lynn's place as she listens to Joyce talk about her feelings toward the candidate for the supervisor's job. What might you be thinking and feeling, and what internal conflicts might you be experiencing? What principles and issues are involved in the situation? What course of action might you recommend that Mary Lynn take to resolve her dilemma, and on what do you base your recommendation?

Analysis

Standard A.6.a. of the Code of Ethics indicates that dual relationships should be avoided when possible. Mary Lynn has taken the necessary steps to secure informed consent and, unfortunately, had no way to foresee the situation that developed. Joyce's actions in discussing her feelings and Bill's interest in seeking the job are both operating in good faith, but their mutual good faith collides in Mary Lynn's conflict between her family and her practice, along with her understanding of the complexity of the dual relationship issue. Mary Lynn wonders whether she has a responsibility to consider the intent of Standard A.11.b., which states that counselors must terminate a counseling relationship if they determine that they are unable to be of professional assistance to a client. Should she suggest to Joyce that she may have to consider once again travelling the 50 miles to see her former counselor in order to continue her grief work?

Mary Lynn will need to respect Joyce's integrity and promote her welfare (A.1.a.). Further, as much as she may wish otherwise, confidentiality standards prohibit her from talking to Bill about the prospect that he may not get the job.

Mary Lynn decides, in accordance with the Code of Ethics (D.2.a.), to consult a counselor with whom she went to graduate school. This counselor lives in another state and serves on that state counseling association's ethics committee.

After a lengthy consultation, Mary Lynn and the consulting counselor decide that Mary Lynn will continue meeting with Joyce, be as supportive as possible to her brother Bill but disclose nothing, and obtain supervision of her work with Joyce. Mary Lynn arranges for supervision and sets up a schedule for face-to-face supervision that coincides with regular travel she makes to the city 50 miles away.

Questions for Further Reflection

1. Do counselors who practice in isolated, rural settings need to take additional precautions regarding dual relationships that are not required of their urban counterparts?

2. Do counselors who practice in sparsely populated areas face unique problems in addition to dual relationship concerns like those described in this case?

Case Study 15

A QUESTION OF BOUNDARIES
Harriet L. Glosoff

Teresa, a professional counselor, moved to a small town in Iowa
with her 13-year-old son. She discovered that, except for a psychiatrist, the closest other mental health professional practiced
approximately 1½ hours away. Initially, she felt isolated and
found it emotionally and financially difficult to establish her
private practice, adjust to small-town living, and develop a personal life.

After almost a year of struggle, her practice was fairly steady,
and her son was doing quite well in his new school. Teresa had become close friends with Evelyn, the principal at her son's school. In
fact, her son and Evelyn's son had also become very close friends
and spent a good deal of time together in each other's homes. Teresa
and Evelyn discovered many commonalities, including that they were
both divorced, received little support from their ex-husbands, and
were originally from large cities. They car pooled, watched each
other's sons, did a number of things together, and became strong
social supports for each other.

Teresa and Evelyn spent a good bit of time commiserating on
the joys and problems of being a single parent and the difficulties of
dealing with a teenage son. Evelyn confided that she was really concerned about her son, Chris, stating that he was having a lot of problems in school and that their relationship at home had become
strained. Chris seemed to be testing authority and often lashed out
at Evelyn. Evelyn thought that most of his problems were caused
by his inconsistent communication with his father and shared that
she was at her wit's end. She thought that Chris needed counseling
and asked Teresa to take him on as a client.

Teresa was initially reluctant and explained to Evelyn that she
was concerned about how this might affect their friendship. They
discussed the differences between friendships and professional relationships and how these differences might manifest themselves in
their almost-daily contacts. Evelyn insisted that she felt comfortable with the duality and that she didn't see a necessity to drive 3
hours round trip when Teresa was qualified to work with her son.
Teresa was concerned that if she refused Evelyn's request, it might
damage their friendship. She was also fairly sure that she would do

no harm in providing counseling and began to see Chris on a weekly basis in her office.

During their second session, Chris shared that he was uncomfortable talking about some of the things that were bothering him, particularly anything to do with his mother. Teresa discussed confidentiality issues, and eventually Chris seemed to relax and open up. During the course of treatment he divulged information about both of his parents that led Teresa to believe that some of Evelyn's behaviors were contributing to her son's problems. It seemed that Evelyn complained to Chris about her ex-husband, and this upset him. Teresa struggled with how to explore this with Evelyn. On the one hand, discussing it in the office with both Evelyn and her son, as she might with other clients, felt too formal. On the other hand, Teresa felt it would be unethical to discuss this with Evelyn over coffee and without Chris. She decided to wait and see what else Chris might bring up in sessions.

Teresa also noticed that when Chris was at her house with her own son, she felt uncomfortable. She realized that she was shifting back and forth between the unconditional positive regard she tried to exhibit in her office and the realities of having to discipline two teenagers who sometimes got a bit out of hand. She brought this up with Chris during their next session, explaining that she was wearing different hats: in the office she was his counselor and at home she was his best friend's mom. He seemed to understand, but Teresa found herself becoming increasingly uneasy as the weeks passed. She decided to consult by phone with the woman who had supervised her in her previous job.

Questions for Thought and Discussion

Regardless of what Teresa's colleague may have told her, how ethical do you consider her behavior? Compared to the tremendous potential for harm that can exist in a sexual dual relationship, how dangerous does this situation seem? Do you believe that Teresa should continue to see Chris as a client?

Analysis

Standard A.6.a. states that counselors "are aware of their influential position with respect to clients, and they avoid exploiting the trust and dependency of clients." It seems clear that Teresa does not intend to exploit Chris' trust, and she does not promote his dependency on her. It could be argued that there are no major power issues at play here. However, many contend that there is always a power differential between counselors and clients. A minor client might be even more subtly affected by this differential, especially when it is combined with Chris' perception of Teresa as his best friend's mother—a person who is very loving but has to discipline him when he stays over at her house. Can both Teresa and Chris change their expectations for their counseling time together? Can Teresa remain objective in her work with Chris when she also sees him in nontherapeutic situations as well as through his mother's eyes?

Standard A.6.a. also states that counselors make every effort to avoid dual relationships "that could impair professional judgment or increase the risk of harm to clients." What would have to be shown for Teresa to be considered in violation of this standard? First, it would have to be demonstrated that she did not make every effort to avoid the dual relationship. Did she offer alternative providers? Does a 3-hour round trip to the next closest provider constitute a great enough hardship for Evelyn to warrant Teresa's risks in establishing a dual relationship? Second, it would have to be shown that the risk of harm to Chris was increased by the dual relationship. Although it does not appear that Chris has suffered any harm at this point, Teresa has stated that her professional judgment might have been influenced at times by her struggles to wear different hats.

Teresa may think that she established informed consent regarding the potential risks in this situation. However, it must be noted that she initially reviewed the potential risks with Evelyn, not with Chris. It could be argued that Chris was old enough to give informed consent, and that Teresa's failure to provide him with all pertinent information when counseling was first initiated is in violation of standard A.3.a., which states that counselors promote the client's freedom to choose whether to enter into a counseling relationship and with whom. Finally, the emphasis of Teresa's conversation with Evelyn was on the risks to *their* friendship, not on any possible ramifications for Chris.

Two questions seem to be at the heart of the matter. First, did Teresa's own personal needs influence her work with Chris? Standard A.5. requires that counselors "avoid actions that seek to meet their personal needs at the expense of clients." Teresa would need to demonstrate to an ethics committee, if she were charged with a violation, that her concern over maintaining her friendship with Evelyn did not influence her treatment of Chris.

Second, what precautions did Teresa take to ensure Chris' well-being? Teresa's use of supervision or consultation with other appropriate professionals would also be an essential matter for an ethics committee to explore. Teresa sought consultation only after Chris had been in counseling for more than 6 weeks. A more ethical behavior might have been to consult with her previous supervisor before agreeing to see Chris professionally. This could have provided an opportunity for her to examine her own needs and weigh the potential risks to Chris. In fact, if she had done this, Teresa might have realized that she was focused on the possibility of damaging her friendship with her one close friend in town. Her colleague might have helped her to anticipate problems likely to occur due to the divergent expectations involved in the dual roles she would be assuming. Ongoing supervision throughout the course of Chris' counseling seems warranted in this case.

Questions for Further Reflection

1. If a dual relationship is unavoidable, what steps can a counselor take to safeguard the client's welfare?

2. Do counselors need to be particularly careful in addressing boundary issues with minor clients?

CHAPTER EIGHT

WORKING WITH SUICIDAL CLIENTS

Robert E. Wubbolding

Suicidal statements made by clients may be the most stressful of all situations faced by counselors (Deutsch, 1984; Farber, 1983). When clients are at risk of suicide, a number of ethical issues are raised for practitioners. These include client autonomy versus becoming a decision maker for the client, the counselor's competence, and the willingness and ability to assume responsibility for life-or-death decisions.

Although some have argued in favor of the right to commit suicide, the codes of ethics of professional organizations are in agreement that helpers must actively attempt to prevent such destructive behavior. The ACA Code of Ethics states that the "general requirement that counselors keep information confidential does not apply when disclosure is required to prevent clear and imminent danger to the client or others" (B.1.c.). When counselors determine that it is necessary to breach confidentiality to protect a client from attempting suicide, they limit disclosure to essential information and, if possible, inform the client before making the disclosure (B.1.f.).

Competence issues certainly need to be addressed when counselors are confronted with clients who may be suicidal. Counselors will need to determine whether they have the appropriate training and experience to work with these clients or whether they should make a referral to another professional (C.2.a.). They will need to consider whether they are skilled in the use of both standardized and nonstandardized instruments to assess suicidal ideation (E.5.a., E.6.a.) and in the application of appropriate intervention strategies.

Counselors need to know how to handle suicide threats in order to prevent clients from ending their lives. They need skills that are practical and that represent the highest level of ethical practice. Even veiled threats should be discussed in a clear and explicit manner. The six generic questions that follow can help to facilitate a frank discussion of the suicidal threat with the client as well as to assess the lethality of the threat, to determine the proximity of rescue, and to provide the data the counselor needs in order to determine the seriousness of the immediate threat and whether further intervention is necessary.

1. *"Are you thinking about killing yourself?"* Clients often give the impression of being suicidal by making indirect threats such as "I can't stand to put up with this situation any longer," "I'd like to end it all," or "They'll be better off without me." When a counselor explicitly asks clients in a calm manner whether they are suicidal, they are often relieved to be able to express their suicidal ideation. The counselor can help the client discuss, often for the first time, the decision in a rational manner.

   The overall future orientation of the client can also be discussed. Can the client articulate future goals, that is, what he or she expects life will be like in a month or a year? The person's medical condition is also a factor. Is there a serious, debilitating disease that might make suicide more attractive?

   Recent loss or threat of loss can add to the lethality of the threat. A failure in business, fear of public embarassment, business or political pressure, the death of a friend or relative, or rejection by a lover can enhance the client's desire to seek a long-term solution to what the counselor believes is a short-term problem.

2. *"Have you attempted suicide in the past?"* A history of attempts presents an added danger and increases the lethality of the threat. If the current threat is the client's first consideration of suicide, the threat is lessened though not removed.

   Along with exploring past suicide attempts the counselor should inquire about the client's past involvement with the mental health system. Has the client been under the care of a psychiatrist or another mental health professional? Does the client have a history of drug or alcohol abuse? Is there any history of domestic or other violence or acting-out behaviors?

3. *"Do you have a plan?"* Clients should be asked exactly how they would kill themselves. Would they use a gun, a rope, pills, asphyxiation, jump from a high place? If they have formulated explicit plans, the lethality of the threat is increased, and the counselor should begin to consider intervention outside of counseling.

4. *"Do you have the means available to you?"* If clients know exactly how they would kill themselves, they are asked if the means are accessible. Do they own a gun? Do they have pills that could be lethal? If they do not have the means, the threat is lessened. If they own a gun, have access to life-threatening drugs, or know how to asphyxiate themselves, the threat increases, and more data point toward intervention.

5. *"Will you make a unilateral no-suicide agreement to stay alive, that is, to not kill yourself accidentally or on purpose for a specified amount of time?"* This question is the cornerstone of the assessment process. The client's commitment is not a promise to stay alive for the sake of the counselor but a commitment made to oneself and for oneself. The empha-sis on the unilateral aspect of the agreement serves to make the commitment more firm and solid in the mind of the client.

   The commitment includes the explicit clarification "to not kill yourself accidentally or on purpose." Some suicidal persons drive recklessly or are overly casual about taking too many sleeping pills, and are thus indirectly attempting to kill themselves.

   A specific amount of time for refraining from suicidal attempts is included in the agreement. It might be a month, 2 weeks, or even 24 hours. The exact amount of time is less important than the counselor's effort to lead the client through this process to the point of making a decision that is opposite of suicide.

6. *"Is there anyone close to you who could prevent you from killing yourself and to whom you could speak when you feel the need to commit suicide?"* Suicidal clients often feel alienated and out of control. Detailed plans should be made to assist the client in making connections with people who can help prevent the suicide. Thus another option can be apparent to the client, and a sense of effective control can be regained.

When clients refuse to make plans to stay alive for a specific amount of time, the lethality of the threat requires that the counselor take action outside the counseling session. Such intervention might include informing the parents, spouse, physician, or a significant person in the client's life.

If clients say that suicide has only occurred to them and they have made no previous attempts, have neither a plan nor the means available, and are willing to make a no-suicide agreement, the lethality of the threat is lessened and the need to intervene is not as urgent. Still, there is no absolute or universal recommendation about whether or not to take further action. The counselor should avoid the impulse to intervene recklessly outside of counseling. Nonetheless, even though a specific client answers all the questions "correctly" and promises to stay alive, the counselor might still sense that there is clear and imminent danger. An intervention is then justified. As Motto (1991) has stated, "When all the questions have been asked and answered, the final decision regarding degree of suicide risk is a subjective one," and there is no substitute for professional judgment.

Case Study 16

A SUICIDAL TEENAGER
Robert E. Wubbolding

Frank, age 17, has been referred to a counselor in private practice because of recent changes in his behavior. He is withdrawn and is uncharacteristically irritable with his parents. He has been an average student, but his grades have recently fallen. He has also given away some of his prized possessions, including a baseball that was very valuable to him because he caught it in the stands at a major league game. Other gifts to friends have included a pair of boots, a school jacket, and a cherished set of baseball cards. His parents don't understand his behavior and are concerned about him, telling the counselor that Frank is given to expressions of hopelessness and anger. They connect these feelings with the fact that his girl friend recently dropped him in favor of a more popular student at school.

During the first session with Frank, the counselor helps him describe why he has been sent. He freely describes his unhappiness at home and school, stating that he is fed up and very angry that his girl friend dropped him. He says that she'll be sorry when it becomes impossible for her to get back with him, adding that soon he'll be free of all this agony. The counselor asks how he has handled disappointments in the past. Frank relates that he always gets upset when he can't get his way, and that if people don't like him he finds little ways to get even. He then feels overwhelmed with guilt over his reactions. The way he chooses to deal with the guilt, hurt, and ubiquitous pain is to get high with a few friends. He adds that his parents are unaware of his drug use, which he denies is a problem. Subsequent dialogue between the counselor and Frank might include the following:

Counselor: Frank, you said earlier that you had a solution to your problems.

Frank: Yeah, I guess so.

Counselor: Tell me more about your thoughts on ways you might best solve your problems.

Frank: Well, I've thought of things.... I just don't want to struggle so much any more.

Counselor: I routinely ask people a simple question when they are upset about something. Are you thinking of killing yourself?

Frank: One of my classmates did that last year.

Counselor: Was this classmate a friend?

Frank: Yeah, kind of.

Counselor: Have you thought about joining your friend?

Frank: I think it would be a good idea.

Counselor: Is that a "yes"?

Frank: Yes, I've thought a lot about it.

Counselor: Have you ever talked about this with anyone?

Frank: No. This is the first time I've said it out loud.

Counselor: Sometimes it helps just to talk about it. I've found that people feel better if they are willing to talk about what is on their minds. I'd like to ask you some more questions about your thoughts on dying. Is that okay?

Frank: Sure, its okay.

Counselor: Have you tried to injure yourself or to commit suicide in the past?

Frank: One time about a year ago I took a razor and cut my arm. But I got scared when I saw the blood and I stopped.

Counselor: Have there been any other times?

Frank: No, that's the only one.

Counselor: If you were to try to kill yourself again, how would you do it?

Frank: I was thinking I'd drive my car into a busy intersection at 4:00 p.m. on Route 12 when the 18-wheelers are out on the road. It would be quick and would look like an accident.

Counselor: I see. So you've thought about a plan and you have your own car?

Frank: Yes, I've had it for about a year.

Counselor: Frank, I believe I can help you feel better. I think I can offer you the possibility of getting past this misery. Would you be interested in thinking about some of these ideas before you make this final decision?

Frank: I might....

Counselor: Good. First, I want to ask you if you can agree to make a firm commitment not to me, but to yourself, to stay alive for a while.

Frank: Yeah, I think so. I haven't tried anything yet.

Counselor: For how long?

Frank: What do you mean?

Counselor: Can you agree to stay alive, not to kill yourself accidentally or intentionally, for a week? A month? Or how long?

Frank: I can do it for a month. What did you mean by *accidentally?*

Counselor: Like driving recklessly or accidentally pulling out in front of an 18-wheeler.

Frank: I see what you mean. Yeah, I won't kill myself.

Counselor: Is there anyone around you with whom you could talk if you start to feel like killing yourself?

Frank: I have an uncle who might listen. I can't talk to my parents.

Counselor: Would you be willing to talk to him if you seriously start to want to kill yourself?

Frank: Yeah, that's okay.

Counselor: Frank, how do you feel right now, after you've talked about this for a few minutes?

Frank: I feel a little better.

Counselor: This shows that life can be better, that you are able to do some things, make plans, and take actions which result in feeling better. Would you be willing to work in that direction?

Frank: Yes, I'm willing.... Do you really think my life can be better?

Counselor: I really think so. I firmly believe that your life can take a turn around.

The purpose of the dialogue has been to illustrate the questions related to assessing the seriousness of a suicide threat. Thus many empathic statements used by the counselor are omitted for the sake of brevity. The counselor asked the questions calmly, clearly, and unambiguously after having established rapport with Frank. It is important that the counselor expressed confidence that Frank will feel better, without minimizing the problems. The counselor tried to instill a sense of hope and yet avoided making a guarantee. The counselor will want to consult with a colleague (C.2.e.) and to document. In documenting, quotes from the counselor and consultant are helpful in assuring that the assessment was both thorough and comprehensive.

After the crisis has passed, the counselor can proceed to explore Frank's drug usage, how he handles stress, the roots of his unhappiness, rational and irrational thinking, self-evaluation, effective fulfillment of needs, personal goals, interpersonal relationships, and myriad other issues.

Questions for Thought and Discussion

What components do you think are essential to include in a no-suicide agreement? Does it need to be in writing?

Do you believe that in Frank's case, intervention outside counseling is necessary? Might it be necessary if Frank had refused to commit to a no-suicide agreement? If so, should the counselor then notify Frank's parents? Frank has said that he can't talk to them. What is the risk that if the parents are brought in Frank will feel angry and betrayed, and the counseling relationship will be destroyed?

Analysis

Counselors who function at the highest level of ethical behavior are aware of specific questions to ask clients who express suicidal ideation. They know how to assess the lethality of the threat and determine the proximity of rescue. They are aware of the need to consult and document as well as the importance of proceeding with counseling related to other issues. They recognize that the ultimate decision as to whether to intervene is subjective and often entails resolving the pull of apparently opposing responsibilities.

In Frank's case two sets of competing needs seem apparent: a responsibility to protect Frank from harm versus his right to privacy, and a possible need to intervene outside counseling versus a need to keep the client engaged in the counseling process. The fact that Frank, at 17, is still legally a minor, is a complicating factor. The Code of Ethics states that confidentiality requirements do "not apply when disclosure is required to prevent clear and imminent danger to the client ... or when legal requirements demand that confidential information be revealed" (B.1.c.). In this case, after a careful assessment, Frank's counselor made the judgment that danger was not imminent. When counseling minors, "counselors act in these clients' best interests" (A.3.c.) and may include parents in the counseling process as appropriate (B.3.). At some later point, considering Frank's continuing drug use and his perception that he can't communicate with his parents, the counselor may want to involve the parents in family counseling sessions if Frank is in accord with this decision.

As Corey et al. (1993) have noted, the crux of the dilemma in dealing with suicidal clients is in knowing when to take a client's hints or verbalizations seriously enough to report the condition. The burden of responsibility to make the right decision is high, and the ethically conscientious counselor will need to call upon a combination of skill and training, careful assessment of risk, consultation and documentation, and sound professional judgment.

Questions for Further Reflection

1. How well do you manage your own stress and deal with the awesome sense of responsibility that can attend working with clients who pose a danger to themselves or others?

2. Sometimes clients do commit suicide. When this happens, survivors may look for someone to blame and bring suit against the counselor for malpractice. What steps do counselors need to take, as they work with suicidal clients, to minimize the risk that such a suit could be successful? What steps do they need to take to deal with feelings of loss and failure they may experience when a client commits suicide?

CHAPTER NINE

COUNSELOR TRAINING AND SUPERVISION

Gerald Corey and Barbara Herlihy

An entire section (Section F) of the Code of Ethics is devoted to the teaching, training, and supervision of counselors. It includes standards for counselor educators and trainers, for counselor preparation programs, and for students and supervisees.

Counselor educators need to be skilled as teachers and practitioners, to be knowledgeable about professional responsibilities, and to conduct training programs in an ethical manner (F.1.a.). As role models for their students, counselor educators demonstrate by example the ideals they wish to impart. Certainly, students will emulate the ethical behaviors they have observed and experienced.

Before students enroll in a graduate program in counseling, they have a right to know what will be expected of them, both academically and personally. The concept of informed consent applies to students as well as to clients. Counselor educators orient prospective students to the program's expectations. According to the Code of Ethics this orientation needs to include the type and level of skill acquisition required to complete the program; subject matter to be covered; bases for evaluation; training components that encourage self-growth or self-disclosure; types of supervision settings and site requirements for required clinical field experiences; policies and procedures for student and supervisee evaluation and dismissal; and current employment prospects for graduates (F.2.a.).

After students enroll, they have the right to expect that their training will meet certain ethical standards. They can expect their professors to provide information about the scientific bases of practice, and to present varied theoretical positions so that students can make comparisons and develop their own personal theoretical stances (F.2.f.). Counselor educators also make students aware of ethical standards and their ethical responsibilities to the profession (F.2.d.). Students and supervisees need to be aware that they have the same obligations to clients that they will have later, when they become fully qualified counselors (F.3.e.).

Training programs are based on the assumption that the counselor's personal qualities make a significant difference in the outcomes of the therapeutic relationship. Therefore, training includes attention to the counselor trainee as a person, and it is essential to focus on the dynamics between trainees and their clients. Students should have ongoing opportunities to identify and explore a range of personal issues that are related to their potential effectiveness as counselors. Students need to be challenged to examine their own personal and countertransference issues that will directly impact their capacity to intervene effectively with clients. Counselor education programs must not only integrate academic study and supervised practice (F.2.b.), but counselor educators must carefully use their professional judgment when designing and conducting training experiences that require student self-growth or self-disclosure. Students are made aware of the possible ramifications of their self-disclosures, and evaluation needs to be kept separate from and independent of students' levels of self-disclosure (F.3.b.).

The integration of personal, experiential components with didactic, academic components of training places a special burden on counselor educators in their role as evaluators. They convey clearly to students what their expectations will be in terms of levels of competency and methods and timing of appraisal and evaluation for both didactic and experiential elements. They provide students "with periodic performance appraisal and evaluation feedback throughout the training program" (F.2.c.).

Through this process of ongoing appraisal, counselor educators will at times become aware of a student's academic and personal limitations that are impeding the student's performance. When this occurs, counselor educators assist the student in securing remedial assistance when needed. However, when efforts at remediation fail, they are obligated to dismiss from the training program students who are unable to provide competent service. To accompany this obligation, the Code of Ethics includes safeguards for students: counselor educators seek professional consultation and document their decisions to dismiss or refer students for assistance, and they assure that students have recourse to address these decisions (F.3.a.).

Counselor educators have a responsibility not only to students but also to the profession. Ethically, they cannot endorse students for certification, licensure, employment, or completion of the program if they believe students are not qualified for the endorsement (F.1.h.).

Another ethical issue that arises when training includes personal and experiential learning involves relationship boundaries between counselor educators and supervisors and their students and supervisees. Counselor educators and supervisors are aware of the power differential that exists and understand that students may not be aware of the ramifications of this difference in power. Therefore, counselor educators and supervisors take responsibility for defining and maintaining "ethical, professional, and social relationship boundaries with their students and supervisees" (F.1.b.). They "do not accept close relatives as students or supervisees" (F.1.e.), nor do they engage in sexual relationships with them or subject them to sexual harassment (F.1.c.). They treat students fairly by giving them credit through appropriate means "for their contributions to research and scholarly projects" (F.1.d.).

The counselor training process provides students with practice in counseling clients under supervision. Supervisory relationships have common qualities with the instructor-student and therapist-client relationships but also have unique features. Counselor educators who supervise must be "adequately prepared in supervision methods and techniques" (F.1.f.) and must work "to ensure that counseling services provided to clients are professional" (F.1.g.). Supervisors play multiple roles in the supervision process, and the boundaries are not always clear. Because supervisory relationships are a complex blend of professional, educational, and therapeutic relationships, supervisors need to work to create and maintain an ethical climate for both skill development and self-exploration. Again, it is the supervisor's responsibility to help trainees identify how their personal dynamics are likely to influence their professional work, but it is not the supervisor's proper role to serve as a personal counselor to supervisees. Other ways in which a dual relationship problem could arise are addressed in the Code of Ethics. Counselor educators do not take on the dual roles of serving as both site supervisor and training program supervisor, and they do not accept any form of compensation from a site for placing students or supervisees at that site (F.2.h.).

In doctoral programs, advanced students are often involved in the supervision of students who are seeking their master's degrees, and when this happens the doctoral students must be adequately prepared and supervised by faculty (F.1.f.).

The supervision of students by students also raises a potential for harmful dual relationships. When students are assigned to lead counseling groups or provide clinical supervision for their peers, counselor educators take steps to ensure that students "placed in these roles do not have personal or adverse relationships with peers and that they fully understand their ethical obligations" (F.2.e.).

When students are involved in field placements, they can expect that program faculty have confirmed that site supervisors are well qualified and understand their responsibilities in this role, and that roles and responsibilities are also clearly stated for the student or supervisee and the program supervisor (F.2.g.). Clients who receive counseling services from students or supervisees are entitled to the information they need in order to give informed consent, which includes the qualifications of the students and supervisees and the limits of confidentiality (F.3.d.).

Training and supervision are ethically complex processes. When boundaries are crossed there can be serious repercussions for all parties involved, as is illustrated by the first case study in this chapter. The supervision of students by students provides the context for this chapter's second case study.

Case Study 17

A DUAL RELATIONSHIP BETWEEN STUDENT AND PROFESSOR
Virginia B. Allen

Jim was admitted to a master's degree program in coun-seling. He had outstanding GRE scores, a high undergraduate GPA, and excellent academic skills. During his first semester, Jim was very successful in his didactic classes. However, he struggled in his beginning hands-on counseling courses, and it became obvious that he had numerous personal issues that severely hindered his counseling abilities. He was encouraged by faculty to come to understand himself better and resolve those issues that were blocking him in becoming a counselor. Jim did manage marginally to complete the hands-on classes, which enabled him to continue on into his first practicum experience.

During the second semester Jim enrolled in Dr. Peterson's practicum section for supervision. He had enjoyed her as a professor and felt she was the best supervisor for him. He met with her for weekly supervision. During the early weeks of supervision, Jim disclosed to her that his personal and marital problems were what was hindering his work as a counselor. Dr. Peterson agreed that he needed to resolve these problems before he could make progress in improving his counseling skills. She worked with him during the supervision hour to overcome his problems and make choices that could promote his personal happiness and thus allow him to become a better counselor.

When the counseling program faculty met to review the progress of first-year students, Jim was mentioned as having difficulties with course components that required the demonstration of interpersonal effectiveness and counseling skills. Dr. Peterson disclosed to her colleagues that he was having personal problems. She also stated that resolution was close at hand, and she thought that once these concerns were resolved he should do fine in the program and become a good counselor.

During his second year in the program Jim continued to have regular meetings with Dr. Peterson to discuss his personal issues. During this semester he solicited the support and signature of this faculty member as his major adviser for his thesis committee.

Dr. Peterson told Jim that she couldn't support him at this time because of his unresolved personal problems. However, she would sign as his major adviser at a later date if he continued to meet with her and show progress toward resolving his personal issues and improving his counseling skills. He continued to meet with her regularly to fulfill this requirement.

The following semester Jim again asked the professor for her support and signature and was again turned down for the same reasons. At this time he filed a complaint with the ACA Ethics Committee charging the professor with violating the Code of Ethics.

Questions for Thought and Discussion

Do you believe Jim has a valid complaint against the professor? If so, what standards do you think she has violated? Do you think that Dr. Peterson was obligated to keep confidential her knowledge of Jim's personal problems? If so, what might be the ramifications of her silence? Because Jim is clearly making a good-faith effort

> *to resolve his personal problems and is deemed to have good potential, should he be allowed to progress through the program and become a counselor?*

Analysis

Standard A.6.a. states that counselors avoid dual relationships whenever possible. Counselors need to be aware of their influential positions with respect to their clients and avoid exploiting their trust and dependency. In this case, the student contended that when the counselor educator took on the role as his counselor, she established a dual relationship that could impair her professional judgment.

Standard A.6.b. states that counselors do not accept as clients persons with whom they have supervisory or evaluative relationships. The student argued that he had indeed become Dr. Peterson's client while they also had a supervisory and evaluative relationship.

Standard F.1.b. requires counselor educators to define clearly relationship boundaries with their students and deals with the power differential that exists in these relationships. The student maintained that the counselor educator never explained the potential for the relationship to become exploitive.

Standard F.1.h. requires counselors to withhold the endorsement of a student for completion of a program if they believe the student is not qualified. The student contended that if in the educator's mind he was not qualified to complete the academic program, he should have been informed of this rather than be led to believe that he might become qualified in the future.

Standard F.3.c. clearly states that counselor educators provide students with appropriate referrals for their personal counseling. Further, the standard requires that counselor educators do not serve as a student's counselor unless it "is a brief role associated with a training experience." The student believed that the counselor educator had in fact established herself as his personal counselor. Dr. Peterson responded that, as part of a supervisory relationship, students' personal issues are often discussed to facilitate their growth potential for becoming better counselors. She further maintained that her judgment about this student was never impaired because, although they discussed personal issues, she was never his counselor but rather was his supervisor utilizing accepted supervision methods.

In considering this case, the ACA Ethics Committee would find the counselor educator in violation of several standards, including A.6.a., A.6.b., F.1.b., and F.3.c. It seems clear that the counselor educator did indeed cross the line between providing supervision and becoming a personal counselor. She established a dual relationship with the student while an evaluative relationship existed. Relevant factors include the extended time period of at least two semesters, the number of hours the counselor educator spent dealing with the student's personal concerns, and the student's belief that he was in fact a client during these supervisory times.

It does not appear that the counselor educator was in violation of standard F.1.h. because the student had received regular feedback regarding both his academic standing in the program and the faculty member's concern about his ability to procure a thesis committee.

Questions for Further Reflection

1. The potential for role conflicts always exists when counselor educators deal with the personal dimensions of student growth. How might a counseling program develop safeguards to avoid dual relationships between faculty members and students?

2. In a supervisory relationship, what are the supervisor's responsibilities and what are the supervisee's responsibilities in maintaining the appropriate boundaries?

Case Study 18

THE SUPERVISION OF STUDENTS BY STUDENTS
Geri Miller

Allied Mental Health Center has a long-established relationship with the local university to serve as a field placement and training setting for university interns in the counseling and clinical psychology graduate programs. The center offers an ongoing therapy group that meets weekly for 1½ hours and is co-led by interns from the university. It is an open group, offered at no charge to community members. One unique feature of this group is that a process observer also attends group meetings. The process observer, who is also a student, records group content and dynamics but remains silent during group sessions. The intern co-leaders are advanced students who are expected to refine their group leadership skills and to mentor and supervise the process observer who is a less-advanced student.

This group leadership structure, although unusual, is standard in the agency. Group members are informed and give consent to the structure before they join the group. In the past, member reactions to process observers have ranged from ignoring them to expressing anger at their silence. These member reactions have been incorporated into the group process by the leaders.

Presently, the group is being co-led by two doctoral interns — a female counseling psychology student and a male clinical psychology intern. Valerie, who is a master's level student in counseling, is serving as the process observer. After the group has met for 6 months, the two intern leaders have an idea that they believe will increase their own learning. They decide to process group sessions publicly after each session. This idea is discussed with group members, who like the idea of watching the leaders talk with each other after the sessions. Ground rules are established that the 30-minute processing sessions will be videotaped and that any group members who choose to attend are to remain silent as observers. They are encouraged to discuss their reactions in the following therapy group session.

For several months, the new format seems to work well. During the public processing sessions, the two co-leaders have been open and honest in their communication with each other. They are pleased with the modeling that they are doing for group members, as well as for Valerie who will be one of the next co-leaders of the group after they complete their internships. As the end of the leaders' internship year draws near, Valerie begins to take on more of a leadership function in the processing sessions. Group members express appreciation for her increased involvement, primarily because they are glad to know that a familiar person will be co-leading their group in the future.

During this period of leader transition, Valerie's leadership anxiety begins to grow. During the public processing, she begins to blame members for group development problems and discusses her anxiety and sense of inadequacy as a leader. The co-leaders feel caught between a protectiveness toward the group members and their commitment to public processing. They try to discuss their concerns with Valerie, but she becomes rigid and defensive. She seems to view the co-leaders as being students like herself, who have no right to confront her. These problematic dynamics begin to have an effect on the therapy group. During therapy sessions following the processing sessions, the group members begin to express feelings of guilt and shame, and anger towards Valerie. They begin to voice their concerns about her competence to lead the group in the near future.

The co-leaders, after recognizing their participation in a power struggle with Valerie, consult with their university supervisor. The supervisor ponders how she might best intervene to correct the situation.

Questions for Thought and Discussion

If you were the university supervisor, what might you do at this point? The supervisor has multiple responsibilities to consider: the welfare of the therapy group members, the individual needs of all three of the student supervisees as well as their relationship difficulties, and her responsibilities to the agency, which has a long history of service to the university as a training site. Whose needs should take precedence? What intervention strategies can you think of that might be most likely to resolve the problems in a satisfactory manner for all the parties involved?

Analysis

The supervisor began meeting weekly with Valerie on an individual basis. Valerie was able to hear the concerns from the supervisor who was not a fellow student. These individual sessions provided Valerie with a sense of safety because she could freely vent her feelings regarding leadership and explore guidelines for her upcoming leadership role. Her leadership behavior shifted to a more supportive stance toward group members, and she did less sharing in group sessions of her leadership anxiety. The supervisor watched Valerie grow in self-confidence and leadership skills. She suggested that they include the two doctoral students in their weekly sessions, instead of continuing to meet individually. Valerie was amenable to the suggestion, and with the supervisor's facilitation, the three students were able to examine their own dynamics and then to focus on transitional issues for the group's leadership.

This case raises questions about the limits of supervision provided by doctoral students to master's students. The Code of Ethics states that counselors "who are doctoral students serving as practicum or internship supervisors to master's level students are adequately prepared and supervised by the training program (F.1.f.). In this case, it appears that there was compliance with the ethical standard in that (a) the doctoral interns had adequate training to view the situation as requiring additional assistance, and (b) the supervisor was available and intervened when it became necessary. However, it is possible that some of the problems might have been prevented if the supervisor had from the outset more closely monitored the work of the doctoral students and Valerie.

Counselor educators and supervisors need to realize that students may have difficulty both supervising and being supervised by other students. Thorough training in both the theoretical and practical aspects of supervision appears to be critical in ensuring its success. In particular, doctoral students need to learn the goals of supervision and how to provide feedback in an honest and respectful manner.

It is essential to consider the needs and rights of all parties involved when students are placed in the position of providing training to, or receiving training from, other students. When training is carefully and thoughtfully organized by the training program, student supervisors and supervisees can learn substantially from a supervision experience. When difficult situations arise, counselor educators can assist doctoral students to find their strengths and weaknesses as supervisors. Counselor educators serving in the role of supervisor to the supervisor can role model effective supervision by intervening in difficult situations and communicating in an honest and supportive manner.

Questions for Further Reflection

1. How do you believe you might react if you were in a situation similar to that of Valerie? Do you think you might listen differently to supervision suggestions offered by a fellow student than you might to suggestions made by a faculty member?

2. Should students be put in the position of supervising other students? What are the risks and benefits of such an arrangement?

CHAPTER TEN

THE RELATIONSHIP BETWEEN LAW AND ETHICS

Theodore P. Remley, Jr.

"Is it ethical to take a particular course of action?" "Even if it is ethical, is it legal?" "What if my employer demands that I do something I consider unethical?" "Can I breach my ethical responsibilities to a client by taking some action that is required by law?" "If I do not follow every requirement set forth in the Code of Ethics, will I be vulnerable to a malpractice suit filed by a client?" These are questions professional counselors ask themselves on a daily basis.

The ACA Code of Ethics and Standards of Practice defer to the law. This acknowledgement that counselors must practice their profession within the requirements of the law sets the stage for exploring the differences between the law and ethics.

A Definition of Legal and Ethical Standards

There are a number of sources of law (Crawford, 1994). The United States Constitution provides the foundation for all other laws. The Constitution cannot be violated by other forms of law, which include the common law, statutes, court decisions that interpret the law, and governmental regulations that implement the law. There are a number of levels of legal authority, including federal, state, and local.

The law is divided into civil and criminal arenas. Civil laws relate to the obligations of citizens to each other. Legal rights of citizens must be affirmatively asserted by individuals before civil laws are enforced by the government. Criminal laws require certain behaviors of citizens and prohibit others and are enforced by governmental legal authorities. Citizens who fail to meet legal standards of conduct can be forced to comply under threat of fines, imprisonment, or even death.

Both civil and criminal law set standards of conduct for citizens who are under the authority of the government. Generally standards set by laws are minimal in nature. They represent the minimum behavior society will tolerate from its citizens (Austin, Moline, & Williams, 1990; Bray, Shepherd, & Hays, 1985; Van Hoose & Kottler, 1985).

Codes of ethics are promulgated by professional associations, national certification boards, and governmental boards that regulate professions. These bodies have authority over only those professional counselors who are members of an association, certified by a board, or regulated by a governmental entity. Entities that have codes of ethics enforce them by requiring those who are members or who hold certificates or licenses to comply or lose the privileges associated with the membership or credential.

The standards of conduct established in professional codes of ethics usually describe best practices of members of the profession and are concerned with ensuring a high quality of practice rather than with establishing minimal acceptable behaviors of members of the profession. Woody (1988b) and Austin et al. (1990) have described professional codes of ethics as idealistic and aspirational.

To summarize, legal standards are minimal in nature and are enforced by the government. The government can order all citizens to comply with legal standards and may punish those who refuse. Ethical standards are aspirational and are enforced by professional associations, national certification boards, and governmental boards that regulate professions. Such entities have jurisdiction only over those who have voluntarily submitted themselves to their authority, and their most severe penalty is to remove professionals from membership or to revoke their certificate or license.

The Use of Ethical Standards to Establish Legal Standards

Generally clients have the legal right to expect that the care they receive from a professional counselor is equivalent to that which would have been provided by other professional counselor practitioners in the same geographical area under similar circumstances (*Burks v. Meredith*, 1977; *Goodman v. Emergency Hospital*, 1978; *McHugh v. Audet*, 1947). It appears, however, that the geographical restriction has given way, and now all professionals, no matter where they practice, are being held to the same national standard of care (Huber, 1994). In the event a counselor renders services that are not of the quality expected of similar professionals and the client is harmed in some way as a result, the client may sue for malpractice.

Expert testimony will be required in a malpractice case to determine the proper standard of care and to establish whether the counselor breached that standard (*Goodman v. Emergency Hospital*, 1978). Any relevant evidence may be introduced regarding the basis of the standard of care, but no one piece of evidence is decisive. All evidence presented will be taken into account by a judge or jury who must determine the standard of care. A professional code of ethics may be introduced as evidence of what the standard of care should be, but the fact that such codes are idealistic and aspirational will probably be considered. The determination of the legal standard of care in a particular case may be influenced by a professional code of ethics, but courts are reluctant to impose idealistic or aspirational standards on practitioners (Woody, 1988a).

Because codes of ethics tend to be idealistic and aspirational and because courts and ethics boards are not inclined to hold counselors to higher standards than are generally being adhered to in the profession, ACA's revised ethical standards contain two documents: the Code of Ethics and Standards of Practice. It is anticipated that only the Standards of Practice will be recognized by courts and ethics boards of licensure and certifying bodies as reflective of the true standards of practice in the profession. The Code of Ethics will be advisory and will define best practices, but will be enforced only by the ACA Ethics Committee.

Other Forces That Guide the Behavior of Counselors

All professional counselors, because of their status as citizens in this society, must obey the law. In addition, counselors who belong to professional associations, are certified by national boards, or hold licenses issued by state boards must practice according to each entity's code of ethics.

Laws and codes of ethics, however, are not the only forces that guide the behavior of counselors. They practice according to many rules and standards that are not related to either law or ethics. Some examples will help illustrate this point. When counselors accept employment, they agree to abide by the rules and regulations that have been developed for the employment setting and to follow the directives of their employer. Counselors who are employed in institutions or agencies that have received accreditation by some outside entity agree to abide by the standards established by that accrediting agency. Those who receive federal or state grants agree to abide by rules and regulations issued by the funding source as a condition of receiving the grant.

When counselors are facing dilemmas regarding their professional behavior, it is important for them to identify the force that is affecting their behavior. Requirements in a job setting often are dictated neither by law nor by ethical principles.

Guidelines for Practice

Counselors who are faced with dilemmas regarding how they should proceed in a particular situation should follow these steps:

1. *Identify the force that is at issue regarding the counselor's behavior.* Is the principle involved legal, ethical, employer imposed, or demanded by some other force?
2. *If a legal question exists, legal advice should be obtained.* If employed in an agency or institution, counselors should request legal guidance from their immediate supervisor. If in private practice, an attorney should be consulted.
3. *If there is a problem in applying an ethical standard to a particular situation or in understanding the requirements of an ethical standard, the best action a counselor could take is to consult* with colleagues and with those perceived to be experts in the counseling field. Once advice is sought and there seems to be a consensus on the appropriate response in an ethical dilemma, it is essential that the counselor take the advice given (Woody, 1988b).
4. *If a force other than law or ethics* (for example, an employer, an accrediting body, or a funding agency) *is suggesting that a counselor take some action he or she perceives to be illegal, the counselor should seek legal advice* to determine whether such action is indeed illegal. If the action seems to be unethical, advice should be sought from colleagues or experts. In the event the counselor determines that an action is illegal or unethical, the counselor should approach the representative of the force in an attempt to resolve the problem in a satisfactory manner. If such an approach is unsuccessful, the

counselor should seek legal advice regarding the next course of action.

In conclusion, legal standards are different from ethical standards. Although the ACA Code of Ethics probably will not be the only evidence used by a court to determine the standard of care a counselor owes to clients, the code may be considered along with other evidence such as expert testimony and other professional documents. However, the ACA Standards of Practice were developed to reflect the realistic standards within which a professional counselor is expected to practice, and a court probably will give significant weight to the Standards of Practice in establishing the standard of care in a particular situation.

Many forces that influence the behavior of counselors are neither legal nor ethical. Counselors must be careful to distinguish the force causing their dilemma when they are facing a difficult practice issue. Legal advice should be sought for legal issues, colleagues and experts should be consulted for ethical issues, and representatives of other forces should be approached when counselors are asked to compromise legal or ethical principles.

Case Study 19

AN ETHICAL DILEMMA OR A LEGAL ISSUE?
Theodore P. Remley, Jr.

When Michael completed his doctorate in counseling, he decided that his career goal was to open a private practice on his own. As a step in that direction, he took a job as a counselor in a very large nonprofit community-based counseling center. The center employs psychiatrists, clinical and counseling psychologists, clinical social workers, and professional counselors. Michael specializes in treating clients with eating disorders, and no other professional on the staff has expertise in that area. The center director is not a mental health professional but holds a master's degree in public administration.

After 5 years of excellent clinical experience, Michael decided it was time for him to leave the counseling center and begin his private practice. He notified the center director that he planned to terminate his employment in 6 months. Michael gave notice of his intention to leave well in advance because he knew that no one else at the center had special skills in treating clients with eating disorders. He wanted to make the transition as smooth as possible for the center and for his clients. The center director gave Michael a letter the day after Michael had notified him that he was leaving. The letter stated that Michael was to take the following actions: terminate his counseling relationships with all of his current clients within the next 2 weeks and transfer his clients to other professionals at the center; turn over to the center director all case notes and records regarding clients he had seen at the center during the past 5 years; comply with the employment agreement he had signed 5 years ago guaranteeing he would not compete with the center for clients for a period of 2 years after he left the center; sign a written statement that he would never accept in his private practice any client or any relative of any client he had counseled at the center; and clean out his desk and accept as his final day of employment 2 weeks from the date of the letter, instead of the 6 months as he had originally intended. The letter indicated that the center would take legal action against Michael if he refused to comply with any of the directives.

Michael was stunned and very angry with the center director. He read the letter from the director early in the morning the day he received it. After a heated discussion with the director, it was clear to Michael that the director was determined to try to enforce his demands.

Michael went from the director's office to his own office where he saw six clients that day. Although unsure what to say to clients, he decided he had better prepare them for his departure. He explained that he might be leaving the center in 2 weeks and indicated to clients that they probably would be transferred to another professional at the center for continued counseling. Every client asked Michael what he intended to do when he left the center, and he responded that he planned to open a private counseling practice. Each client indicated a desire to continue to receive counseling from Michael and wanted to go with him to his new practice. Michael said that he did not think that was possible, but that he would investigate the situation and get back to them. One of the clients told the receptionist that she was sorry that Michael was leaving but that she planned to transfer to Michael's private practice when he left. The receptionist innocently mentioned the conversation to the center director.

Questions for Thought and Discussion

If you were in Michael's place, what do you think you might do about the situation? Can you identify elements of his situation that involve legal issues? Ethical issues? What issues does this case raise for you, as you consider whether you might ever be in a position to accept employment in a community counseling center?

Analysis

This case involves both ethical and legal issues that are intertwined but should be separated if Michael is to maintain his professional reputation and accomplish his goal of beginning his independent private practice. Before addressing the ethical issues, Michael should resolve the legal questions he has regarding the situation. However, he should first identify all of the relevant standards of practice and ethical standards that might apply.

Michael should immediately consult an attorney who either represents mental health professionals in their private practices or, if such a person is not available, an attorney who represents other professionals such as physicians or accountants in their private practices. He should inform his attorney of the relevant ACA Standards of Practice and provisions in the Code of Ethics and should then pose the following questions to his attorney: Is he legally required to turn over to the center director all case notes and records regarding his clients? Is the employment contract provision promising not to compete valid and enforceable? Can he accept clients or relatives of clients in his new private practice? Can the center terminate his employment in 2 weeks because he gave notice that he intended to leave and open a private practice in 6 months?

After resolving the legal issues, Michael can turn his attention to the ethical issues involved. There are numerous standards in the Code of Ethics that are relevant to this situation. These include client welfare, client rights, termination and referral, right to privacy, records, advertising and soliciting clients, and relationships with employers and employees.

Michael will be justified in his concern for the continued welfare of his clients (A.1.a.) if he should be required to transfer them to other professionals in the center who do not have expertise in treating eating disorders. The method of terminating and transferring his clients that is being required by the center director is ethically questionable. Clients do have the right of freedom of choice to "determine which professional(s) will provide counseling" (A.3.b.), and Michael will want to apprise his attorney of this standard.

If Michael's clients decide to discontinue their counseling at the center, the question then becomes one of whether they can see Michael in his private practice. This is a question his attorney should help him answer. An ethical question is whether Michael violated the standard that states that counselors do not use their places of employment to recruit or gain clients for their private practices (C.3.d.) when he told clients of his intentions to go into private practice on his own.

Several standards under Relationships With Employers and Employees (D.1.) are relevant to this situation. Working agreements must be specified in advance, and Michael did sign a contract containing a no-compete clause. His attorney will need to determine whether the clause is enforceable. Although the center director's actions may be ethically questionable, the director is not a counseling professional and is not accountable to the same ethical standards as is Michael.

Michael should follow his attorney's advice regarding his relationship with the center and the center director. Once the legal issues have been addressed, Michael should ensure that whatever course of action he has control over and pursues does not violate any of his ethical obligations.

Questions for Further Reflection

1. If you were ever in a professional situation where you felt you needed an attorney, how might you go about finding and selecting one?

2. What kinds of legal knowledge do you think counselors need to possess in order to be able to work safely and effectively in today's complex world of counseling practice?

PART IV

HIGHLIGHTS
OF ETHICAL
PRACTICE

n these concluding comments, we summarize much of the material in the casebook by putting into focus some principles that we believe are important for counselors to review throughout their professional lives. The emphasis is on considering the cultural context of ethical decision making. Because we work in a pluralistic society, it is essential that we increase our consciousness of ways to apply the ethical standards from a perspective that recognizes and respects diversity.

Ethics From a Multicultural Perspective

Respecting diversity means that you are committed to acquiring the knowledge, skills, personal awareness, and sensitivity that are essential to working effectively with diverse client populations. Highlights of this perspective that we encourage you to reflect on as you examine the ethical standards and apply them to a range of different situations include the following:

✦ Becoming an effective counselor in working with a wide range of client populations begins with becoming aware of your own personal needs, values, and world view. It is your responsibility to consider any prejudices or biases you may have, even though many of them may be subtle.

✦ If you have not received adequate training in counseling persons from diverse backgrounds, realize that ethical practice demands that you find a way to acquire this competence. It is important that you consider your limitations in working with diverse client groups and take steps toward increasing your competence as an effective multicultural counselor. The reality of working in a pluralistic society entails learning a variety of perspectives to meet the unique needs of clients.

✦ If you have not been adequately prepared to work with diversity, it will not be ethical for you to provide direct counseling services to certain clients. Learning where and how to refer clients to appropriate resources is a key ethical mandate. Seeking consultation is an excellent way to begin developing increased knowledge and skills in multicultural counseling. You may need to acquire specialized training in working with persons from diverse cultural, ethnic, and racial backgrounds such as individuals from various socioeconomic groups, gay men or lesbians, or clients from different religious backgrounds. The role of gender socialization is also critical in the counseling process.

✦ Continuing education is a pathway toward achieving competence in working with diversity. Professional development opportunities might include activities that examine cultural, social, psychological, political, economic, and historical dimensions.

✦ In the area of teaching, training, and supervision of counselors, it is essential that those responsible for counselor education programs make an honest effort to infuse material related to human diversity into all courses. This includes infusing material related to cultural, ethnic, racial, gender, and sexual orientation, and socioeconomic differences. The implications of these differences need to be explored as they pertain to counseling practice, research, and training. Ethical practice demands that counselor educators discuss the cultural limitations and biases associated with traditional counseling theories, techniques, and research findings.

As we mentioned in the Introduction, there is a difference between ethical functioning geared toward mandatory versus aspirational aims. The Standards of Practice reflect the minimal behaviors expected of professionals. Hopefully, your stance toward practice will be to strive for the highest level of ethical functioning, that is, toward aspirational ethics. This includes keeping the client's best interest foremost. Certainly, aspirational ethics involves considering situations from a multicultural perspective and all of the standards in the Code of Ethics can be interpreted against a framework of diversity.

The Challenge of Developing Your Personal Ethics

As a professional counselor, you are expected to know the ethical standards of your professional organizations, and you are also expected to exercise good judgment in applying these principles to particular cases. You will find that interpreting the ethical guidelines and applying them to particular situations demand the utmost ethical sensitivity. Even responsible practitioners differ over how to apply established ethical principles to specific situations. You will be challenged to deal with questions that do not always have obvious answers. You will need to struggle within yourself to decide how to act in ways that will further the best interests of your clients.

Resolving the ethical dilemmas you will face requires a commitment to questioning your own behavior and motives. A sign of your good faith is the willingness to share struggles openly with colleagues or fellow students. Such consultation can be of great help in clarifying issues by giving you other perspectives. It is essential that you keep yourself informed about laws affecting your practice, keep up to date in your specialty field, stay abreast of developments in ethical practice, reflect on the impact that your values have on your practice, and be willing to engage in honest self-examination.

It is our hope that you will think about the guidelines and principles explored in this casebook, apply them to yourself, and attempt to formulate your own views and positions on the topics raised in this casebook, and that you will do the work necessary to develop and refine your personal ethics. The task of developing a sense of professional and ethical responsibility is never really finished. As we have seen, ethical thinking is not simply a matter of black-or-white categorization. As you are confronted by new ethical challenges, you will need to reflect continually on the implications of these issues.

REFERENCES

American Association for Counseling and Development. (1988). *Ethical standards*. Alexandria, VA: Author.

American Association for Marriage and Family Therapy. (1991). *AAMFT code of ethics*. Washington, DC: Author.

American Counseling Association. (1995). *Code of ethics and standards of practice*. Alexandria, VA: Author.

American Counseling Association. (1994). *Policies and procedures for processing complaints of ethical violations*. Alexandria, VA: Author.

American Psychological Association. (1991). *Legal liability related to confidentiality and the prevention of HIV transmission*. Washington, DC: Author.

Association for Specialists in Group Work. (1989). *Ethical guidelines for group counselors*. Alexandria, VA: Author.

Association for Specialists in Group Work. (1991, Fall). Professional standards for the training of group workers. *Together, 20*(1), 9-14. Alexandria, VA: Author.

Atkinson, D.R., Thompson, C.E., & Grant, S.K. (1993). A three-dimensional model for counseling racial/ethnic minorities. *The Counseling Psychologist. 21*, 257-277.

Austin, K.M., Moline, M.E., & Williams, G.T. (1990). *Confronting malpractice: Legal and ethical dilemmas in psychotherapy*. Newbury Park, CA: Sage.

Bray, H.J., Shepherd, J.N., & Hays, J.R. (1985). Legal and ethical issues in informed consent to psychotherapy. *American Journal of Family Therapy, 13*(2), 50-60.

Burks v. Meredith, 546 S.W.2d. 366 (1977).

Corey, G., Corey, M.S., & Callanan, P. (1993). *Issues and ethics in the helping professions* (4th ed.) Pacific Grove, CA: Brooks/Cole.

Corey, G., Corey, M.S., & Callanan, P. (1990). Role of group leader's values in group counseling. *Journal for Specialists in Group Work, 15*, 68-74.

Crawford, R.J. (1994). *Avoiding counselor malpractice*. Alexandria, VA: American Counseling Association.

Davis, J.L., & Mickelson, D.J. (1994). School counselors: Are you aware of ethical and legal aspects of counseling? *The School Counselor, 42*, 5-13.

Deutsch, C.J. (1984). Self-reported sources of stress among psychotherapists. *Professional Psychology: Research and Practice, 15*(6), 833-845.

Farber, B.A. (1983). *Stress and burnout in the human service professions.* New York: Pergamon Press.

Forester-Miller, H., & Davis, T.E. (1996). *A practitioners guide to ethical decision making.* Alexandria, VA: American Counseling Association.

Forester-Miller, H., & Rubenstein, R.L. (1992). Group counseling: Ethics and professional issues. In D. Capuzzi & D.R. Gross (Eds.), *Introduction to group counseling* (pp. 307-323). Denver: Love.

Golden, L. (1992). Dual role relationships in private practice. In B. Herlihy & G. Corey, *Dual relationships in counseling* (pp. 130-133). Alexandria, VA: American Association for Counseling and Development.

Goodman v. Emergency Hospital, 96 Misc.2d. 1116; 410 N.Y.S.2d 511 (1978).

Haas, L.J., & Malouf, J.L. (1995). *Keeping up the good work: A practitioner's guide to mental health ethics* (2nd ed.). Sarasota, FL: Professional Resource Press.

Harding, A.K., Gray, L.A., & Neal, M. (1993). Confidentiality limits with clients who have HIV: A review of ethical and legal guidelines and professional policies. *Journal of Counseling and Development, 71,* 297-305.

Hayman, P., & Covert, J. (1986). Ethical dilemmas in college counseling centers. *Journal of Counseling and Development, 64*(5), 315-317.

Herlihy, B., & Corey, G. (1994). Codes of ethics as catalysts for improving practice. *Ethical Issues in Professional Counseling, 2*(3), 2-12.

Herlihy, B., & Corey, G. (1992). *Dual relationships in counseling.* Alexandria, VA: American Association for Counseling and Development.

Herlihy, B., & Remley, T.P., Jr. (in press). Unified ethical standards: A challenge for professionalism. *Journal of Counseling and Development.*

Huber, C.H. (1994). *Ethical, legal, and professional issues in the practice of marriage and family therapy* (2nd ed.). New York: Macmillan.

Huey, W.C., & Remley, T.P., Jr. (Eds.). (1989). *Ethical and legal issues in school counseling.* Alexandria, VA: American School Counselor Association.

Hughes, R., & Friedman, A. (1994). AIDS-related ethical and legal issues for mental health professionals. *Journal of Mental Health Counseling, 16,* 445-458.

Ibrahim, F.A., & Arredondo, P. (1990). Ethical issues in multicultural counseling. In B. Herlihy & L. Golden (Eds.), *AACD Ethical standards casebook*, (4th ed., pp. 137-145). Alexandria, VA: American Association for Counseling and Development.

Keith-Spiegel, P., & Koocher, G.P. (1985). *Ethics in psychology: Professional standards and cases.* New York: Random House.

Kitchener, K.S. (1984). Intuition, critical evaluation, and ethical principles: The foundation for ethical decisions in counseling psychology. *Counseling Psychologist, 12*(3), 43-55.

Kitchener, K.S., & Harding, S.S. (1990). Dual role relationships. In B. Herlihy & L. Golden (Eds.), *Ethical standards casebook* (4th ed., pp. 146-154). Alexandria, VA: American Association for Counseling and Development.

Lakin, M. (1994). Morality in group and family therapies: Multiperson therapies and the 1992 code. *Professional Psychology: Research and Practice, 25*(4), 344- 348.

McHugh v. Audet et al., 72 F. Supp. 394 (1947).

Motto, J. (1991). An integrated approach to estimating suicide risk. *Suicide and Life-Threatening Behavior, 21*(1), 74-85.

Neukrug, E.S., Healy, M., & Herlihy, B. (1992). Ethical practices of licensed professional counselors: An updated survey of state licensing boards. *Counselor Education and Supervision, 32*(2), 130-141.

Paniagua, F.A. (1994). *Assessing and treating culturally diverse clients.* Thousand Oaks, CA: Sage.

Ponterotto, J.G., & Casas, J.M. (1991). *Handbook of racial/ethnic minority counseling research.* Springfield, IL: Charles C Thomas.

Pope, K.S., & Vasquez, M.J.T. (1991). *Ethics in psychotherapy and counseling.* San Francisco: Jossey-Bass.

Remley, T.P., Jr. (1990). *Safeguarding against ethical and legal dangerpoints.* Ann Arbor, MI: ERIC/CAPS Workshop.

Rinas, J., & Clyne-Jackson, S. (1988). *Professional conduct and legal concerns in mental health practice.* East Norwalk, CT: Appleton & Lange.

Salo, M.M., & Shumate, S.G. (1993). *Counseling minor clients.* Alexandria, VA: American Counseling Association.

Sileo, F., & Kopala, M. (1993). An A-B-C-D-E worksheet for promoting beneficence when considering ethical issues. *Counseling and Values, 37,* 89-95.

Sleek, S. (1994, December). Ethical dilemmas plague rural practice. *APA Monitor,* pp. 26-27.

Sonne, J.L., & Pope, K.S. (1991). Treating victims of therapist-patient sexual involvement. *Psychotherapy, 28,* 174-187.

Stadler, H.A. (1986). Making hard choices: Clarifying controversial ethical issues. *Journal of Counseling and Human Development, 19,* 1-10.

Sue, D.W. (1993). Confronting ourselves: The white and racial/ethnic minority researcher. *The Counseling Psychologist, 21,* 244-249.

Sue, D.W., Arredondo, P., & McDavis, R.J. (1992). Multicultural competencies/standards: A pressing need. *Journal of Counseling and Development, 70*(4), 477-486.

Sue, D.W., Ivey, A., & Pedersen, P. (1996). *Multicultural counseling and therapy.* Pacific Grove, CA: Brooks/Cole.

Sue, D.W., & Sue, D. (1990). *Counseling the culturally different: Theory and practice.* New York: John Wiley & Sons.

Super, D.E. (1990). A life-space approach to career development. In D. Brown & L. Brooks (Eds.), *Career choice and development: Applying contemporary theories to practice.* San Francisco: Jossey-Bass.

Tarasoff v. Regents of University of California, 13c.3D177, 529 p.2D553; 118 California Reporter, 129 (1974).

Tomm, K. (1993, January/February). The ethics of dual relationships. *The California Therapist,* pp. 7-19.

Van Hoose, W.H., & Kottler, J.A. (1985). *Ethical and legal issues in counseling and psychotherapy* (2nd ed.). San Francisco: Jossey-Bass.

Van Hoose, W.H., & Paradise, L.V. (1979). *Ethics in counseling and psychotherapy: Perspectives in issues and decision making.* Cranston, RI: Carroll Press.

Wittmer, J., & Remley, T.P., Jr. (1994, Summer). A counselor-client contract. *NBCC NewsNotes, 11*(1), p. 12.

Woody, R.H. (1988a). *Fifty ways to avoid malpractice.* Sarasota, FL: Professional Resource Exchange.

Woody, R.H. (1988b). *Protecting your mental health practice.* San Francisco: Jossey-Bass.

APPENDIXES

APPENDIX

A

POLICIES AND PROCEDURES FOR PROCESSING COMPLAINTS OF ETHICAL VIOLATIONS

Section A:
General

1. The American Counseling Association, hereafter referred to as the "Association" or "ACA," is dedicated to enhancing human development throughout the life-span and promoting the counseling profession.

2. The Association, in furthering its objectives, administers the Code of Ethics that has been developed and approved by the ACA Governing Council.

3. The purpose of this document is to facilitate the work of the ACA Ethics Committee ("Committee") by specifying the procedures for processing cases of alleged violations of the ACA Code of Ethics, codifying options for sanctioning members, and stating appeals procedures. The intent of the Association is to monitor the professional conduct of its members to promote sound ethical practices. ACA does not, however, warrant the performance of any individual.

Section B:
Ethics Committee Members

1. The Ethics Committee is a standing committee of the Association. The Committee consists of six (6) appointed members, including two (2) Co-Chairs whose terms overlap. Two members are appointed annually for three (3) year terms by the Presi-

dent-Elect; appointments are subject to confirmation by the ACA Governing Council. Any vacancy occurring on the Committee will be filled by the President in the same manner, and the person appointed shall serve the unexpired term of the member whose place he or she took. Committee members may be reappointed to not more than one (1) additional consecutive term.

2. One (1) of the Committee Co-Chairs is appointed annually by the President-Elect from among the Committee members who have two (2) years of service remaining and serves as Co-Chair for two (2) years, subject to confirmation by the ACA Governing Council.

Section C:
Role and Function

1. The Ethics Committee is responsible for:
    a. Educating the membership as to the Association's Code of Ethics;
    b. Periodically reviewing and recommending changes in the Code of Ethics of the Association as well as the Policies and Procedures for Processing Complaints of Ethical Violations;
    c. Receiving and processing complaints of alleged violations of the Code of Ethics of the Association; and
    d. Receiving and processing questions.

2. The Committee shall meet in person or by telephone conference a minimum of three (3) times per year for processing complaints.

3. In processing complaints about alleged ethical misconduct, the Committee will compile an objective, factual account of the dispute in question and make the best possible recommendation for the resolution of the case. The Committee, in taking any action, shall do so only for cause, shall only take the degree of disciplinary action that is reasonable, shall utilize these procedures with objectivity and fairness, and in general shall act only to further the interests and objectives of the Association and its membership.

4. Of the six (6) voting members of the Committee, a vote of four (4) is necessary to conduct business. In the event a Co-Chair or any other member of the Committee has a personal interest in the case, he or she shall withdraw from reviewing the case.

5. In the event Committee members recuse themselves from a com-

plaint and insufficient voting members are available to conduct business, the President shall appoint former Committee members to decide the complaint.

Section D:
Responsibilities of the Committee

1. The Committee members have an obligation to act in an unbiased manner, to work expeditiously, to safeguard the confidentiality of the Committee's activities, and to follow procedures established to protect the rights of all individuals involved.

Section E:
Responsibilities of the Co-Chairs Administering the Complaint

1. In the event that one of the Co-Chairs administering the complaint has a conflict of interest in a particular case, the other Co-Chair shall administer the complaint. The Co-Chair administering the complaint shall not have a vote in the decision.

2. In addition to the above guidelines for members of the Committee, the Co-Chairs, in conjunction with the Headquarters staff liaison, have the responsibilities of:
   a. Receiving, via ACA Headquarters, complaints that have been certified for membership status of the accused;
   b. Determining whether the alleged behavior(s), if true, would violate ACA's Code of Ethics and whether the Committee should review the complaint under these rules;
   c. Notifying the complainant and the accused member of receipt of the case by certified mail return receipt requested;
   d. Notifying the members of the Committee of the case;
   e. Requesting additional information from complainants, accused members, and others;
   f. Presiding over the meetings of the Committee;
   g. Preparing and sending, by certified mail, communications to the complainant and accused member on the recommendations and decisions of the Committee; and
   h. Arranging for legal advice with assistance and financial approval of the ACA Executive Director.

Section F:
Jurisdiction

1. The Committee will consider whether individuals have violated the ACA Code of Ethics if those individuals:
   a. Are current members of the American Counseling Association; or
   b. Were ACA members when the alleged violations occurred.

2. Ethics committees of divisions, branches, corporate affiliates, or other ACA entities must refer all ethical complaints involving ACA members to the Committee.

Section G:
Eligibility to File Complaints

1. The Committee will receive complaints that ACA members have violated one or more sections of the ACA Code of Ethics from the following individuals:
   a. Members of the general public who have reason to believe that ACA members have violated the ACA Code of Ethics.
   b. ACA members, or members of other helping professions, who have reason to believe that other ACA members have violated the ACA Code of Ethics.
   c. The Co-Chair of the Committee on behalf of the ACA membership when the Co-Chair has reason to believe through information received by the Committee that ACA members have violated the ACA Code of Ethics.

2. If possible, individuals should attempt to resolve complaints directly with accused members before filing ethical complaints.

Section H:
Time Lines

1. The time lines set forth in these standards are guidelines only and have been established to provide a reasonable time framework for processing complaints.

2. Complainants or accused members may request extensions of deadlines when appropriate. Extensions of deadlines will be granted by the Committee only when justified by unusual circumstance.

Section I:
Nature of Communication

1. Only written communications regarding ethical complaints against members will be acceptable. If telephone inquiries from individuals are received regarding the filing of complaints, responding to complaints, or providing information regarding complaints, the individuals calling will be informed of the written communication requirement and asked to comply.

2. All correspondence related to an ethical complaint must be addressed to the Ethics Committee, ACA Headquarters, 5999 Stevenson Avenue, Alexandria, VA 22304, and must be marked "confidential." This process is necessary to protect the confidentiality of the complainant and the accused member.

Section J:
Filing Complaints

1. Only written complaints, signed by complainants, will be considered.

2. Individuals eligible to file complaints will send a letter outlining the nature of the complaint to the Committee at the ACA Headquarters.

3. The ACA staff liaison to the Committee will communicate in writing with complainants. Receipt of complaints and confirmation of membership status of accused members as defined in Section F.1. will be acknowledged to the complainant. Proposed formal complaints will be sent to complainants after receipt of complaints have been acknowledged.

4. If the complaint does not involve a member as defined in Section F.1., the staff liaison shall inform the complainant.

5. The Committee Co-Chair administering a complaint will determine whether the complaint, if true, would violate one or more sections of the Code of Ethics or if the complaint could be properly decided if accepted. If not, the complaint will not be accepted, and the complainant shall be notified.

6. If the Committee Co-Chair administering the complaint determines that there is insufficient information to make a fair deter-

mination of whether the behavior alleged in the complaint would be cause for action by the Committee, the ACA staff liaison to the Committee may request further information from the complainant or others.

7. When complaints are accepted, complainants will be informed that copies of the formal complaints plus evidence and documents submitted in support of the complaint will be provided to the accused member and that the complainant must authorize release of such information to the accused member before the complaint process may proceed.

8. The ACA staff liaison, after receiving approval of the Committee Co-Chair administering a complaint, will formulate a formal complaint that will be presented to the complainants for their signature.
   a. The correspondence from complainants will be received, and the staff liaison and Committee Co-Chair administering the complaint will identify all ACA Code of Ethics sections that might have been violated if the accusations are true.
   b. The formal complaint will be sent to complainants with a copy of these Policies and Procedures, a copy of the ACA Code of Ethics, a verification affidavit form, and an authorization and release of information form. Complainants will be asked to sign and return the completed complaint, verification affidavit form, and authorization and release of information form. It will be explained to complainants that sections of the code that might have been violated may be added or deleted by the complainant before signing the formal statement.
   c. If complainants elect to add or delete sections of the Code of Ethics included in the formal complaint, the unsigned formal complaint shall be returned to ACA Headquarters with changes noted and a revised formal complaint will be sent to the complainants for their signature.

9. When the completed formal complaint, verification affidavit form and authorization and release of information form are presented to complainants for their signature, they will be asked to submit all evidence and documents they wish to be considered by the Committee in reviewing the complaint.

Section K:
Notification of Accused Members

1. Once signed formal complaints have been received, accused members will be sent a copy of the formal complaint and copies of all evidence and documents submitted in support of the complaint.

2. Accused members will be asked to respond to the complaint against them. They will be asked to address each section of the ACA Code of Ethics they have been accused of having violated. They will be informed that if they wish to respond they must do so in writing within sixty (60) working days.

3. Accused members will be informed that they must submit all evidence and documents they wish to be considered by the Committee in reviewing the complaint within sixty (60) working days.

4. After accused members have received notification that a complaint has been brought against them, they will be given sixty (60) working days to notify the Committee Co-Chair (via ACA Headquarters) in writing, by certified mail, if they wish to request a formal face-to-face hearing before the Committee. Accused members may waive their right to a formal hearing before the Committee. (See Section P: Hearings).

5. If the Committee Co-Chair determines that there is insufficient information to make a fair determination of whether the behavior alleged in the complaint would be cause for action by the Committee, the ACA staff liaison to the Committee may request further information from the accused member or others. The accused member shall be given thirty (30) working days from receipt of the request to respond.

6. All requests for additional information from others will be accompanied by a verification affidavit form that the information provider will be asked to complete and return.

7. The Committee may, in its discretion, delay or postpone its review of the case with good cause, including if the Committee wishes to obtain additional information. The accused member may request that the Committee delay or postpone its review of the case for good cause if done so in writing.

Section L:
Disposition of Complaints

1. After receiving the responses of accused members, Committee members will be provided copies of (a) the complaint, (b) supporting evidence and documents sent to accused members, (c) the response, and (d) supporting evidence and documents provided by accused members and others.

2. Decisions will be rendered based on the evidence and documents provided by the complainant and accused member or others.

3. The Committee Co-Chair administering a complaint will not participate in deliberations or decisions regarding that particular complaint.

4. At the next meeting of the Committee held no sooner than fifteen (15) working days after members received copies of documents related to a complaint, the Committee will discuss the complaint, response, and supporting documentation, if any, and determine the outcome of the complaint.

5. The Committee will determine whether each section of the Code of Ethics the member has been accused of having violated was violated based on the information provided.

6. After deliberations, the Committee may decide to dismiss the complaint or to dismiss charges within the complaint.

7. In the event it is determined that any sections of the ACA Code of Ethics have been violated, the Committee will impose for the entire complaint one or a combination of the possible sanctions allowed.

Section M:
Withdrawal of Complaints

1. If the complainant and accused member both agree to discontinue the complaint process, the Committee may, at its discretion, complete the adjudication process if available evidence indicates that this is warranted. The Co-Chair of the Committee, on behalf of the ACA membership, shall act as complainant.

Section N:
Possible Sanctions

1. Reprimand Remedial requirements may be stipulated by the Committee.

2. Probation for a specified period of time subject to Committee review of compliance. Remedial requirements may be imposed to be completed within a specified period of time.

3. Suspension from ACA membership for a specified period of time subject to Committee review of compliance. Remedial requirements may be imposed to be completed within a specified period of time.

4. Permanent expulsion from ACA membership. This sanction requires a unanimous vote of those voting.

5. The penalty for failing to fulfill in a satisfactory manner a remedial requirement imposed by the Committee as a result of a probation sanction will be automatic suspension until the requirement is met, unless the Committee determines that the remedial requirement should be modified based on good cause shown prior to the end of the probationary period.

6. The penalty for failing to fulfill in a satisfactory manner a remedial requirement imposed by the Committee as a result of a suspension sanction will be automatic permanent expulsion unless the Committee determines that the remedial requirement should be modified based on good cause shown prior to the end of the suspension period.

7. Other corrective action.

Section O:
Notification of Results

1. Accused members shall be notified of Committee decisions regarding complaints against them.

2. Complainants will be notified of Committee decisions after the deadline for accused members to file appeals or, in the event an appeal is filed, after a filed appeal decision has been rendered.

3. After complainants are notified of the results of their complaints as provided in Section O.2., if a violation has been found and accused members have been suspended or expelled, counselor licensure, certification, or registry boards, other mental health licensure, certification, or registry boards, voluntary national certification boards, and appropriate professional associations will also be notified of the results. In addition, ACA divisions, state branches, the ACA Insurance Trust, and other ACA-related entities will also be notified of the results.

4. After complainants have been notified of the results of their complaint as provided in Section O.2., if a violation has been found and accused members have been suspended or expelled, a notice of the Committee action that includes the sections of the ACA ethical standards Code of Ethics that were found to have been violated and the sanctions imposed will be published in the ACA newsletter.

Section P:
Hearings

1. At the discretion of the Committee, a hearing may be conducted when the results of the Committee's preliminary determination indicate that additional information is needed.

2. When accused members, within sixty (60) working days of notification of the complaint, request a formal face-to-face or telephone conference hearing before the Committee a hearing shall be conducted. (See Section K.6.)

3. The accused shall bear all expenses associated with attendance at hearings requested by the accused.

4. The Committee Co-Chair shall schedule a formal hearing on the case at the next scheduled Committee meeting and notify both the complainant and the accused member of their right to attend the hearing in person or by telephone conference call.

5. The hearing will be held before a panel made up of the Committee and, if the accused member chooses, a representative of the accused member's primary division. This representative will be identified by the division president and will have voting privileges.

Section Q:
Hearing Procedures

1. **Purpose.**
   a. A hearing will be conducted to determine whether a breach of the Code of Ethics has occurred and, if so, to determine appropriate disciplinary action.
   b. The Committee will be guided in its deliberations by principles of basic fairness and professionalism, and will keep its deliberations as confidential as possible, except as provided herein.

2. **Notice.**
   a. The accused members shall be advised in writing by the Co-Chair administering the complaint of the time and place of the hearing and the charges involved at least forty-five (45) working days before the hearing. Notice shall include a formal statement of the complaints lodged against the accused member and supporting evidence.
   b. The accused member is under no duty to respond to the notice, but the Committee will not be obligated to delay or postpone its hearing unless the accused so requests in writing, with good cause reviewed at least fifteen (15) working days in advance. In the absence of such 15 day advance notice and postponement by the Committee, if the accused fails to appear at the hearing, the Committee shall decide the complaint on record. Failure of the accused member to appear at the hearing shall not be viewed by the Committee as sufficient grounds alone for taking disciplinary action.

3. **Conduct of the Hearing.**
   a. Accommodations. The location of the hearing shall be determined at the discretion of the Committee. The Committee shall provide a private room to conduct the hearing, and no observers or recording devices other than a recording device used by the Committee shall be permitted.
   b. Presiding Officer. The Co-Chair in charge of the case shall preside over the hearing and deliberations of the Committee. At the conclusion of the hearing and deliberations of the Committee, the Co-Chair shall promptly notify the accused member and complainant of the Committee's decision in writing as provided in Sections O.1. and O.2.

c. Record. A record of the hearing shall be made and preserved, together with any documents presented in evidence, at ACA Headquarters for a period of three (3) years. The record shall consist of a summary of testimony received or a verbatim transcript, at the discretion of the Committee.

d. Right to Counsel. The accused member shall be entitled to have legal counsel present to advise and represent him or her throughout the hearing. Legal counsel for ACA shall also be present at the hearing to advise the Committee and shall have the privilege of the floor.

e. Witnesses. Either party shall have the right to call witnesses to substantiate his or her version of the case.

f. The Committee shall have the right to call witnesses it believes may provide further insight into the matter. ACA shall, in its sole discretion, determine the number and identity of witnesses to be heard.

g. Witnesses shall not be present during the hearing except when they are called upon to testify and shall be excused upon completion of their testimony and any cross-examination.

h. The Co-Chair administering the complaint shall allow questions to be asked of any witness by the opposition or members of the Committee if such questions and testimony are relevant to the issues in the case.

i. The Co-Chair administering the complaint will determine what questions and testimony are relevant to the case. Should the hearing be disturbed by irrelevant testimony, the Co-Chair administering the complaint may call a brief recess until order can be restored.

j. All expenses associated with counsel on behalf of the parties shall be borne by the respective parties. All expenses associated with witnesses on behalf of the accused shall be borne by the accused when the accused requests a hearing. If the Committee requests the hearing, all expenses associated with witnesses shall be borne by ACA.

4. **Presentation of Evidence.**
    a. The staff liaison or the Co-Chair administering the complaint shall be called upon first to present the charge(s) made against the accused and to briefly describe the evidence supporting the charge. The person presenting the charges shall also be responsible for examining and cross-examining witnesses on

behalf of the complainant and for otherwise presenting the matter during the hearing.

b. The complainant or a member of the Committee shall then be called upon to present the case against the accused. Witnesses who can substantiate the case may be called upon to testify and answer questions of the accused and the Committee.

c. If the accused has exercised the right to be present at the hearing, he or she shall be called upon last to present any evidence that refutes the charges against him or her. This includes witnesses as in Section Q.3.

d. The accused will not be found guilty simply for refusing to testify. Once the accused member chooses to testify, however, he or she may be cross-examined by the complainant and members of the Committee.

e. The Committee will endeavor to conclude the hearing within a period of approximately three (3) hours. The parties will be requested to be considerate of this time frame in planning their testimony.

f. Testimony that is merely cumulative or repetitious may, at the discretion of the Co-Chair administering the complaint, be excluded.

5. **Relevancy of Evidence.**

a. The Hearing Committee is not a court of law and is not required to observe formal rules of evidence. Evidence that would be inadmissible in a court of law may be admissible in the hearing before the Committee, if it is relevant to the case. That is, if the evidence offered tends to explain, clarify, or refute any of the important facts of the case, it should generally be considered.

b. The Committee will not consider evidence or testimony for the purpose of supporting any charge that was not set forth in the notice of the hearing or that is not relevant to the issues of the case.

6. **Burden of Proof.**

a. The burden of proving a violation of the Code of Ethics is on the complainant and/or the Committee. It is not up to the accused to prove his or her innocence of any wrong-doing.

b. Although the charge(s) need not be proved "beyond a reasonable doubt," the Committee will not find the accused guilty in the absence of substantial, objective, and believable evidence to sustain the charge(s).

7. **Deliberation of the Committee.**
   a. After the hearing is completed, the Committee shall meet in a closed session to review the evidence presented and reach a conclusion. ACA legal counsel may attend the closed session to advise the Committee if the Committee so desires.
   b. The Committee shall be the sole trier of the facts and shall weigh the evidence presented and assess the credibility of the witnesses. The act of a majority of the members of the Committee present shall be the decision of the Committee. A unanimous vote of those voting is required for permanent expulsion from ACA membership.
   c. Only members of the Committee who were present throughout the entire hearing shall be eligible to vote.

8. **Decision of the Committee.**
   a. The Committee will first resolve the issue of the guilt or innocence of the accused on each charge. Applying the burden of proof in Section Q.5., above, the Committee will vote by secret ballot, unless the members of the Committee consent to an oral vote.
   b. In the event a majority of the members of the Committee do not find the accused guilty, the charges shall be dismissed. If the Committee finds the accused member has violated the Code of Ethics, it must then determine what sanctions, in accordance with Section N.: Possible Sanctions, shall be imposed.
   c. As provided in Section O., the Co-Chair administering the complaint shall notify the accused member and complainant of the Committee's decision in writing.

Section R:
Appeals

1. Decisions of the ACA Ethics Committee that members have violated the ACA Code of Ethics may be appealed by the member found to have been in violation based on one or both of the following grounds:
   a. The Committee violated its policies and procedures for processing complaints of ethical violations; and/or

    b. The decision of the Committee was arbitrary and capricious and was not supported by the materials provided by the complainant and accused member.

2. After members have received notification that they have been found in violation of one or more sections of the ACA Code of Ethics, they will be given thirty (30) working days to notify the Committee in writing by certified mail that they are appealing the decision.

3. An appeal may consist only of a letter stating one or both of the grounds of appeal listed in Section R.1. and the reasons for the appeal.

4. Appealing members will be asked to identify the primary ACA division to which he or she belongs. The ACA President will appoint a three (3) person appeals panel consisting of two (2) former ACA Ethics Committee Chairs and the President of the identified division. The ACA attorney shall serve as legal adviser and have the privilege of the floor.

5. The three (3) member appeals panel will be given copies of the materials available to the Committee when it made its decision, a copy of the hearing transcript if a hearing was held, plus a copy of the letter filed by the appealing member.

6. The appeals panel generally will render its decision regarding an appeal, which must receive a majority vote, within sixty (60) working days of its receipt of the above materials.

7. The decision of the appeals panel may include one of the following:
    a. The decision of the Committee is upheld.
    b. The decision of the Committee is reversed and remanded with guidance to the Committee for a new decision. The reason for this decision will be given to the Committee in detail in writing.

8. When a Committee decision is reversed and remanded, the complainant and accused member will be informed in writing, and additional information may be requested first from the complainant and then from the accused member. The Committee will then render another decision without a hearing.

9. Decisions of the appeals panel to uphold the Committee decision are final.

Section S:
Substantial New Evidence

1. In the event substantial new evidence is presented in a case in which an appeal was not filed, or in a case in which a final decision has been rendered, the case may be reopened by the Committee.

2. The Committee will consider substantial new evidence, and if it is found to be substantiated and capable of exonerating a member who was expelled, the Committee will reopen the case and go through the entire complaint process again.

Section T:
Records

1. The records of the Committee regarding complaints are confidential except as provided herein.

2. Original copies of complaint records will be maintained in locked files at ACA Headquarters or at an off-site location chosen by ACA.

3. Members of the Committee will keep copies of complaint records confidential and will destroy copies of records after a case has been closed or when they are no longer a member of the Committee.

Section U:
Legal Actions Related to Complaints

1. Complainants and accused members are required to notify the Committee if they learn of any type of legal action (civil or criminal) being filed related to the complaint.

2. In the event any type of legal action is filed regarding an accepted complaint, all actions related to the complaint will be stayed until the legal action has been concluded. The Committee will consult with legal counsel concerning whether the processing of the complaint will be stayed if the legal action does not involve the same complainant and the same facts complained of.

3. If actions on a complaint are stayed, the complainant and accused member will be notified.

4. When actions on a complaint are continued after a legal action has been concluded, the complainant and accused member will be notified.

POLICIES AND PROCEDURES FOR RESPONDING TO MEMBERS' REQUESTS FOR INTERPRETATIONS OF THE CODE OF ETHICS

Revised by Governing Council April 1994
Effective July 1, 1994

Section A:
Appropriate Requests

1. ACA members may request that the Committee issue formal interpretations of the ACA Code of Ethics for the purpose of guiding the member's own professional behavior.

2. Requests for interpretations will not be considered in the following situations:
    a. The individual requesting the interpretation is not an ACA member; or
    b. The request is intended to determine whether the behavior of another mental health professional is unethical. In the event an ACA member believes the behavior of another mental health professional is unethical, the ACA member should resolve the issue directly with the professional, if possible, and should file an ethical complaint if appropriate.

Section B:
Procedures

1. Members must send written requests for interpretations to the Committee at ACA Headquarters.

2. Questions should be submitted in the following format: "Does (counselor behavior) violate Sections _____ or any other sections of the ACA Code of Ethics?" Questions should avoid

unique details, be general in nature to the extent possible, and be brief.

3. The Committee staff liaison will revise the question, if necessary, and submit it to the Committee Co-Chair for approval.

4. The question will be sent to Committee members who will be asked to respond individually.

5. The Committee Co-Chair will develop a consensus interpretation on behalf of the Committee.

6. The consensus interpretation will be sent to members of the Committee for final approval.

7. The formal interpretation will be sent to the member who submitted the inquiry.

8. The question and the formal interpretation will be published in the ACA newsletter, but the identity of the member requesting the interpretation will not be disclosed.